From the Footlights
to the Tenderloin

From the Footlights to the Tenderloin

The Tragic Life of Actress Edna Loftus

DAVID GRASSÉ

McFarland & Company, Inc., Publishers
Jefferson, North Carolina

Also by David Grassé

The Bisbee Massacre: Robbery, Murder and Retribution in the Arizona Territory, 1883–1884 (McFarland, 2017)

Frontispiece: Publicity photograph of Edna Loftus in a Grecian-style gown (author's collection).

Library of Congress Cataloging-in-Publication Data

Names: Grassé, David, author.
Title: From the footlights to the Tenderloin : the tragic life of actress Edna Loftus / David Grassé.
Description: Jefferson, North Carolina : McFarland & Company, Inc., Publishers, 2024. | Includes bibliographical references and index.
Identifiers: LCCN 2024023295 | ISBN 9781476694887 (paperback : acid free paper) ∞
ISBN 9781476652887 (ebook)
Subjects: LCSH: Loftus, Edna, 1891-1916. | Actors—Great Britain Biography. | Actors—United States Biography.
Classification: LCC PN2598.L6325 G73 2024 | DDC 792.02/8092 [B]—dc23/eng/20240604
LC record available at https://lccn.loc.gov/2024023295

British Library cataloguing data are available
ISBN (print) 978-1-4766-9488-7
ISBN (ebook) 978-1-4766-5288-7

© 2024 David Grassé. All rights reserved

No part of this book may be reproduced or transmitted in any form or by any means, electronic or mechanical, including photocopying or recording, or by any information storage and retrieval system, without permission in writing from the publisher.

Front cover image: postcard image of Edna Loftus in furs (author's collection)

Printed in the United States of America

*McFarland & Company, Inc., Publishers
Box 611, Jefferson, North Carolina 28640
www.mcfarlandpub.com*

To Jessie Ownbey

Acknowledgments

Judi Leff, Board Member, San Francisco Historical Association

Beth Behnam, Reference Archivist, California State Archives

David Castillo, Archives Specialist/Textual Reference Archives II, at the National Archives at College Park, Maryland

Tom Carey, Librarian/Archivist at the San Francisco History Center, San Francisco Public Library

Christina Moretta, Photo Curator, at the San Francisco History Center, San Francisco Public Library

Jim Dempsey, Research and Preservation Director of the Hamilton County Ohio Genealogy Society

Chris and Nicky Vierhaus at the American Monumental Co., Colma, California

Taylor Wallpe, Reference Librarian, Cincinnati Public Library

Jan Eaton

Jennifer Claybourne, Digital Projects Specialist, University of Minnesota Libraries

Jessica Howe, Project Manager, Legacy Tree

Jamie Kay, Researcher, Legacy Tree

Josefine Zachert at the Landesarchiv Berlin

Dominik Draheim at the Landesarchiv Berlin

David A. Langbart, Research Services, National Archives at College Park, Maryland

Jean Kelley, Windover Historical Research & Genealogical Services

Arabeth Balasko, Curator of Photographs, Prints & Media, Cincinnati Museum Center

Louisa Emmons, Indexer Extrordinaire

Table of Contents

Acknowledgments vi
Prologue 1

Chapter One. Origins 11
Chapter Two. The High Life 16
Chapter Three. Enter Harry Rheinstrom 44
Chapter Four. Into the West 84
Chapter Five. Spiraling Downward 120
Chapter Six. Dissipation and Death 139

Chapter Notes 171
Bibliography 180
Index 181

"History is orphan. It can speak, but cannot hear. It can give, but cannot take. Its wounds and tragedies can be read and known, but cannot be avoided or cured."
—Kedar Joshi

"When all trace of our existence is gone, for whom then will this be a tragedy?"
—Cormac McCarthy, *Stella Maris*

Prologue

My forte is deconstructing the myths associated with Arizona territorial history, and giving voice to the maligned and oppressed. Though the subject of this book is not a "westerner" per se, I am still looking at the life of Edna Loftus with the same critical insight and cogitation I applied in my other writings. I am not inclined to pull my punches when confronting the inherent prejudices and the institutionalized discrimination which were rampant in Victorian/Edwardian culture. With few exceptions, if one was not a male of Anglo-Saxon extraction, with Protestant proclivities, and, at minimum, of upper-middle-class affluence, in this era, during which the subjects of my writings lived, life was harsh.

This study of the life of Edna Loftus is a study of institutionalized patriarchy, sexism, classism, and religious intolerance. It was these cultural prejudices which put her in the spotlight, pulled her from in front of it, and then sank her to the depths of poverty and despair.

After she fell out of favor, the press of the era branded Edna a "gold digger"—a woman from a middle-class or working-class background who attempted to better her position within society by utilizing her sexual desirability to entice a man of means to marry her and support her throughout her life. "Gold-digging" is, speaking plainly, a form of prostitution, with the woman providing sexual favors and, perhaps, progeny production, in exchange for financial gain and social standing. There were a number of "showgirls" who managed this quite nicely, including some of Ms. Loftus' contemporaries, like Beatrice "Minnie" Ashley, who wed William Astor "Willie" Chanler; Belle Bilton, who became the Countess of Clancart; and Lady Seagrave, who had formerly been Doris Mary Stocker.

Ms. Loftus was not so fortunate.

Unlike the press of the Edwardian era, with its adherence to strict social mores and convention, this modern era may consider Ms. Loftus' story from a more nuanced perspective, taking into consideration the challenges women faced during this reactionary, rigorously

Publicity photograph of Edna Loftus reading a letter (author's collection).

classist, patriarchal, prejudiced epoch. The Victorian bourgeoisie construct of "true womanhood" persisted into the early decades of the 1900s in Europe and the United States. The role women were relegated to in these preponderant, subjugating male cultures, namely that of wife and mother, was extremely restrictive. As historians Sara Dalamont and Lorna Duffin asserted, "the woman who deviated from the retiring domestic ideal was at constant peril: at any moment she might become one of the threatening, dangerous, unsexed, monsters incarnate, so abhorred by the conservative press."[1]

As an actress, Edna was in a doubly precarious position. In her study on actresses and prostitutes in Victorian London, author Tracy C. Davis observed, "Despite the tendency for Victorian performers to be credited with increasing respectability and middle-class status and for actors to receive the highest official commendations, the popular association between actresses and prostitutes and belief in actresses' inappropriate sexual conduct endured throughout the nineteenth century." Davis postulates that "Victorians recognized that acting and whoring were occupations of self-sufficient women," and this flew in the face of the patriarchy, and was viewed by moralists "as unwomanly, anti-family, and anti-male." Davis wrote, "The actresses' contravention of men's rules for feminine behavior likened her to prostitutes not only in terms of public profile, but also in her perceived anti-domestic choice."[2]

I would argue that, though actresses and prostitutes might seem to have been liberated and "self-sufficient," in fact, both these professions served the existing patriarchal structure. The women who became actresses and/or prostitutes were still absolutely reliant for their livelihood on a male "audience." Edna was fortunate in that she was beautiful and had a good singing voice. In addition, she had an education, and a background in theater (she stated she came from a family of show people). This allowed her the unique opportunity to make her way to the stage when she left the convent in her late teens.

It is worth noting that had any of these attributes been missing, especially her beauty (read: sexual desirability), Edna likely never would have become a star.

In his book, *The Lords and the New Creatures*, Jim Morrison, a film school graduate, asserted, "cinema is created by men for the consolation of men." This was certainly true of the music halls of the Victorian/Edwardian era. It was men who built the theaters, men who created the entertainments, men who cast these entertainments (most often with a bevy of showgirls), and men who were the core of the audience. Especially in the early days, the acts were openly suggestive, and designed to appeal primarily to men.

Music hall star Marie Lloyd made a career out of bawdy songs filled with double-entendres. Later acts, like the Barrington Sisters and Lottie Collins, continued this ribald tradition. Despite the fact that, over time, the music hall took on an air of refinement, and became more legitimized and socially acceptable, it never quite lost the underpinning of winking salaciousness. It is not surprising that prostitutes regularly frequented the music halls, even the more upscale establishments, in search of customers.[3]

Of course, concepts like "the male gaze," "gender roles" and "sexual politics" were still decades away, and it is highly unlikely Edna and the majority of her contemporaries ever stopped to analyze the patriarchal cultural construct which was the English music hall scene. It would not have occurred to these women, except maybe in the vaguest fashion, as chorus girls, dancers, singers, variety artists, and actresses, they were not only playing well-defined roles on stage, but also playing well-defined roles within the parameters of the English social system. These performers were selling their charms and beauty (as evidenced by the lucrative postcard trade which grew up around them) as much as they were selling their talents. Being on the stage was a way to make a living and, for some, like Edna, a rather good one.

However, as Edna was to discover, though she commanded a good salary as a performer and enjoyed immense privilege, she was still at the mercy of men. After Edna bore him a child, her first husband unceremoniously threw her over for another actress, resulting in her being stranded in New York City without means. Her second husband, who had grown up with wealth, but had no ownership of it, could not provide a living for himself or his wife. The press did not fault the husband, though. Instead, it was Edna who was blamed for his failures. It was not his lack of business acumen, but her extravagant and luxurious tastes which were reported to have doomed their marriage, and resulted in his being sent to an asylum.

Later, when Edna was involved in an automobile accident with her doctor, she was accused by his wife of alienating the doctor's affections, and named as co-respondent in the wife's divorce suit. The press did not condemn the physician for his alleged infidelity. It was Edna who was denounced and cast in the role of the wanton homewrecker. As showgirl Evelyn Nesbit observed when her husband, Harry Thaw, was prosecuted for the killing of architect Stanford White in a jealous rage, "I, and not Harry Thaw, stood trial."[4]

The patriarchal culture was not the only thing which doomed Edna. There was also the issue of classism. In the Victorian/Edwardian era, class distinction was clearly an issue in England and on the

Postcard image of Edna Loftus on a ladder (author's collection).

continent, with nearly impermeable distinctions between the various social classes. At the apex of society was the "upper class," consisting of about 300 families. who tended to be of the nobility, and did not work. Beneath them in the social hierarchy was the "middle class," which made up about 15 percent of the population. Historian Sally Mitchell observed, "The middle class was a diverse group that included everyone between the working class and the elite class," from successful industrialists to clerical workers. "Income was not the defining factor of [this] class, the source was." Next was the "working class," which included all manual laborers—skilled or unskilled. Lastly, there was the "underclass"—the poor, the indigent, and the destitute. These class divisions were present in most European countries which were monarchies, including Germany, Italy, Austria, and Russia.[5]

The United States was divided into the same general classes, but the classes were solely based on finances, not titles, and were more permeable. At the top were the extremely wealthy, which included the likes of the Astors, the Vanderbilts, and the Carnegies. On the tier below there was the middle class, which was a very inclusive category. As in Europe, the occupations which would place one in the middle class were quite varied. The distinction between the middle class and those beneath them in the hierarchy was that the middle class did not engage in manual labor. Below the middle class were the working class folks, which included skilled tradesman, unskilled factory and farm workers, and the like—persons who sold their labor, and worked primarily with their hands. Their lives did not differentiate much from their counterparts across the Atlantic. Finally, the lowest in the social stratum were the indigent.

Except in certain instances, a woman's social class was determined by whom she married, and typically a woman married within the class she had been born into. This is understandable, as the people of her class, be it upper, middle, or working class, were who she would have typically socialized with. A serving girl would necessarily live in a working class neighborhood, and her husband would likely be chosen from among the local men. The middle class woman would be introduced into society in a more formal manner and her suitors would be middle class men who had the means to keep her in the manner she was accustomed to. The upper classes had much more rigid rules concerning courtship and marriage. Often, their marriages had to do with the acquisition or preservation of land, as land was the lifeblood of aristocratic wealth and secured one's high station in society. The upper class woman's choice of potential mates was severely curtailed by her social status and this concern with real estate. Very few women could marry into a higher class, and they would avoid at all costs marrying someone society judged to be beneath them in social standing.[6]

Showgirls and actresses were the exception.

Showgirls, like Edna, Evelyn Nesbit, and Anna Held, who were born into either middle class or working-class families, due to their profession could marry well above their station and, as was noted earlier, a few did. As these women were young and generally considered to be among the most beautiful in the world, affluent men of all ages—men who could well afford to lavish them with expensive gifts, and take them to the finest restaurants and clubs—pursued them. The fact these women had their own money, and were not reliant on any particular man for their livelihood (except, maybe, the theater owners), meant they could afford also to pick and choose from their numerous suitors.

Edna appears to have had a solid middle-class education and upbringing. She stated her family were respectable theater people, and that she had attended a convent school before taking to the stage. Her first husband, though he made a fortune on the racing circuit in Europe, had grown up poverty-stricken in a working-class neighborhood in the Bronx, New York, He was barely literate. Comparatively, Edna, with her middle-class breeding and manners, must have seemed to him to be the epitome of refinement and sophistication. This may have also been why the marriage did not last. After he divorced Edna, he married a woman of a more similar, and compatible, class background.

In contrast, Edna's second husband was the son of a wealthy distiller. To say the young man's mother was classist would be an understatement. Though the family was not wealthy enough to be among the elite class of the country, the matriarch (the father was dead) was very protective of their privileged position among the upper echelon of the middle class, and the family's wealth which insured it. The matriarch saw Edna, with her middle-class roots, her career as an actress, and her previous marriage, as well beneath her in social ranking. It did not matter that at the height of her career, Edna had made more money in a month than the salary the mother paid her son each year to manage the family business. Nor did it matter that Edna, while she was on the stage, and after she married, had moved within Europe's high society, and kept company with nobility.

There was also the issue of the religious intolerance of the family matriarch. Edna's second husband was Jewish and she was a Gentile. Edna repeatedly stated this was the reason the mother of the young man she married rejected her as a suitable mate for her son. Much has been written about anti–Semitism in the Victorian/Edwardian age (there is no denying anti–Semitism was an issue in this period). However, except for modern essays by a few progressive Jewish scholars, the historical issue of Jewish prejudice against Gentiles has rarely been explored. The author does not intend to explore it here, except to say the matriarch of the family Edna married into appears to have harbored an unreasonable hatred for her new daughter-in-law, which was, at least in part, founded on a difference in religious belief systems.[7]

Edna was once quoted as saying, "Millions are stronger than maids, especially merry, merry maids." The story of her life proves it was not just moneyed interests, but also institutionalized sexism, classism, and religious intolerance which worked to destroy her. This is not to say Edna did not make some fearfully bad choices along the way. When she told her friend, the French actress Gaby Deslys, she intended to marry, and was going to give up the stage, Gaby counseled against it. Gaby pointed out to Edna that her career on the stage was really just beginning, and she had the potential to become a much bigger star. Gaby had a head for business, and made a fortune as an actress. Gaby was also fiercely independent.

Edna also should have recognized her soon-to-be husband was not the most responsible of men when it came to his finances, and was what they would have called "a rounder," i.e., a heavy drinker. He also was engaged in a profession—as a jockey—which, though quite lucrative, was not sustainable. Like actresses, athletes have decidedly brief careers, eventually becoming too old and/or too injured to continue to perform as they had in their prime. Certainly, her future husband could have parlayed his knowledge of horses and racing into a career as a trainer or become a stable owner, but, as he readily admitted in his memoir, he was not financially responsible, and spent recklessly and invested poorly.

Her second marriage also was a poor choice on Edna's part. She should have realized, when the family matriarch attempted to have her son incarcerated in an asylum just to prevent his marrying Edna, the woman was never going to reconsider or relent, no matter how hard Edna worked to prove herself to be a worthy wife. Edna also should have realized the son, having been born into and lived a life of luxury and affluence, was not going to be able to live without it. The role of the millionaire playboy was the role he was accustomed to playing. He had no marketable skills outside of managing the family business. He was not suited to any other profession, especially one which required him to engage in manual labor for subsistence wages.

However, before condemning Edna for her poor choices, three things should be taken into consideration—her youth, her unique position, and her upbringing. Evelyn Nesbit, who had grown up in impoverished circumstances, and had, as a young girl, led a rather sheltered existence, reacted to her burgeoning fame, saying, "A strange new life for me. A fairyland, glamourous, glittering and exciting!" Edna had also become renowned at an early age, and what a romantic life she led—the notoriety and recognition, the celebrity treatment, nights out on the town, dinners at posh restaurants, gambling in casinos, the best seats at the theaters, traveling across the continent, expensive gifts from admirers, and all the other amenities which came with being a star of the stage. It must have been surreal for a young woman in her late teens/early twenties, and a bit overwhelming.

Not that Edna's position was completely unique. Obviously, there were other actresses, like Evelyn, who had suddenly ascended to the pinnacle of acclaim and experienced the same high emotion and bedazzlement. Unfortunately, like Edna, most of these other women were also young and inexperienced, and in no position to give sage advice (the career-driven Gaby Deslys being an exception). Older actresses, who knew the perils and the pitfalls inherent to the profession, were few and far between, and usually did not keep company with their younger counterparts. Nor did there exist counsellors, therapists, or any other professionals to advise these up-and-coming performers in the event they needed guidance. In the end, these young women were very much on their own, and the decisions they made concerning their careers and their personal lives were not always for the best.

Further, it was expected a young woman of that era and of that culture would marry and bear children. Women, especially those of the middle classes, were trained by the culture specifically for this role from a very early age, and Edna was no different from the other women of this era. Even though she had become an actress, achieved a certain degree of fame in that profession, and enjoyed an autonomy most women never experienced, Edna was still a product of a middle class upbringing. Doubtlessly, since childhood, she had been programmed, by society, the church, and her family and friends to believe a woman's greatest attainment was to become a wife and mother, not an independent actress. It is no wonder then that this is exactly what Edna did.

Many things about Edna are now lost to us. We do not know what she sounded like when she sang or spoke, as there are no recordings of her extant. We know from a smattering of reviews in the period trade papers that she had some talent as a singer and actress, but do not know how talented in comparison to her contemporaries. As far as is known, Edna did not keep a journal or diary, and there are no remembrances of her from her family and friends, so her innermost thoughts remain a mystery to us. There are a handful of interviews which were conducted with her but, as shall be seen, these were usually conducted when her life was in a state of upheaval, and she was obsessing with what was happening to her. She did provide some revelations—some insight as to the workings of her mind and her emotions—when talking to reporters, but they were few and far between.

In the end, what is left to us of Edna are some picture postcards, some legal documents, quite a few newspaper articles of questionable veracity (some of which are downright biased against her), and a lonely headstone in the Cypress Lawn Cemetery in Colma, California. Still, it is enough to paint an Impressionist-style portrait from of a woman of the Belle Époque era, who climbed near the heights of fame and fortune, and then, due to a combination of bad choices, institutionalized patriarchy, sexism, classism, and religious intolerance, sank into the depths of degradation and despair, and, eventually, drowned.

Postcard image of Edna Loftus with roses (author's collection).

After one of her run-ins with the law, Edna was quoted as saying, "They don't know how to treat a lady in this town." More to the point, society in general did not treat Edna Loftus very well.

Chapter One

Origins

Edna Loftus was always rather reticent about her background. In January of 1910, during an interview, she said:

> I was born in England and my parents are well-to-do respectable people. My family has been connected with the stage for years and some of my relatives are high up in the profession. I would rather not mention any names, for there is no reason for dragging them into print. I was 16 years of age when I first went on the stage and played ingénue parts in London and the provinces. I learned to dance, but I do not follow that particular line, and am not a professional dancer, as has been stated. I was in England for about a year, when I went to France and remained for about three years. It was there that I learned to dance, while studying the language. Later, I took part in a number of French dramatic productions. I have been to Australia and many parts of the world.... I am not a "woman with a past," and I know that no one can say a thing to stain my character....[1]

It does not give the researcher much to go on. Worse, another newspaper said she was Irish, and a third asserted she was born in the United States.[2]

Several newspapers of that era stated Edna was the sister of the famous Scottish music hall singer and impersonator Marie Cecilia "Cissie" Loftus, which would make Edna the daughter of Marie Loftus, who was also wildly popular and often billed as the "Sarah Bernhardt of the Music Halls." At 19, Marie eloped with Ben Brown, who was part of the variety group, Brown, Newland & Le Clerc. Cissie was born to the couple in 1876. There is no record indicating Marie Loftus had any other children during her lifetime.[3]

A newspaper article from November of 1907 stated Edna "hailed from Southwark, Lancashire." Finally, in September 1910, a reporter from *The San Francisco Examiner* was provided a more nuanced biography than Edna ever was inclined to:

> Edna Loftus is the daughter of Mr. and Mrs. John Loftus of Manchester, England. She is the granddaughter of the famous Manchester gun-maker of

Southwark, London, England.

that name. She is also the divorced wife of Winnie O'Connor, the jockey.... A daughter was born to Mr. and Mrs. O'Connor, and the child is now with Edna Loftus' mother in Lancashire. The O'Connors were divorced a year ago last August in Paris. The young woman made her professional debut in "Sergeant Breu" [sic] at The Strand Theater, London. Later, she played successfully in "Madame Lengerie," as the Lancashire Lass, in "The Folie [sic] Marigny" and "Les Ambaseuders [sic]."[4]

In another interview, conducted in April of 1913, Edna stated, "I left Sacred Heart Convent in France before I was 17. At 18, I was a star. I never played small parts; I never 'suped.' I made a hit right from the start." Unfortunately, she did not specify where in France, nor did she say why she had been sent to a convent. Also, Edna contradicted the statement she made in 1910, when she said she first appeared on stage at age 16 in London and the provinces in "ingénue parts." Three years later, Edna asserted she became a "star" almost immediately, and "never played small parts." Taking the two interviews together, it may be deduced Edna left the convent at age 16, and went to England, where she began her career. Then, a year or so later, at 17, she returned to France, where she said she stayed for about three years.[5]

The problem with this timeline is *Sergeant Brue* opened in June of 1904 at The Strand Theater. Her name does not appear among the dramatis personae. Of course, the author of her brief biography in *The Examiner* may have been mistaken about Edna appearing in this particular musical comedy. The English press first took notice of Edna in

February of 1906, when she was appearing in the musical comedy *The Catch of the Season* at the Vaudeville Theater in London. If this timeline is correct, she would have been 21 years of age. This also implies she became a "star" in France first.[6]

On a passenger manifest from 1907, Edna's age is listed as 21. Assuming she provided the ship's officer with accurate information, it would mean Edna was born in the year 1885. However, in an interview with *The Sacramento Star* conducted in April of 1913, Edna claimed to have been 19 in 1907 when she married Winnie O'Connor. Of course, it was not unheard of for actresses to lie about their ages. Edna's friend, the French music hall star Gaby Deslys, regularly shaved about five years off her actual age when she was asked how old she was.[7]

After searching numerous genealogical databases in England for both "John Loftus" and "Edna Loftus," in both Lancashire and Manchester, and finding no definitive matched, this author concluded "Edna Loftus" was probably a stage name, and not the woman's given name. "Aside from the aforementioned Marie and Cissie, there were other actors and actresses, including Kitty and Alexander, who

Actress Cecilia "Cissie" Loftus.

employed the surname Loftus." Edna may well have chosen the surname "Loftus" because of its association with these already established stars of the stage.

On the aforementioned passenger manifest, Edna's husband was listed as "Mr. O'Connor, Winnie, (age) 25, (occupation) jockey." Edna was listed as "Mrs. O'Connor, J., (age) 22, (occupation) none." It may be assumed that Edna was traveling under her birth name. This would explain the "J." Unfortunately, this is all the information the manifest provided. Further, no U.S. passport was issued in 1907 to any female named "O'Connor." Genealogical researcher Jessica Howe observed, "Because Winnie's wife was listed as a citizen of the United States, it would seem necessary for her to have obtained a passport using her married name sometime in 1907. However, it is possible she traveled on her British passport from before her marriage ... (which) was likely to have been issued using her birth name."[8]

Edna married O'Connor on June 26 in Berlin, but they had to be re-married by the U.S. Consul-General, Daniel Harper, in Chantilly, France, "because they were of different religious faiths." This author contacted the Berlin State Archive (Landesarchiv Berlin) to see if that institution might have any record of the marriage. They did not have any record of the Winfield O'Connor marriage. This author also contacted the National Archives in College Park, Maryland, in the hopes the U.S. Consul General might have a record of the re-marriage that took place

Postcard image of Edna Loftus lounging in a chair (author's collection).

Chapter One. Origins

in France. Again, there were no records to be found. Further, historical archives in Chantilly were contacted, but to no avail.[9]

The records from the United States Citizenship and Immigration Services Genealogy Program concerning her deportation case of 1913 includes an interview with Edna conducted by Inspector Frank H. Ainsworth. When asked, Edna stated her maiden name was "Edna Loftus." She stated she was 25 years-of-age, meaning she was actually born in 1888. She asserted she was born in "Lancashire, England, Liverpool." Unfortunately, Ainsworth did not ask the names of her parents. Further, she said she was a singer, and started in her career at age 16. When asked whom she lived with prior to marrying the first time, she stated she lived with her mother in Liverpool, and also in London and France. She said her marriage to O'Connor was "consummated" in Chantilly.

Again, there are contradictions between these statements and other records. By way of example, on the 1907 ship's manifest mentioned previously, Edna stated she was 22, which would mean Edna was born in the year 1885. In the 1913 interview with *The Sacramento Star*, Edna stated she was 19 when she married O'Connor, which would mean she was born in 1888, which would be in agreement with what she told Inspector Ainsworth. Also, in agreement with all the other available sources, is that Edna was born in Lancashire. She was, indeed, a "Lancashire Lass."

However, a number of questions remain unanswered: Was she born in 1885 or 1888? Was she born Edna Loftus or was this a stage name? Who were her parents? Did she have any siblings? What convent was she schooled in, and why was she sent there? Did she make her stage debut in London or Paris? What became of Edna's daughter, whom she left with her mother? Does Edna have any descendants living today? Unfortunately, many of these questions remain unanswered, and, possibly, are unanswerable.[10]

Chapter Two

The High Life

Edna Loftus came to fame towards the end of the heyday of the English music hall scene. Historian Jacky Bratton noted the "signs of the end were the 1907 performers' strike and the 1912 Royal Command performance." Additionally, there was the burgeoning motion picture industry, which would eventually usurp some of the grand old theaters and playhouses. However, the music halls in the early 1900s were still going strong, mostly due to the immense popularity of the new "musical comedy" genre.[1]

Tracing the roots and rise of the music halls could be a book unto itself. Though the tradition dates back to the 1500s in drinking taverns, the music halls came of age in Britain in the 1840s in pubs and saloons, when the owners began bringing in singers, dancers, and other variety acts to entertain their newly-urbanized, working-class customers. These entertainments proved so popular, the owners began building separate halls to house them, while still serving drinks and food. By the 1860s, the music hall business was booming in Britain, and had begun to spread to the continent. The French would take the concept and adapt it, creating the cabaret. Some of the more famous French music halls included the Moulin Rouge and the Follies Bergère. The phenomenon also spread to the United States, where it evolved into vaudeville.

Back in Britain, the music hall eventually moved beyond its working-class roots, and become an egalitarian entertainment. As Bratton notes, this change was by design, as theater owners and managers sought to attract the middle and upper classes and their money. By 1870, in London alone, there were 31 music halls, including The Gaiety, the Alhambra, and the London Pavilion, and 384 scattered throughout the rest of the United Kingdom. As historian Steven Gerrard observed, "The Music Hall became the mass populist entertainment for the population. Every town had one, where everyone could be entertained by variety acts showing off the performer's skills." In London's West End, the entertainments in the music halls gradually changed, and became more suited to the new upper and middle class clientele. "The publicans sought elevation to the higher echelons of polite society, and as dramatic episodes were performed in the Music Halls, so their reputations as procurers of highbrow entertainment was assured."

Though the halls could be quite lavish in their décor and furnishings, the entertainments were still very much designed to appeal to the proletariat and middle classes, satirizing British culture and customs, with a fair amount of sexual innuendo thrown in for good measure. "Despite their risqué songs and routines," said Gerrard, "the music hall was a place advertised for *all* the family; a communal area of fun, frivolity, and enjoyment." The entertainments presented therein appealed to all social classes, with the exception of the nobility. For the common working folks, it was a place to escape the hardships of life and the daily toil. For the upper classes it was a place where they could escape strict social mores, and indulge their taste for the bawdy. The middle classes attended in emulation of the bourgeoisie. "Despite their being a delineate boundary between the classes, the Music Hall was one aspect of British society that allowed for *all* to become part of the Utopian-collective for the briefest of moments."

The performances presented were quite varied, and could include singers, dancers, monologists, magicians, acrobats, impersonators, clowns, minstrels, comedians, chorus girls, actors and actresses—and the audience. In fact, audience participation was a key factor in the success of the Music Hall. The audience was encouraged to sing along with popular songs, and performers such as the comedians and magicians would engage directly with audience members. "This affinity between the audience and performer ... proved to be the cornerstone of the halls' achievements," stated Gerrard. Songs and jokes were calculated to resonate with the audience members, and spoke to topics with which they were familiar, including labor, poverty, class divisions, domestic relations, government bureaucracy, drunkenness, and, of course, sex.[2]

By the early 1900s, when Edna made her debut, the musical comedy had become the prevailing entertainment in the music halls. George Joseph "The Guv'nor" Edwardes, who bought The Gaiety Theater in the 1880s, is commonly credited with inventing this wildly popular genre. Realizing that audiences were tiring of the operettas of Gilbert and Sullivan as well as the more raucous music hall burlesques, which had been the mainstay of The Gaiety, Edwardes, and his musical director, Ivan Caryll, created a "mash-up." The duo combined the catchy musical numbers which were a feature of the burlesques with a narrative which was common to the operettas. They also toned down the more risqué aspects of the burlesques, replacing the scantily-clad dancing girls with fashionably-attired show girls and the like, in order to appeal to the more austere tastes of the upper classes. In 1892, Edwardes premiered *In Town*, which was a smash hit. This was followed up by *The Gaiety Girl* in 1893, The latter proved so popular, the show was taken on a world tour the following year. *The Shop Girl*, which was first staged at The Gaiety in November of 1894, had a run of 546 performances—a record for the era. It did not take long for the owners and managers of other theaters to begin copying Edwardes' successful formula.[3]

Most of the critics lambasted the new musical comedies as not being "legitimate drama." A reviewer for *Theatre* magazine derided them as a "formless, vacuous kind of stage entertainment." New

Gaiety Theater, London, England (author's collection).

York–based critic Alan Dale lamented that the "only national drama ... is that beautiful, flip and classic commodity known as musical comedy." However, the condemnation of musical comedies had little effect on public opinion. Every evening all across England, the United States, and Europe the masses turned out in droves to see these entertainments, and the theaters regularly sold-out. The popularity of the genre was undeniable, and the musical comedy quickly became the mainstay of Edwardian-era theater.[4]

Edna began her theater career as a show girl in the musical comedy genre. It was reported in 1910, she made her professional stage debut in a show called *Sergeant Brue* at The Strand Theater in London. However, Edna's name is not mentioned in the review which appeared in *The London Opinion* on June 25, 1904, or any others. Only the principal actors, including Willie Edouin, Arthur Williams, and the up-and-coming Zena Dare, were credited as having appeared in the play. Then again, if Edna was cast in a bit part, such as the role of "barber girl" or was simply one of the numerous show girls, her appearance would not have been commented on or even acknowledged. The musical farce, as *Sergeant Brue* was described, was not well received by the critics and, within a month of opening, it closed at The Strand and was moved to the Prince of Wales Theater. It did not last long there either, and was soon only being played at theaters in the provinces.[5]

The show girl of the Edwardian era was a much different creature from what we would call a show girl today. In 1903, a reporter for *The Sun*, a New York City newspaper, described the show girl thus:

> She may be called without exaggeration the comely foundation on which musical comedy rests. The musical plays created the show girl. But without her they could not exist to-day. Her importance seems really great when one realizes that the phrase "show girl" only became part of the theatre's slang a year or more ago. The phrase was coined to describe the handsome young women who stand in the front rows of the chorus in all the musical plays and stun the spectators with their opulent loveliness.
>
> They are midway between the chorus and the principles. Sometimes they have a few lines to speak, but this importance is rarely given them. They are meant to serve a merely spectacular purpose with the addition of certain charms of manner that are a part of the successful show girl's outfit. She must look happy and she must move with spirit and abandon. She must really seem to be having as good a time as she pretends to. But above all, she must possess lavish physical pulchritude and display it freely as the exigencies of modern stage demand.
>
> It will be seen that the show girl is a person of importance. She is practically indispensable to musical performances, and the demand for the right kind of girls still continues greater than the supply. The chorus can easily

be recruited from season to season. The ordinary chorus girl, with a salary ranging from $15 to $20 a week, usually comes along in sufficient numbers to fill up the ranks without trouble. But the dazzling show girl is a different person. She is so different that her salary ranges from $35 to $60 a week....

Every musical performance nowadays must have its group of [show girls], and the first night audience invariably gazes with an especially critical eye at the contingent among the women.... They await eagerly the first appearance of the group. The members are studied cautiously through opera glasses by all but those fortunate enough to be seated in the first or second row. And on this judgement depends much of the success of a musical play....

Although it is possible to establish a reputation as a show girl, it will be seen that from the very nature of the duties one cannot remain a show girl very long. A veteran show girl would, for instance, be an intolerable anomaly. She must be ever young, fresh, and ever beautiful, So the show girl can count on no more than five or six years at utmost....

Edna seems to have had the good fortune of having some natural talent for singing and acting in addition to being beautiful, as evidenced by the fact she quickly moved from being just another show girl into supporting roles in these musical comedy productions.[6]

Edna first came to the general public's attention in February of 1906, when she was featured on the cover of *The Tatler* magazine. At the time, Edna was appearing in a play called *The Catch of the Season*. Oddly, there was no article accompanying the cover image. *The Catch of the Season* was first staged at the Vaudeville Theater in September of 1904. The "comedy with music" was written by Seymour Hicks and Cosmo Hamilton, and was an updated version of the Cinderella story, with "the old world spirit of the fairy tale retained in spite of its modern setting." In its review of the original play, *The Morning Post* said, "The success of the piece was never in question from almost the very beginning, and if ever a musical play deserved a long run, this one assuredly does."[7]

In what would be classified today as a romantic comedy, *The Catch of the Season* told the story, in two acts, of Lady Crystal's neglected stepdaughter Angela. In addition to Angela, Lady Crystal has two daughters, who are described as beautiful, but "disagreeable." The "catch of the season" is the handsome and affluent Duke of St. Jermyn's, whom all the young beauties are chasing after. The first act takes place in Lady Crystal's drawing room, which is crowded with visitors. When the company depart the scene, only Angela is left, drinking tea and eating buttered bread off kitchen crockery, as she bemoans her situation. A young page, named Bucket, comes in and declares his love for Angela. However, another has spied Angela through the window, and moments later the Duke makes his appearance. Smitten by Angela, he declares his love

Chapter Two. The High Life 21

Edna Loftus on the cover of *The Tatler* (author's collection).

for her. Eventually, the Duke departs without ever revealing his true identity.

The event for which everyone is gathered is the grand ball, celebrating the Duke's coming-of-age, which is to take place that very night. Of course, poor Angela has not received an invitation. That evening, Lady Crystal, her daughters, and the rest set out for the ball, and Angela, left alone, prepares to retire. Suddenly, there is a pounding on the door, and Lady Caterham, Angela's aunt, arrives on the scene. She has brought along a small army of milliners and seamstresses, and soon Angela is outfitted in a resplendent gown. Lady Caterham plans to take Angela to the ball, but Angela must pretend to be the aunt's young Irish friend, Molly O'Halloran, in order to fool the stepmother.

Act two begins at the ball. The Duke is in a blue funk. Despite being surrounded by a bevy of young beauties all offering themselves up to him, he is still pining for Angela. However, Angela soon arrives, and though the subterfuge cooked up by Lady Caterham fools Lady Crystal, The Duke is not long deceived. He continues to press his suit. Finally, Angela slips away, but in her haste, she leaves in her wake her crystal slipper. The Duke finds the errant footwear soon afterward, and then goes in search of his beloved. The second scene of the second act takes place at the church, where Angela is marrying the Duke. At the wedding, Lady Crystal remarks, "Angela, you've got the catch of the season." The Duke corrects Lady Crystal, saying, "No! *I've* got the catch of the season."

In the original 1904 production, the part of Angela was played by actress Zena Dare. Among the other dramatis persona are the Rev. William Gibson and his wife Enid, who are the proud parents of eight daughters, known as the Gibson Girls. These characters were based on and outfitted to resemble Charles Dana Gibson's popular illustrations, and the parts were played by a handful of up-and-coming actresses—basically, show girls. When she joined the cast, Edna was cast in one of these roles. She eventually became the lead show girl of the troupe.[8]

As reported in *The Folkestone Express* in January of 1906, *The Catch of the Season* was still drawing large audiences at The Vaudeville despite having played over 550 times since its opening two years earlier. By the time, the lead in the production was being played by Madge Crichton. Being one of the Gibson Girls, Edna was not named in the advertisements for or in the reviews of the show, though, as evidenced by her photo appearing on the cover of *The Tatler*, she was certainly being noticed.[9]

The Vaudeville's troupe of Gibson Girls, including Edna, were eventually invited to appear at the Théâtre Marigny in Paris. Of course, the invitation was accepted, and the women took a steamship across the channel, and landed in France. A reviewer for *The Referee*, who signed himself "Percival," wrote a review of their performance at the Folies Marigny. He noted the management of the Marigny "has engaged, among other attractions, a bevy of British Gibson girlies, who are so pretty that they have to lock them in during rehearsal ... to keep out the admirers who will not be denied." Said Percival, "The leader of these lovely ladies is Miss Edna Loftus, blue-eyed and graceful as the dear gazelle I never

Publicity photograph of Miss Madge Crichton.

Théâtre de Marigny, Paris, France (author's collection).

loved, and most divinely fair. Miss Loftus is, I learn, to play a part in the Porte Saint-Martin version of 'Cinderella' in Drury Lane in autumn. Well, chin chin."[10]

Edna had not only made an impression on the critics, but the audiences adored her as well. So much so, that is October of 1906, it was announced Edna had a co-starring role in the play entitled "The New Aladdin" at Edwardes' Gaiety Theater. *The Tatler*, which was among the first to give notice of the production, featured a full-page photo of Edna under the headline "A Beauty in 'The New Aladdin' at the Gaiety." The journal reminded its readers "Miss Loftus ... played at the Vaudeville during the run of 'The Catch of the Day.'" Edna's star was in its ascendency.[11]

The New Aladdin, which was written by James T. Tanner and W.H. Risque, was also a musical comedy, and told the story of "the sentimental nephew of a Bondstreet dealer in antiques. The young man seeks the idol of his dreams—the fair princess, and he finds her after a voyage in an airship in far Cathay.... He also becomes possessed of the [magic] lamp, by means of which [the audience] were treated to an 'Ideal London.'" Though Edna did have a starring role in the production, playing the character of Madge Oliphant, she was not the lead. The Princess was played by newcomer Lily Elsie, who would go on to be quite the sensation. Elsie had not been slated to star in the production, but when Gertie Millar's husband fell ill, Elsie had replaced her.

Also included in the cast was a young French actress named Gaby Deslys. According to her biographer, James Gardiner, Gaby, who had already made quite the name for herself in Paris, was spotted by actor George Grossmith, who regularly appeared in productions at The Gaiety, and was a close associate of Edwardes. Grossmith convinced Edwardes to visit Paris with him to see Deslys. Edwardes was equally impressed by Gaby's beauty and performance, and offered her a role in this new extravaganza. Gaby, who spoke very little English, played the Charm of Paris, and performed two songs. By the end of the run of *The New Aladdin*, Gaby was as well-known in London as she was in Paris. She would go on to become one of the biggest stars of the early 20th Century.

Edna would later state she and Gaby became good friends during this time. "And who do you suppose I worked with at the Gaiety in Paris? Gaby Deslys! I taught her to speak English on the stage. We were chums.... Gaby told me not to [marry], but I wouldn't listen to her. She said: 'You are foolish to marry. You are young and you have a wonderful chance.' She was right. Gaby called me 'ma petite Edna.' It was her pet name for me. I can hear her now laughing in her cheery way, chiding, mocking playfully at those about her as she 'made up' for her act." Gardiner made no mention of Edna in his biography of Gaby but, then, Edna did not become as big a star as Gaby did, and her career on the stage was rather brief.[12]

The Sporting Life magazine made mention of Edna's appearance in *The New Aladdin*, saying she had "created quite a sensation last spring at the Folies Marigny, Paris, as leader of the British Gibson girls." The journal also reported she had been "offered a part at the Saint-Martin [theater] in the Gallic version of the Drury Lane pantomime, *Cinderella*, recently successfully produced," but that she had declined to take the role in the play at The Gaiety. *Lloyd's Weekly* revealed the reason Edna had refused the role in Cinderella was she had not felt sure of her French. The review the newspaper gave Cinderella was generally good, but it was also said "they were given too much of a good thing and it was but a remnant of the original audience that saw the conclusion of the pantomime at one o'clock on Sunday morning. Five solid hours of amusement is too much even for pleasure-loving Parisians."[13]

The review given *The New Aladdin* in *The Stage* was not favorable. The critic wrote, "'The New Aladdin' is a weak, disappointing piece. There is plenty of rippling, pleasing music, which runs its course without being particularly impressive in any individual numbers ... [the play] commenced well and finished badly, dragged considerably. So far as story is concerned, the piece may be said to end with the first act. The second act in one of irrelevant turns, entertaining, do doubt, but only in a detached manner."

Publicity photograph of Miss Lily Elsie (author's collection).

The reviewer praised Lily Elsie, calling her "captivating and pleasing," and said she carried herself "admirably." Of Gaby Deslys he said, "She is a bundle, and a pretty one, of vivacity and expression," but conceded she did not have much of a singing voice. Edna's performance was not reviewed.[14]

Even before she was given the role in *The New Aladdin*, Edna had discovered the perks of being a show girl. Whereas most middle-class women in the Edwardian era were still restrained by strict social mores and conventions, which were introduced during the Victorian era, and which severely curtailed their liberty, showgirls and actresses had much more independence. This was primarily due to the fact these women made their own money and were not reliant on husbands or fathers for support. Frequenting casinos and gambling with strange men were not something most women of the Edwardian era due to the societal constraints placed upon them. *The Sporting Times* reported the previous summer, Edna had been frequenting the gambling tables in Ostend, Belgium. One evening, she had been quite fortunate, and had reportedly won £2,000. "The Duke of Orleans [Prince Phillipe], who followed the fair English girl's luck, presented her with a pearl and diamond ring as a souvenir of the occasion."[15]

Edna's fame was certainly spreading. On Saturday, September 8, her photograph had appeared within the pages of *The Illustrated Sporting and Dramatic News* alongside several other actresses. The paper identified Edna as being "of the light opera stage." The photograph was credited to Ellis & Walery, Ltd. In its November 10 edition, *The Illustrated Sporting and*

Prince Philippe, Duke of Orléans.

Dramatic News again featured Edna's photo alongside those of several other actresses including Billie Burke, Mabel Greene, and the Palace Girls—the chorus line which appeared at the Palace Theater where Miss Burke was performing. The caption below the photo read simply, "5. Miss Edna Loftus, who appears as Madge Oliphant in 'The New Aladdin' at the Gaiety Theater." Of course, the photos were nothing more than titillation for the largely male consumers of the paper, but it gives some indication how popular Edna was becoming in the British music hall scene.[16]

This is a good point at which to speak to the postcard business which flourished during this era. Don Gillan, who wrote about the history of the postcard for the website Stage Beauty, stated the postcard, as distinct from a letter, was first used in Austria in 1869, and was introduced in England the following year. "The idea behind their introduction was to provide a cheap means for brief communication" at a lower postal rate. By the following year, the postcard phenomenon had spread across Europe. In England, the first postcards were blank on both sides. The message was written on one side and the address on the other. These were issued by the post office and came pre-stamped. However, in 1894, the post office "relinquished its monopoly on the publishing of postcards, and allowed their private publication for use with an adhesive stamp." Suddenly, a new industry was born—the illustrated postcard.

However, as Gillan noted, the post office still insisted one side of the card be used for the address and the other for the message, which meant the space for the illustration was limited. It was not until 1902 that the post offices allowed the back of the card to be divided, with the address on one side and the message on the other. "This simple innovation of the divided back card led to a massive proliferation of the types of cards available as the publishers explored different subject matter." One of the most popular themes with the public was the theater. "Theatre cards encompassed photographs of theatre buildings, scenes from plays, and posed portraits of players. Of these, it was the actresses, who included some of the most beautiful women of the day, that sold the most."

"The theatre itself welcomed the advent of the photo postcard with open arms," observed Gillan. "It elevated many of their players to be the superstars of their day and made their faces instantly recognizable to the public at large, whether they had seen any of their plays or not. This fueled a desire to see their favourites in action which then swelled the box-offices at the many theatres," Edna's visage appeared on at least a dozen different postcards. As many of these show her in different outfits, it may be assumed she spent a good amount of time posing for photographers. It was well worth the effort, though, as monochrome postcards sold for two pence and hand-colored ones sold for three. "For the stars themselves," said Gillan, "it was a welcome form of extra income as the more financially astute among them signed often quite lucrative contracts with the postcard companies."

The upside of the postcard phenomenon for historians writing about Edwardian-era theater is that there are numerous images of these subjects which can be utilized to illustrate a book such as this one.[17]

"A fine portrait of Miss Edna Loftus forms the front piece of the *Illustrated Sporting and Dramatic News*," noted *The Belfast News-Letter* in its October 1 edition. The Irish newspaper also noted the other portraits featured in the journal, but it was Edna's photo that seemed to have caught the attention of the reporter.[18]

In November, there was a significant change in the cast of *The New Aladdin*, as Gertie Millar, who was originally slated to play the lead role, replaced Lily Elsie as *The Princess*. *The American Register* stated the authors had written the role with Millar in mind. Across the Atlantic, *The Philadelphia Inquirer* also noted Millar had succeeded Elsie in the play. The newspaper said, "When this play was produced at the Gaiety Theatre, Miss Edna Loftus made a successful appearance and showed that she is a charming a young actress as she is pretty." Above the notice was a large picture of Edna.[19]

The following month, *The Scotsman*, an Edinburgh newspaper, reported The Theater Royal was closed for the final rehearsals of John B. Howard and Frederick W.P. Wyndham's new pantomime, entitled *The Babes in the Wood*, authored by J. Hickory Wood. It was stated the production was being produced "under the personal supervision of F.W.

Edna Loftus on the cover of *Illustrated Sporting and Dramatic News* 1906 (author's collection).

Wyndham, and was to open on the 13th of December." The cast was to include Gwladys Elvey, Gladys Cooper. Mildred Claire, Daisy Dormer, Baby Betty Green, and Edna Loftus. This announcement ran in the newspaper's editions of December 3rd, 5th, and the 10th. On the 13th, it

Carte de visite of Daisy Dormer in *The Babes in the Wood*.

was announced the run of the play would commence at 7:00 p.m. at the Theatre Royal.[20]

The review for the new production, which appeared in the next edition of *The Scotsman*, was generally positive. "There has been so admirable a succession of pantomimes at the Royal. And the public expect so much there nowadays. That it must be increasingly difficult for the management to yearly go one better on previous efforts. In this task, however, Mr. F.W. Wyndham, with his large experience and genius for organizing this class of entertainment, seldom fails, and upon the success of his latest work of theatrical art, which was submitted last night to a crowded and enthusiastic house, he may be heartily congratulated." The newspaper went on to give a synopsis of the plot and praised the songs and dancing, the "pretty faces, handsome dresses, and well-designed scenery." Said the reviewer, "It is a pantomime which makes a hearty appeal to both old and young."[21]

The pantomime was based on a very old fairytale, first published in 1595 by Thomas Millington. The original story was about a villainous uncle who employs a couple of thugs to dispose of his orphaned niece and nephew, so he might obtain the fortune which the children are to inherit. The would-be murderers kidnap the children, and take them into the woods to kill them, but have a change of heart. Instead, the thugs quarrel, and the young children escape into the forest. Lost, the children continue to wander in the wilderness, starve, and finally perish. Not exactly a happy story, and certainly without appeal to music hall audiences, who preferred much lighter, more amusing entertainments.

To make the tale more palatable, in 1867, at The Covent Garden, the folk-hero Robin Hood was introduced into the story. After the children are abandoned in the wood, which became Sherwood Forest, Robin and Maid Marion find them, and take them back to the encampment. Maid Marion becomes their governess. The Sheriff of Nottingham takes the place of the wicked uncle, and Robin Hood's Merry Men (who were often played by women clad in close-fitting tights) provided a chorus and comic relief. In contrast to the fairy-tale, in the pantomime, the children are rescued, and returned to their rightful place, and the machinations of the wicked uncle/Sheriff are exposed.

As the Robin Hood legend predates the *Babes in the Wood* story by about 200 years, it is not certain how they became intertwined. However, because the storyline of *Babes in the Wood* is rather simplistic, the introduction of the Robin Hood legend, which English audiences were already quite familiar with added much needed drama and suspense to the original story. Also, the relationship between Robin and Marion added a romantic aspect, and allowed for musical "love duets."

Further, the inclusion of the Nottingham Fair scene in Act Two, and the famous archery contest, added a fair amount of action to the story.[22]

Edna, who had the part of the miller's daughter, Molly, was said to have played it "nicely." *The Era*, in its review of the production, which was also quite complimentary, said, "Miss Mildred Claire as Allan-a-Dale and Miss Edna Loftus as Molly, are a pair of captivating sweethearts." It is not known why Edna chose to leave *The New Aladdin* production at the Gaiety in London to appear in *The Babes in the Wood* in Edinburgh. Perhaps she saw it as a better opportunity. Certainly, she was receiving more press, her name being mentioned in every advertisement for the pantomime which appeared in the various newspapers.[23]

The Stage, a newspaper catering specifically to those who worked in theater and the performing arts, contained a column which advertised letters which they had received and were holding for various persons. The listing reads like a who was who of the music hall scene. On the 10th of January 1907, Edna Loftus' name first appeared on the list, indicating a letter or letters were being held for her at *The Stage's* offices at The Covent Garden, in London. Unfortunately, there is no further information available about these missives.[24]

On February 16, 1907, *The Era* announced that *The Babes in the*

The Theater Royal in Edinburgh, Scotland (on the left).

Winfield "Winnie" O'Connor in 1901 (author's collection).

Wood was in its closing weeks. "The company has worked well together," said the reporter, and went on to speak to the performances given by the various cast members. "Miss Mildred Claire as Allan-a-Dale, and Miss Edna Loftus as Molly have gained a host of admirers by their clever, charming acting."[25]

After *The Babes in the Wood* closed, the English newspapers carried no more news about Edna until December of 1907. At that time, it was announced in *The Sportsman* that Edna had married the American jockey, Winnie O'Connor, in June. The newspaper, which identified 19-year-old Edna as "an English lady," stated the couple had been married in Berlin, and O'Connor had taken his new bride back to New York on the French ocean liner *La Provence*. The correspondent, who was more interested in the activities of the jockey than those of his wife, said, "O'Connor ... has grown considerably since he rode here, and is evidently up in the ways and methods Continental." What the English newspaper failed to mention was how rough the journey had been.[26]

"The French liner La Provence," said *The Evening Star*, the Washington, D.C., newspaper, "which arrived in port today, ran into heavy weather on the way over." On Wednesday, November 27, the ship ran into a gale, and it was said Edna, who was standing on deck, was almost swept into the ocean. "Mrs. Winnie O'Connor, newly married, had a narrow escape from going overboard. She was swept from her feet and fell against the rail. A French sailor caught her just in time." *The Evening Star* noted Mr. O'Connor had been "riding with great success in France." Edna, who the newspaper stressed was not related to Cecilia "Cissie" Loftus—though it was said they were friends—had married the jockey on June 26 in Berlin, but they had to be re-married by the U.S. Consul-General, Daniel Harper, in Chantilly, France, "because they were of different religious faiths," O'Connor being a Catholic and Edna a Protestant.[27]

The Meridian Daily Journal and New York's *Standard Union* also picked up the story of Edna's near fatal mishap. The latter reported the incident in more detail, saying, "During one of the hardest blows, she went from the saloon to the promenade deck. The blast caught her, driving her along the deck for some distance, and then hurling her against the rails. A seaman went to her assistance as she was about to slide through the opening." None of the newspapers indicated that Edna had been injured in any way, but it must have been quite a harrowing experience for her.

The New York newspaper also expounded on Mr. O'Connor's successes on the track, saying, during the previous season in France, he had "ranked third in the list of winners, with 62 first and 250 second and third places to his credit." Edna was simply described as "a concert hall singer of Berlin." None of the newspapers disclosed where Edna had performed or made any mention of her previous successes in London, Paris, and Edinburgh. In the end, the U.S. newspapers raised more questions than they answered. Unfortunately, O'Connor, in his autobiography, did not elaborate on his relationship with Edna either. In fact, he did not mention her at all, as though she never existed.[28]

The steam ship's "alien" passenger manifest, which was completed November 23, listed Mr. Winnie O'Connor, age 25, occupation jockey, among the passengers aboard *La Provence*, which arrived in New York on November 30, having sailed from the port of Le Havre. Traveling with O'Connor was "Mrs. O'Connor (Edna)," age 22. However, in the column where her given name should have appeared, there was just the initial "J," and her occupation was listed as "none." It would appear, complying with the dictates of Victorian/Edwardian society, after marrying O'Connor, Edna had foresworn her previous occupation, that of an actress, to play the traditional role of wife and mother. Historian Amanda Wilkinson posited, "For most women, the luxury of being a housewife, simply caring for children, cooking and cleaning and creating a peaceful haven for the hard-worked husband who brought home the bread at the end of the day, was only ever an illusion created by the middle classes." However, for Edna, as part of the middle class, this "illusion" was a reality, and she accepted this was to be her life.[29]

According to his biography at the National Museum of Racing and Hall of Fame (into which he was inducted in 1956), Winfred Scott "Winnie" O'Connor was a runaway, who learned to ride under the tutelage of trainer William C. "Father Bill" or "Pa" Daly, who trained numerous other future Hall of Fame jockeys as well. O'Connor won his first race in 1896, and quickly achieved fame on the racing circuit in the United States. Reportedly, he won 117 races in 1900, and was ranked as the seventh best jockey in the country. "In an era when jockeys would perhaps receive a $50 gratuity for winning important races ... trainer John E. Madden paid O'Connor $10,000 win or lose, just to ride Yankee in the 1901 Futurity." O'Connor won.[30]

Tracing O'Connor's roots back a bit further, one finds he was born July 6, 1881, in Brooklyn, New York, to Francis H. and Annie O'Connor. Winfield was the third of four children born to the couple. He had two older brothers. Francis Jr. and Joseph, and a younger sister named Florence. The New York State Census of 1905 did not reveal the occupation of Francis O'Connor, Sr. The younger O'Connor stated his father was "both a broker and a skatorial king." His other two sons, Francis Jr. and Joseph were both employed as assistant foremen. Also residing with the O'Connor family was Mary Wells, a cousin, and Julia McCormack, a boarder. Even though Winnie O'Connor had run away from home in his youth, as has been asserted, the family must have forgiven his impulsiveness, and welcomed back, as evidenced by this 1905 census, which includes him as a member of the O'Connor household. Then again, by this time O'Connor had made quite a name for himself in the United States and Europe.[31]

In his dictated memoir, O'Connor admitted he only briefly attended the Brooklyn Public Schools, and "never got beyond the first school reader." In short, he was functionally illiterate. One might wonder, given Edna possessed a convent education and was fully literate, if this was a point of contention between them. After running away from home at the age of nine, O'Connor's grandfather. George, met with "Father" Daly, and gave permission for his grandson to work at the Brighton Beach track. O'Connor's first job was as a stable boy. "That meant that I could lead the runners around the ring and sleep in the stalls with them. Happy? I had the whole world in my pocket."

After apprenticing for a year or so under "Father" Daly, whom he described as "strict disciplinarian," O'Connor had his first race in Canada. He lost the race, but was not deterred. Soon after, O'Connor won his first race at the Aqueduct track in Queens, New York. Though it had been "Father" Daly whom O'Connor credited with teaching him all he knew, he admitted it was Alfred Featherstone, the bicycle manufacturing tycoon, who gave him his big break in the world of horse racing. Featherstone bought out the contract O'Connor had with "Father" Daly for $10.000. "Somehow, (Featherstone) had gotten the idea that I was about the best jockey in the world." O'Connor did not disappoint his new patron, winning 115 races during that season, 1898–1899, at the New Orleans fairground track.

By 1902, O'Connor was ranked fifth in rider standing in the U.S. That same year he signed a "lucrative contract" with Baron Alphonso James de Rothschild, the French financier and vineyard owner, to ride in races across the continent. He departed for Europe in the fall of that year. Unfortunately, O'Connor filled this part of his memoir with humorous anecdotes about steeplechases and the shenanigans of the expatriate jockeys, and provided little information otherwise. He did state that Chantilly, where he and Edna had a chateau, was "the prettiest place he had ever known." Since 1834, the Chantilly region was renowned for horseracing, and remains the principal equestrian training center in France.

From France, O'Connor went to Germany to ride for Carl von Weinberg, who made his fortune in dye manufacturing. Again,

O'Connor's narrative is filled with anecdotes, such as meeting the Kaiser and a sumptuous dinner he held at the restaurant in the Hamburger Hotel to which he invited twenty-five "horse-fanciers and race followers." He also spoke of visiting England, meeting King Edward VII. and his new interest in bicycle racing (which O'Connor was not particularly skilled at). It was during this period of his life that O'Connor met Edna, and had a child by her—a daughter—but he made mention of neither of them in his memoir. The child was most likely born after the couple's trip to the United States, as there is not a child listed as traveling with the couple on the passenger manifest from the *La Provence* in November of 1907.[32]

In February of 1908, Winnie O'Connor brought a $50,000 libel suit against *The Graphic*, a weekly newspaper published by Turf News Publishing Company of Manhattan. *The Brooklyn Daily Eagle*, which broke the story, stated O'Connor was represented by attorney Joseph J. Reither and said the action was being brought to the supreme court of King's County, though the newspaper did not give any details. It was expected the case would go to trial "some time within the next two years." In the interim, O'Connor was said to be planning to return to France for the racing season "but next year he plans to return permanently to this country and race a string of foreign-bred horses over the Jockey Club tracks."[33]

The Chicago Tribune reported that George Walker, an American horse trainer residing in Germany, had signed O'Connor to a contract to ride for the Weinberg stable for two years. "O'Connor," said the newspaper, "rode for the stable on 1906, being succeeded on 1907 by Willie Shaw." It may be assumed, when Winnie boarded the ship for Europe, Edna was with him, though none of the newspapers mentioned her.[34]

Florence O'Connor, Winnie's only sister, died on May 15, 1908, in New York, the victim of a "peculiar accident." Two years prior, while Winnie was riding in France, he had invited his mother, brother, and sister to join him there for a holiday, and spend a few months. "He and his sister were boon companions, and Winnie took her everywhere." One morning, they went shooting at a hunting reserve outside of Paris, "and, in drawing a bead on some sort of an animal, the gun held by Florence, who was quite a good shot, kicked and struck her on the chest. The blow was hard one and the girl collapsed."

Florence was taken to a hospital. Soon after, the vacation was ended, and the family returned to Brooklyn. "The French physicians said that cancer had developed, and when noted specialists [in New York] made an examination they confirmed this." Over the next two years, there were repeated operations, "and the once healthy and robust young woman became a mere shadow." A few weeks before her death, Florence was taken to the home of her parents, where she succumbed to the cancer. On Monday the 18th, her funeral was held at the Church of Our Lady of the Angels, and her remains were interred at Holy Cross Cemetery in Brooklyn. She was 21. Winnie, who was in Germany, was notified by cable of the death.[35]

There was a short article in *The New York Times* about a month after it reported Florence O'Connor's death, speaking to the expatriate jockeys in Germany. Winnie was named among several riders from the United States, Australia, and England who were to be there for the season. "Berlin sadly needs something which will elevate the sport of kings to the level it enjoys in other countries. The immense salaries which American riders and trainers this year, for the first time, are commanding here does more than anything else to induce turf patrons to reorganize the whole game on a better and higher level."

The newspapers in the United States, from New York to California, continued to report on Winnie O'Connor's success on the European racing circuit. Later in June, *The San Francisco Examiner* reported he had ridden *Sauge Pour Pres* in the prestigious Grand Prix in Paris, as did *The Brooklyn Eagle* and *The Winnipeg Tribune*. O'Connor finished second. In August, *The San Francisco Call* reported jockey Eddie Jones had returned to the states from Europe "According to Jones, Henry Spencer, Johnny Reiff, and Winnie O'Connor are riding well in Germany." Later in the month, O'Connor was named in *The Commercial Appeal* of Tennessee. It was stated he was in "the best form he has ever shown," and had "won nearly a million marks for the Weinberg Brothers." The following month, the newspaper reported O'Connor, aboard Faust, had clinched the Grand Prize at Frankfort-am-Main, and included a photo of the race. By the close of the season, in October, O'Connor was reported by *The Oakland Tribune* as being the third winningest jockey in Germany. On December 24, *The Tribune* reported that O'Connor had left Germany for India, "where he has an engagement for the winter." He was expected to return to France in the spring.[36]

And what was Edna doing during this year? There is no mention of her in the available newspapers of the United States, France, or the United Kingdom during 1908. However, some idea of what Edna's life was like during the brief time she was married to Winnie O'Connor may be derived from a gossip column item penned by Bert Dorman. Dorman was the London correspondent for *The Hartford Daily Courant*. In his column, dated August 5, 1909, he spoke of Edna in the most glowing terms:

> Mrs. Edna O'Connor, wife of Winnie O'Connor, the American jockey, known in stageland as Edna Loftus, has received some very flattering offers to return to the stage. Mrs. O'Connor is one of the most beautiful English women I have ever seen. She has a superb figure, a grand voice, and is one of the best gowned women in Paris. When you see her at the Longchamps races, she is the most admired lady on the course. Mrs. O'Connor is a charming hostess and is always pleased to meet friends at her chateau in Chantilly. She is a good shot, a great horsewoman, a fine bowler, an excellent angler and archer, and one of the best sportswomen I have ever met.

Dorman seems to have been on good terms with Mr. and Mrs. O'Connor, giving them mention in his columns several times between April and July of 1909.[37]

Judging by Dorman's accounts, Edna was enjoying a life of upper middle-class luxury. However, as Evelyn Nesbit observed, marriage meant an end to a show girl's freedom and autonomy. In her autobiography, Evelyn lamented, "For it [marriage] meant the end of all my high hopes and ambitions. Never again the thrill and excitement of opening night, the hard but congenial work, the smell of grease paint, the sense of freedom and self-reliance of the self-supporter. Simply because I was marrying a rich man, every one of my friends took it for granted that I was getting the breaks, that I was a very lucky girl." It will be recalled, Gaby Deslys had also warned Edna against marrying, saying Edna was throwing away a "wonderful chance."[38]

Despite appearances of domestic felicity in the O'Connor household, there was trouble, and its name was Miss Neva Aymar. *The Los Angeles Times* reported Joe Hart's "Rain Dears" vaudeville troupe had arrived back in New York on the afternoon of June 19, after a tour of England. However, the show's star performer, Miss Aymar was not on board the ship, even though her name was on the passenger list. The wardrobe woman, Mrs. Blanche Townsend, told the newspaper that Miss Aymar had broken with her two other suitors—pugilist James "Jimmy" Britt and Norman Dunbarton, son of Lord Dunbarton of Manchester—in order to marry Winnie O'Connor. "When urged to sail on the St. Louis, she sent a message reading as follows: 'It is impossible. Send my trunks to Paris. I am waiting for Winnie O'Connor to get a divorce. Then I will marry him.'"[39]

The San Francisco Call elaborated on the story, saying. Miss Aymar had been engaged to Jimmy Britt when she left for England with Hart's troupe. "Then came stories from London that Miss Aymar was engaged to the Hon. Lieutenant Norman Dunbarton, son of the earl of Dunbarton, who lives in Lancashire." When the news reached Britt, he traveled to London and "busted it up." After breaking up his fiancée's romance with Dunbarton, Britt took Miss Aymar to Epson Downs to see the races. It was to be Britt's undoing.

Miss Aymar bet on a horse ridden by Winnie O'Connor, and won a sizable sum. Afterwards, she asked to meet the jockey. "She got an introduction to O'Connor, who comes up to about the actress' waist, and lost her heart to him. Then she joined him in Paris." Francis Sullivan, the manager of Rain Dears, wired Miss Aymar, saying, "You must come. Joe Hart will meet you in New York. He wants you to go right out with the company," to which she replied with the "send my trunks" message. This article was reprinted nearly verbatim in *The Cincinnati Enquirer* the following day, June 21, 1909.[40]

This same day, in Mr. Dorman's column in *The Courant*, he stated Winnie O'Connor, riding *Sauge Pour Pres*, had won *Le Prix La Rochette* on June 16. "The race was won by the shortest of heads and the victory was due to the superior horsemanship of Winnie O'Connor." Dorman also revealed, the following winter, O'Connor was to star in a racing sketch called "Won and Lost," supported by the American comedienne "Miss Neva Aymar." There was no mention of Edna in any of the newspapers which carried the story.[41]

Two days after Dorman's column appeared, *The Leavenworth Post* stated a "big scandal" had developed in Paris over "fake fights," and heavyweight pugilist Jim Barry and Dorman, who was also a boxing promoter, were involved. "At least, this is the gist of the rumors that are floating to this country ... and Bert Dorman ... is accused of trying to get Jim Barry to fake a fight with the purpose, it is said, of trimming Winnie O'Connor, the American jockey, out of a sum of $3,000." The story turned out to be a canard, though Dorman indicated Barry had been involved in some underhanded activities. Dorman stated the Parisian sportsmen had had enough of Barry, "and the sooner he gets to carrying hod the better...."[42]

As the discerning reader may well have noticed, Mr. Dorman's column praising Edna, was printed in August, after the news that Miss Aymar was plotting to steal her husband away went public. First Dorman asserted he and O'Connor had joined forces and "shown Barry up in the letters to the *New York Telegraph*." A month later, Dorman is lauding Edna in his column. It must be assumed the rumor about Dorman attempting to cheat O'Connor was untrue, but what of the rumors about Neva Aymar? When did these initially begin to circulate?

Finally, in late August, Edna was given her day in the U.S. press. In a special dispatch to *The Cincinnati Enquirer*, it was reported she had arrived in New York from France on the steamship *La Touraine* on the 20th of the month. When confronted with the rumors, Edna "denied that she was going to ask for a divorce or separation from her husband as had been intimated in cable reports." Said Edna, "Our troubles are all due to a certain vaudeville actress [whom Edna named, but whose name the newspaper did not print]. She tried to separate Winnie and me, and when I see her I intend to horsewhip her." Needless to say, Edna's threatening to horsewhip Miss Aymar caused quite a sensation in the press. The story got as far as Kansas, being reprinted in *The Leavenworth Times*, under the byline "She'll Get It If She Doesn't Stop Talking About Mrs. O'Connor."[43]

Despite her denials that divorce was imminent, a very short notice appeared in the French newspaper *Le Journal* on September 24, which read: *Un divorce. Le tribunal civil de Senlis vient de prononcer par défaut le divorce entre le jockey bien connu Winnie O'Connor, et la dame Edna Loftus, aujourd'hui sans domicile ni residence....*[44]

From all appearances, it seems O'Connor and Miss Aymar waited until Edna had departed France before initializing divorce proceedings against her

"Cabinet card of Neva Aymar" (2021) (courtesy Cabell-Wayne Historical Society Vertical Files, Marshall University Special Collections, Huntington, WV).

Chapter Two. The High Life 41

on the grounds of her being without a home or residence, implying she was a vagrant, or worse. Sadly, as she was defending her marriage to the newspapers, Winnie was stabbing her in the back. Edna would later say the grounds for divorce were "desertion," but who deserted whom? Edna stated she had sailed for New York for the purpose of meeting with Mrs. O'Connor, her husband's mother, though she never did. Was Edna hoping Mrs. O'Connor would dissuade her son from throwing her and their daughter over for Aymar? If Edna was hoping to earn Mrs. O'Connor's sympathy, why did she not bring the child—Mrs. O'Connor's granddaughter?

Obviously, Edna did not learn O'Connor had divorced her until she had already landed in the United States. By then, it was too late to have Mrs. O'Connor intercede on her behalf with her husband. When she was asked if she had opposed the divorce, Edna replied, "No I never bothered." Instinctively, Edna must have known she had lost O'Connor to Aymar, and there would be no chance of a reconciliation. Further, as she had been indisposed at the time O'Connor filed for divorce in France, and had not appeared in court to answer the charges, the court found in O'Connor's favor. To challenge the decision of the court after the fact would have been extremely difficult, if not impossible. Edna must have understood this as well.[45]

There was no further news of Edna in the newspapers in England or the United States that year, nor any notice of the divorce. O'Connor was still making headlines for his riding abilities, but nothing else was mentioned. It is known he married Neva Aymar, and they remained together until her death in 1932. In his autobiography, published in 1930, two years before her death, O'Connor said about his wife: "She is one of the most agreeable women I have ever known, In the twenty-one years we have been married, she has never been anything but helpful and cheerful. The only debates I can start at home are with Winnie O'Connor, the long time jockey."[46]

In December of 1909, the U.S. newspapers began running a story about Winnie O'Connor's daughter, and the sacrifices he made for her. *The Muskogee Times* ran the story on the 18th of the month, W.C. "Pa" Daly, who had trained O'Connor, described the jockey in verse:

> "Just a tinge of wickedness,
> With a touch of devil-may-care;
> Just a little bit of bone and meat,
> With plenty of nerve to dare."

After proving himself to Daly at the Futurity and Brooklyn, O'Connor went on to become one of the greats of horseracing, but the newspaper revealed O'Connor actually hated racing. He had also tried his hand at boxing, acting, and cycling, but proved a failure at all of these. Always he was forced to return to the saddle to make a living.

As O'Connor had lately gained too much weight to continue flat racing, it was said he was going to take up cross country steeple chasing for Eugene Fischoff, a wealthy horse breeder and art dealer. "And for why?" asked the newspaper rhetorically. "Well, because 'Winnie' O'Connor desires to educate his daughter, Eileen, a sweet-faced little colleen about whom his every thought is wrapped. 'Winnie' was back of the door when they passed out the education stuff, but he is determined Eileen shall not lack that which he never had, and is risking his life daily to give the apple of his eye every possible advantage."

This story was subsequently published in *The Omaha Daily News* on December 19, *The Pittsburg Press* and *The Evening Mail* (Nova Scotia), on December 20, *The Brooklyn Citizen* on December 22, *The Tacoma Times* on December 30, and several others. What none of these newspapers bothered to address was the question of maternity. Who was Eileen's mother?

It is known Edna and O'Connor had a daughter together. In 1910, this was revealed by the press in the U.S., which also stated "the child [was] with Edna Loftus' mother in Lancashire." In 1913, Edna publicly acknowledged she had a daughter, saying, "How I long for my little girl. She is six years old now and I haven't seen her for nearly five years." This would imply she had not seen her daughter since 1908. At that time, Edna was still married to O'Connor. This being the case, it may be safely assumed the child spoken of in the article, Eileen, was Edna's daughter by O'Connor. The question remains: what became of Eileen Loftus-O'Connor?[47]

Also, in December 1909, there was a collision between two trains on the Lake Shore and Michigan Southern railroad in Pennsylvania. "Plunging forward through a blizzard at the rate of over sixty miles an hour, the eastbound New York Central Limited from St. Louis crashed into the rear of train No. 10 on the Lake Shore railroad," despite the fact a warning light had been placed on the track to alert the crew of the danger ahead. The engineer of the former train, L.M. Berger, had been unable to see the light due to the snow flurries. When he saw the lights of the No. 10, Berger applied the airbrakes, but to no avail.

Damage to the New York Central train was minimal, However, the engine hit the smoking car at the rear of the No. 10, killing three men, and injuring fifteen more, seven of them seriously. *The Newark Evening Star* reported one Miss Edna Loftus of New York being among the latter. She received a minor blow to the head. However, *The Detroit Times*,

The Morris County Chronicle, and *The Washington Times*, which also reported on the collision, all identified the injured woman as "Mrs. Edna Loftus." No further information was given.

Could the injured woman have been the former actress and wife of Winnie O'Connor? Certainly, Edna's name was fairly unique, but to state as a veritable fact the injured woman and our subject were one and the same person—especially at this remove—would be disingenuous.[48]

Chapter Three

Enter Harry Rheinstrom

The new decade began with no little amount of excitement for Edna. Having been unceremoniously jilted by Winnie O'Connor in September while she was out of the country, she virtually disappeared from the newspapers for about three months. What she was doing during this time is unknown, but certainly, having been left high and dry and without means by O'Connor, she was doing her best to make ends meet. Edna later stated she had joined a theater company which was performing *The Morals of Marcus*.

The four-act play *The Morals of Marcus* was written by William Locke, based on his novel of the same name. It is the story of a middle-aged ex-schoolmaster named Sir Marcus Ordeyne, who unexpectedly inherits money and a title. Walking through a park he finds a young girl, Carlotta, weeping on a bench. Carlotta is a former harem girl from Syria, who was brought to London for an arranged marriage, whose betrothed deserted her. Not knowing what else to do, Sir Marcus brings her to his home under the protection of his guardianship. Havoc ensues as Carlotta upends Marcus' carefully ordered life. The play opened in New York at the Lyceum Theater in August of 1909, with the American actress Marie Doro in the lead role of Carlotta, though she was only engaged for a few weeks' time. The show closed in early September. It is not known when Edna joined the cast or what role she was given.

It also seems as if Edna was reduced to acting as the Edwardian equivalent of a spokesmodel. It was said she took a hot air balloon ride with a man to promote a brand of wine. It should be remembered though that she did not have the name recognition in the United States that she had had in Paris and London. Edna had also been out of circulation for nearly two years, and many had forgotten her.[1]

Then in late November, fortune seemed to smile upon Edna. In an interview conducted in late December, she said, "I met [Harry A. Rheinstrom] about six weeks ago at a party." Rheinstrom elaborated on Edna's story, stating he had been in a restaurant in New York with a friend named Chuck Freeman, who was a reporter for a theatrical paper. "I saw this girl and thought she was the most beautiful I had ever seen. She didn't make much of a show of clothes then, for she didn't have them, but every one took a second look at her." Rheinstrom asked who the woman was, and Freeman offered to introduce him to "the pretty song-and-dance actress." Rheinstrom said, "I met her the next night; we went to where she lived. We were together a good deal after that."

Aside from his attentions, Rheinstrom lavished gifts upon Edna, including a "swell" sealskin coat, and a diamond ring, which he stated cost "$400 or $500." The smitten man readily admitted he had spent a "good deal of money" on Edna, "probably about $2,000" (this number would be inflated to $5,000 in other news reports). In answer to a query, Rheinstrom said, "I brought her here [to Cincinnati] and have been paying her expenses." Edna stated Rheinstrom had wanted to marry her in New York, "but I told him that it would be more honorable to wait until I met his mother." Various newspapers alleged the lovers "stopped at one city in the east" for three weeks before returning to Cincinnati together.

Postcard image of Edna Loftus in large hat (author's collection).

Publicity photograph of Miss Marie Doro.

The Commercial Tribune described their affair as "a lurid six weeks' session on New York's Great White Way" and referred to Edna as "a siren." The Cincinnati newspaper stated that Rheinstrom had spent $2,500 on Edna "and was determined to marry her, even though he knew that she had been through some of the shadiest experiences that come to women of her class in the metropolis." She allegedly had told him she was a singer and a dancer, and "never lacked engagements." When pressed to name the companies she had performed with, Edna said "they were too numerous for her to remember." Despite the condemnation of the press and others, Rheinstrom believed Edna to be "a woman of good moral character."

In fact, after meeting Edna, Harry Rheinstrom had returned to Cincinnati alone. He told his mother about Edna, "and he seemed infatuated with her." Mrs. Minna W. Rheinstrom, who was the widow of a distiller, Abraham Rheinstrom, claimed she had not opposed her son, and had not tried to stop him when he said he was going to return to New York. She stated that she had actually encouraged him to go. However, a Dr. Carl Hiller was called upon to accompany the young man, to make certain he did not marry Edna while he was visiting. The doctor later admitted that "he planned, in the event the young man tried to marry the girl, to place his watch in [Rheinstrom's] pocket and then cause his arrest in order to prevent the marriage."[2]

Why the Widow Rheinstrom exhibited such an immediate dislike is a matter of speculation. Years later, Evelyn Nesbit, the showgirl who became embroiled in the "Crime of the Century," namely the murder of her former lover, the architect Stanford White, by her husband Harry Thaw, observed in her autobiography that "In those far off days, people of the theater were more or less socially taboo." Performers and entertainers, especially women, were suspect, and regularly accused of impropriety and promiscuousness.[3]

Music hall historian Tracy C. Davis stated, "The notion persisted ... because Victorians recognized that acting and whoring were the occupations of self-sufficient women, who plied their trade in public places, and because Victorians believed that actresses' male colleagues and patrons inevitably complicated transient lifestyles, economic insecurity, and night hours with sexual activity." However, the Widow Rheinstrom's animosity towards Edna may have run deeper than a simple distrust of people of the theater.[4]

Upon returning to Cincinnati, Rheinstrom and Edna checked into the Havlin Hotel. They registered as Mr. and Mrs. Rheinstrom. Accompanying the couple were Captain Herbert H.B. Holland and his wife, Minnie. It is uncertain if the Hollands came from New York with them, if they were friends of Edna's, or exactly how they insinuated themselves into the lovers' lives. During an interview, Rheinstrom said of the Captain. "He's a mighty clever fellow whom I met a few days ago, He's interested in lumber lands down in Honduras, and wants to form a company, and make me President of it. He's got 5,000,000 feet of mahogany down there, and it looks good to me." However, judging by Holland's later actions, he was probably a grifter, trying to run a game on what he believed was a rich mark.

Rheinstrom did not visit his family upon his return to Cincinnati, but the rumor he intended to marry Edna soon reached his mother's ears, and she took immediate steps to prevent this. About noon on December 31, 1910, the Widow Rheinstrom appeared at the Probate Court in Cincinnati, accompanied by her son-in-law, Henry S. Fechheimer; Karl Kiefer; and the family attorney, A. Julius Freiberg. The widow told Probate Judge William H. Lueders that her son, Harry, "had suddenly gone insane...[and] she decided that it would be best to have him placed in an asylum or sanitarium." She went on to say her son had "delusions of grandeur," and he intended to marry a woman the family knew nothing about. The mother asserted Rheinstrom had overworked himself into this nervous condition.

The Widow Rheinstrom then swore to a lunacy warrant for her son, and this instrument was placed in the hands of Deputy Sheriff Albert "Al" Wecht to be served. The deputy quickly located his man at the office of the S. Kuhn & Sons Bank. Rheinstrom was taken into custody, and removed to the courthouse. His mother, not wanting her son to be incarcerated in the county jail, asked Judge Lueders for a special hearing. This was scheduled for 2:30 that very afternoon. While he was waiting, Rheinstrom was approached by a reporter from *The Cincinnati Enquirer*, with whom he spoke with at some length. "Well, what do you think of such a dirty trick against a man?" Rheinstrom asked the reporter, rhetorically. "It is all the fault of my relatives."

The reporter asked Rheinstrom what specifically was the matter. The young man replied, "Oh, I'm crazy. Can't you see?" while comically grimacing and moving his hands about in a sporadic manner. Then Rheinstrom grew serious, saying, "But, no, you can see how serious this thing is. It is all on account of the girl I love. They don't like her and they want to separate us. Well, my mother thinks that she is going to 'save' a son, but instead she's lost one, for I'll never have anything more to do with any of my folks. I cut them all out now. I may not have anything, but I don't care. I can get along."

The reporter then asked about the girl in question. Rheinstrom answered, "Oh, she's Edna Loftus. You know, of Winnie O'Connor, the jockey? Well, she's his divorced wife. She's a beauty. She's the most beautiful woman any one ever saw, and I'm crazy about her, and she is about me. We are entirely suited to each other in every way. Our tastes are the same and so are our dislikes. She's known all over the world—in London and Paris. Why, she was the scream. It's her beauty. She never enters a swell restaurant or hotel but what every one turns to look at her. She's a queen, and I don't see what she ever saw in me when millionaires and men with title have been crazy after her, while I haven't got a dollar."

When asked why his family opposed the union, Rheinstrom said, "The only reason that they are down on the girl is because she is not of my religion. She is a Catholic, but she is willing to accept my faith for me, even. She will do anything for me." The young man continued, "They may send me to an asylum, but they will find out that she will get even. She won't give me up, and I won't give her up." Rheinstrom continued, asking rhetorically, "Do I look like a crazy man? I have been managing a business here, and it has been booming too. This would be funny, if it wasn't such an outrage, and what makes it more serious is I believe that it is my mother's doings. They want me to break off with the girl." Rheinstrom then asserted he and Edna had been married in New York the day before Christmas. They had not.

The interview was interrupted by a telephone call from Captain Holland. After Rheinstrom's arrest. Holland had returned to the Havlin Hotel to inform Edna about what had happened to Rheinstrom. The two men spoke for a moment, then Rheinstrom asked to speak to Edna. He asked Edna to come to the courthouse, and she said she would. After the call was ended, Rheinstrom asked Deputy Wecht to escort him to the local barber so he might get a shave before the examination. While they were out, Edna and Mrs. Holland arrived by taxicab. She refused to speak with the reporters gathered there. When Rheinstrom returned, Edna was said to have greeted him "effusively." Rheinstrom's attorney, Froome Morris, was sent for, and the three of them spoke until the case was called to court. The reporter observed that Rheinstrom seemed completely lucid, albeit worried.

When interviewed by a reporter from *The Commercial Tribune*, Rheinstrom gushed over Edna. "Why, that girl knows more people in New York than anybody in this room knows in Cincinnati. She is immensely popular in theatrical circles and could have her pick of several rich men who wanted to keep her in luxury. I remember she made a daring ascension in a balloon with an agent for a well-known brand of wine, and got a great deal of notoriety that way."

Rheinstrom continued, "Many people have offered to take her on trips to London and Paris, but she refused. I had a hard time cutting out a young fellow named Gimbel, who belongs to the family that owns the big Philadelphia department store. The last three days Gimbel called her up twenty-five times on the long-distance phone and wanted her to come to him, but she stuck to me and I will stick to her." The reporter described Edna as "a striking young lady of about thirty and with more than ordinary good looks. She is a decided natural blonde of about medium height and has a fine figure." It was said she was wearing the sealskin sacque Rheinstrom had bought for her, a "fur hat trimmed in purple velvet," and rings on all her fingers.

The hearing began with testimony being given by H.S. Fechheimer and Attorney Freiberg, who both stated Rheinstrom's "main delusion" was that he was married to Edna. They also said he had "delusions of strength ... and had caused disturbances in hotels and cafes by his eccentricities." Allegedly, Rheinstrom had been ejected from a banquet being held at the Sifton Hotel, after he caused a scene, smashed some champagne glasses, and slapped a waiter. Additionally, Rheinstrom had stood one of his employees on his head "just because he became angry and wanted to show his strength." The two witnesses claimed he had cursed his own mother, and the family lived in fear of him. "He was a mild-mannered fellow up to a year ago, they said, and then he began to show signs of mental distress."

However, it seems that the family's concerns had more to do with financial liabilities than Rheinstrom's mental health. Attorney Freiberg testified that Rheinstrom had brought Holland to his office, and had proposed forming a company "to operate the Captain's lumber interests" in South America. After the meeting, Freiberg had investigated the Captain, and found "no one in the city seemed to know Holland, and that Rheinstrom had known him but a few days." Freiberg also said Rheinstrom had spent $200 on Edna and another $200 on Mrs. Holland at H. & S. Pogue's department store.

The Widow Rheinstrom, who *The Commercial Tribune* noted had dramatically dressed in mourning, was the next to take that stand. The newspaper alleged "the Widow was on the verge of a nervous breakdown and wept continually as she told her story." She stated the young man had "endeavored to take upon himself all of his father's work after the latter's death." She said he had handled the business "splendidly," but had overworked himself, "became nervous and irritable, and finally ... his mind was overbalanced." She further stated he became "Rough and uncouth to her and treated her most disrespectfully by frequently cursing at her." As to Edna, the widow claimed her son had only known her about a month, and "seemed infatuated," but she had not opposed her son when he announced he was going to New York before Christmas to see Edna. The reporter for *The Enquirer* observed Mrs. Rheinstrom had been in tears during her time on the stand.

Following the Widow Rheinstrom on the stand was Dr. Hiller, who stated he had accompanied Rheinstrom to New York, and revealed his plan to sabotage any attempt Rheinstrom made to marry Edna. The doctor stated Rheinstrom had talked of Edna incessantly during their trip, Though Hiller had returned from New York before Rheinstrom, he said he was convinced the couple had not been married.

Edna was the next to be called before the court, but refused to testify until the newspaper reporters were removed from the room. She began by giving a brief account of her life in Europe, and her sojourn to the United States. She stated that she had met Rheinstrom at a party six weeks prior, and insisted he was not insane, "and there was no reason for anyone thinking that he was." Under questioning, Edna admitted they were not married in New York, as Rheinstrom had asserted, but that they planned to be. "[Edna] was very calm and self-possessed while giving her testimony," said *The Commercial Tribune*, "and laughed at intervals as if something had struck her as humorous had developed."

It was further revealed that Freiberg, on hearing that they had been married, had investigated the matter only to discover it was not true. The family then sent notices to marriage license clerks in Cincinnati, Newport, and Covington, Kentucky, not to issue a license to Rheinstrom. Then the lunacy warrant was filed against Rheinstrom by his mother. After she had given testimony, Edna and Mrs. Holland returned to the hotel.

Rheinstrom then took the stand in his own defense. "He seemed perfectly sane," observed the reporter, "and nothing was noticeable save a rather exalted ego, which was much in evidence when speaking of his feats of strength or his business ability." First, Rheinstrom reiterated the story

Edna Loftus in *The Cincinnati Post*, January 1910.

Chapter Three. Enter Harry Rheinstrom

of meeting Edna in New York, and readily admitted showering her with expensive gifts. When asked if he had married Edna, he contradicted what he had told the reporter earlier, saying, "No, we're not married, but we are going to be to-day, if it will be possible." Rheinstrom, obviously smitten, continued on about Edna, saying, "I know that she is all right and no one can tell me anything against her."

He asserted that his friend, Chuck Freeman, who had introduced him to Edna, had also been enamored of her, and "then he began to run her down to me, thinking he'd get me out of the way. But I'm a pretty good judge of people and I know that what she tells me is true and that I can trust her." Rheinstrom said Edna had plenty of men chasing after her, including a millionaire named Grimball of Philadelphia, who had offered her $2,500 "to come to him." As evidence of Edna's loyalty, Rheinstrom stated, "Here I am without a dollar outside of what I earn and she's sticking to me."

When asked about his personal habits, Rheinstrom admitted to drinking, but not to excess. He did state he smoked between forty and fifty cigarettes a day, and for the past "several months" was unable to sleep more than four hours a night. He also admitted to drinking "considerable absinthe of late."

When questioned about the incident at the club, Rheinstrom said he had been invited to the "Senior Princeton stag," but had decided against going. Then he changed his mind, and went anyway, showing up, not in evening clothes, but in a grey suit. He said he sat down with the other attendees, "and they were glad to see me, and everything was all right until tomatoes were served." Rheinstrom said, when the fellow across the table from him cut into his tomato, seeds and juice squirted out, and all over Rheinstrom's suit. "I laughed, but the fellow next to me suggested that it would be a ____ of a lot of fun if I would hit the fellow back with my tomato. Well, I picked it up and threw it and it smashed him in the face alright. Then there was some doings and they tried to throw me out, but I was too much for the bunch of them and they decided that I could stay if I would behave."

His behaviors obviously caused further consternation among the guests and staff, as finally one of the waiters told him he would have to go. Rheinstrom said he slapped that man across the face, and then kicked over a tray full of champagne glasses, "and sent the mess flying up toward the ceiling." The police were called, and when Rheinstrom left the club, he was stopped on the sidewalk. "Yes. I met a policeman outside," he stated, "and he wanted to arrest me, but I told him he would get what he didn't want and lose his job, and he let me alone."

The reporter was on the money when he commented on

Rheinstrom's egotism, but, as will be seen, for all his bravado, Rheinstrom was not as tough as he pretended to be.

Judge Lueders then asked Rheinstrom if he did not think "he had better look into the antecedents of Miss Loftus before he went any further" in regard to the proposed marriage. Rheinstrom replied he was "satisfied with her and that they might be separated for a time, but would finally be married." At this point in the hearing, Drs. Davis and Kendig had a brief consultation. They agreed Rheinstrom was not mentally ill, and should not be confined to the Longview State Asylum. However, they did recommend, due to "overwork and worry, as well as abuses of living, that he should take a rest-cure somewhere." They informed Attorney Morris of their opinion, and another consultation was held between the attorney and Rheinstrom. In the end, the young man agreed to check himself into the College Hill Sanitarium "for a few days or even weeks."

A car was summoned, and, soon after, Rheinstrom and Attorney Morris, in the company of Deputy Sheriffs O.W. Finn and Albert Wecht, departed for College Hill. Upon his arrival, Rheinstrom asked that a message be sent to Edna to call at the facility the following morning. "As against this, the family telephoned strict orders to the physicians in charge not to allow anyone to visit him and especially refuse any woman admittance." The family also called the Havlin Hotel and settled the bill there, but stated that any further charges incurred by Edna and the Hollands would be their responsibility. "It is the belief of the relatives that if the young man is kept away from Miss Loftus for a few weeks and allowed to recover the strength of his nerves and mind, he will be weaned away from her."

The entirety of the estate of Abraham Rheinstrom had been left to the Widow Rheinstrom, and it was she who controlled it. The Rheinstrom business was continued, with sons Harry and James managing it. Rheinstrom received a salary of $7,500 a year. At a time when the average wage of a U.S. worker was between $200 and $400 a year, this was a princely sum. In addition, the family had accounts with many retailers, which Harry and James, and their sisters, Elsa and Ruth, could take advantage of. *The Enquirer* stated it was the intention of the Widow Rheinstrom to make an application to the Probate Court the following Monday, January 3, to have a guardian appointed for Harry. "If this is done, young Rheinstrom will be kept in restraint until he has fully recovered his health and has lost his desire for the young actress."

The newspaper went on to report "an exciting scene of the Rheinstrom story" had played out at the Hotel Havlin the day before the hearing. On the 28th of December, Edna and the Hollands had checked into the hotel and were assigned rooms 718 and 720. Mr. Holland, the newspaper said, was "a fine-looking fellow, apparently about 38 or 40 years of age, who dresses in the height of fashion and speaks with a decided foreign accent." However, it was also noted he had told "several conflicting stories about his residence and occupation." After arriving in Cincinnati, the trio had contacted Rheinstrom, and he called on them at the Havlin, and paid their bill through noon on December 31. "The trio at once proceeded to get busy."

According to *The Enquirer*, Edna and the Hollands visited H. & S. Pogue's first, and bought about $400 worth of goods, which they charged to the Rheinstrom account. However, at Burkhardt Brothers, on his own account, Captain Holland charged $30 worth of men's wear. Later that afternoon, Edna, "representing herself as Mrs. Rheinstrom," visited Herechede's jewelry store, where she bought three diamond rings and a diamond pin, worth $800. These too were charged to the Rheinstrom account.

"In some way, word reached the H. & S. Pogue Company of the proceedings against Harry Rheinstrom, and they swore out a warrant before Squire Myers ... for the replevin of the goods sold to Holland and the so-called Mrs. Rheinstrom." The warrant was given over to Constable Joseph Thon, who, accompanied by Harry Hess, the attorney for the Pogue Company, camped outside the rooms at the Havlin Hotel until the trio returned. "They first met Holland, who surrendered all he had. Later in the afternoon, Miss Loftus arrived, and the replevin yielded all the purchased goods." Edna then called the courthouse to ask after Rheinstrom. When she was told he had been taken to the sanitarium, "she uttered a loud scream and fell over in the arms of Constable Thon. She grew hysterical and abusive of those who had taken part in separating her from Harry and she was particularly vindictive against the young man's mother."

This was not the end to the drama at the Havlin Hotel. Among the items confiscated from Captain Holland were six suits of pajamas, a pair of slippers, two robes, six handkerchiefs, one suit, a pair of shoes, boot trees, a shirt, and six pairs of socks. "The goods were of the best quality," said the newspaper. "Fair Edna had $300 worth of goods, which had been charged to F.A. Rheinstrom, as follows: Three shirtwaists, three skirts, three ties, six collars, a fur coat, two traveling bags, one corset, one shirt, three combination suits, two gowns, and two hats, worth $45. Miss Loftus made a vigorous kick against surrendering the property, but when threatened with a warrant for arrest, she became subdued. In the woman's room was found another big lot of things which she would have bought but for the sudden interruption of her plans."

Someone contacted jeweler Frank Hereschede as well, inquiring whether the $800 worth of goods sold to Mrs. Rheinstrom had been paid for. He replied in the negative, and proceeded to swear out a writ of replevin "for the sparklers before Squire Meyers and Constable Thon." The newspaper reported the officers "had a hard time ... but after many tearful threats and protestations, Miss Loftus, who proclaimed that she was being cruelly wronged, turned them over to the constable, except one $300 ring, for which she had a pawn ticket."

Captain Holland was said to have been "much agitated over the turn of affairs." He claimed he and Rheinstrom were to go into the lumber business together, and claimed he had previously been in that business in Kansas City. However, he also stated he had been with the Holland Company, perfumers in Buffalo, New York, and presented the Havlin clerks with a pamphlet from said company. When told a replevin suit had been set for January 6, Holland became "greatly excited," and "insisted that the entire proceedings, including the incarceration of Harry Rheinstrom and the replevin suit, were high-handed and outrageous. Holland asserted that there would be something doing before the affair was over."

Despite Holland's pronouncement that he would secure Rheinstrom's release, "and take legal steps to maintain their rights," the newspaper reported that the trio had left town. This course of action was proceeded by Captain Holland being told by the authorities, that, unless he departed immediately, a warrant would be issued for his arrest. "He concluded that it was best to make a quick get-away." *The Enquirer* was mistaken in its reporting, as only the Captain seems to have left town. Edna and Mrs. Holland remained in Cincinnati.

As to Edna, the newspaper said she was "a handsome woman," who bore "a striking resemblance to Evelyn Thaw [née Nesbit], of which fact she is proud." Though she passed herself off as being married to Rheinstrom, when pressed about the matter in court, she admitted the truth, and stated she was the former wife of Winnie O'Connor. The reporter then took a swipe at Edna, saying, "She is evidently an English woman, as she drops and adds her 'h's' in the approved Cockney style."

Since splitting with O'Connor and traveling to the United States, had Edna become a grifter, as the Hollands seemed to be, or did she, as Rheinstrom's fianceé, feel she was entitled to use his accounts at the stores she visited? Perhaps a bit of both. Had she simply been purchasing things for herself, it would be easy to dismiss the incident as an overblown sense of entitlement on her part. However, the fact that Holland had also bought numerous items on the Rheinstrom account gives credence to the argument she was teamed with the Hollands and was on the grift. Then again, after being left high and dry by O'Connor, when he divorced her *in absentia*, Edna was obliged to do what she could to make a living. The fact she pawned one of the pieces of jewelry indicates she was in dire financial straits. Edna did indicate she had been part of an acting troupe, but she did not enjoy the name recognition in the states she had in England and France, so it may be assumed she was cast simply as a chorus girl, and being a chorus girl was not going to keep her in the style she had become accustomed to during her time on the stage and her marriage to O'Connor.

The news of the Rheinstrom-Loftus affair was reprinted in newspapers across the Eastern Seaboard, from Connecticut to Michigan to Tennessee. Even *The Stage*, a theater periodical published in London, picked up the story. Oddly, the paper identified Edna, not as an Englishwoman, but as "an actress hailing from New York." Of course, it had been a few years since Edna had appeared on an English stage, and the press and public had largely forgotten about her.[5]

The following Monday, January 3, there was a new development in the affair, as Edna countered the Widow Rheinstrom machinations by presenting a writ of habeas corpus to Judge John O'Connell to procure her lover's release. News of this latest act in the drama was disseminated across Ohio, and the rest of the United States by the United Press. *The Cincinnati Enquirer* again printed the most comprehensive story of what occurred, beside a large, if rather unflattering, picture of Edna in a shirtwaist and dark skirt. On January 4, the newspaper summed up the events of Monday and Tuesday thus:

> First came a writ of habeas corpus, secured by the woman in the case, demanding the release of Rheinstrom from custody. This was followed by an application by the relatives to have Harry S. Fechheimer appointed as guardian for the young man. On the heels of this came an entirely unexpected move on the part of the relatives, which resulted in warrants being sworn out for Miss Loftus and her friends, Captain H.B. Holland and his wife, May Holland [*sic*].

The complaint was filed by attorney Rufus B. Smith and G.W. Werden, who was described as a "trusted employee of the Rheinstrom Brothers Company."

If the affair had heretofore been of primarily regional interest, the arrest of Edna and May Holland on a charge of "loitering," a common charge used by the police when they wanted to detain prostitutes or gamblers, made the story much more of a sensation. News of the arrest was carried by *The Lincoln Star*, *The Boston Globe*, *The Tennessee Journal and Tribune*, *The Baltimore Sun*, *The Washington Times*, the *New York Tribune*, *The Chicago Tribune*, *The Tampa Tribune*, and numerous others, which had previously had little interest in the drama unfolding in Cincinnati.

As the report was carried by the United Press, and their information was sketchy at best, it was stated Edna and Mrs. Holland were arrested for "vagrancy." Edna, it was said, "became hysterical when arrested and professed that she was penniless." This was an exaggeration, but this was the age of yellow journalism after all, and the more sensational a story could be made, the better it sold.

The application for guardianship was the first order of business brought before the court when it reconvened on Monday. Deputy Wecht was detailed to serve Rheinstrom the papers for this, as well as the writ of habeas corpus, and to bring the young man to the courthouse. Initially, the guardianship hearing was scheduled for Friday, January 7, but as the attorneys and Samuel and Harry Fechheimer were present in Judge O'Connell's court, it was decided the hearing should proceed. Attorney Smith opined that the court had no jurisdiction, as the matter had been heard the previous Friday before Judge Lueders, who had continued the insanity investigation. Attorney M.C. Lykins, who was representing Edna, countered, stating no order had been made committing Rheinstrom anywhere. Judge Lueders had told Rheinstrom he would not commit him "because of the stigma attached to such a step," but told the young man he would have to agree to admit himself to the sanitarium.

Lykins then addressed the court, saying,

> We have no fears as to the outcome of any lunacy investigation, for the young man is as sane as anyone here.... This is purely a religious difference. The young man is a Hebrew and Miss Loftus is a Gentile, and the members of the family have declared that they would rather see him dead than married to a Gentile. Just because the young man has fallen in love with this woman, and she has returned that love, they are harassing her in every possible manner. They have ordered her to get out of town, and have threatened to have her arrested; in fact, a warrant is out for her now, charging her with loitering. That is the conduct in Russia, but not recognized by the courts here!

Lykins made a motion to stop the proceedings until Rheinstrom had arrived. "I want the Court to see him; to talk to him; and then judge." Judge O'Connell concurred, but stated he would "not presume to pass on a man's sanity from merely talking to him myself." He said nothing further could be done until the Probate Court had concluded its investigation.

"Judge, may I speak?" asked Edna, who had been in the courtroom watching the proceedings.

Judge O'Connell allowed this. "Judge," exclaimed Edna,

Chapter Three. Enter Harry Rheinstrom 57

This is an outrage. I think that my position is outrageous. I have been called an adventuress and have been accused of trying to take Harry's money. I am denied the right to see him or even talk to him over the telephone. He is not insane, and I know it. They have arrested him merely because he loves me and I love him. If this case is continued, what am I to do? I came to the city from New York, with Harry, in good faith and we were to have been married last Friday night. Now I have no friends here and everyone seems against me. His family objects merely because I am a Gentile and he is a Jew. He is not crazy, but he will be if he is kept in that sanitarium, and so will I.

The reporter for *The Commercial Tribune* recorded Edna's statement differently:

Judge, this is an outrage, this way I have been treated [Edna had been put under arrest immediately upon entering the courthouse by Detectives Pflug and Hueftlein]! Harry loves me and I love Harry. I came to Cincinnati in good faith to see his folks when he asked me to marry him. I am not to see him? He is not crazy, but he will be if he is kept in a sanitarium. I am nearly crazy myself. I am threatened by this strange man and then another. They say they will arrest me for nothing. It is outrageous! I know no one here. Where am I to go until Monday? Why can I not see him?[6]

In fact, the North American Jews have a Yiddish word for Gentile women who have attracted a Jewish man. The term is "shiksa." It is derived partly from the Hebrew term שקץ (shekets), meaning "abomination," "impure," or "object of loathing." Typically, the term is a pejorative. An 1890 slang dictionary defines shiksa as of "a certain class of the demi-monde." Journalist Ariela Pelaia stated, "The shiksa represents an exotic 'other' to the Jewish man, someone who is theoretically forbidden and, thus, incredibly desirable." However, the shiksa is seen as a danger to the very foundations of faith and the family by the Orthodox Jewish authorities. "The possibility of a non–Jewish woman marrying into a Jewish family has long been seen as a threat," observed Pelaia. "Any children she bore would not be considered Jewish, so that family's line would effectively end with her."

Just as Edna finished her plea, Deputy Wecht arrived with Rheinstrom. Upon seeing one another, they started toward each other, but Rheinstrom demurred, and greeted her with a simple "Hello, dear." *The Enquirer* reporter remarked that Rheinstrom "looked peculiar, and his eyes had a staring, sleepy expression," as though he were drugged. *The Commercial Tribune* also noted Rheinstrom "looked weary and dazed." The reporter stated, "He recognized the girl of his choice ... but seemed afraid to make any move towards her." Attorney Frieberg, who had accompanied Rheinstrom into the courtroom, positioned himself between the young man and Edna. Rheinstrom then took a seat beside

Attorney Lykins, and Edna seated herself on the other side of the table. "She smiled and spoke to him, but his smile was peculiar, and he seemed trying to avoid being seen smiling at her."

Lykins appealed to the judge, asking him to speak with Rheinstrom, but the Judge stated it was not necessary, as the case would be heard the following Monday, and judged on its own merits. When Rheinstrom asked if he might speak to Edna, the Judge stated he was in the custody of the Sheriff's department, and the Court could make no order in this regard. Rheinstrom then stood and approached the bench. "Judge," he said,

> I want to speak with you. I am not crazy. When I was in Court Friday, I was nervous, but I have had plenty of sleep since then and I am alright now. I am in love with this girl and she is in love with me. She's the sweetest girl in this world and as true as my mother. This is too hard on her. I'm 26 years old. What's the reason I cannot speak to her? She is not an adventuress. I am broke and she knows it. She's not going to take any money away from me. She knows that I haven't got a dollar in this world. It isn't right that I should be held this way. Can't you order me released?

Judge O'Connell replied in the negative, saying Rheinstrom could not speak with Edna, and he would have to go with the deputy.

Dejected, Rheinstrom turned away, and walked to the door flanked by Deputy Wecht and Attorney Freiberg. Edna stood, and approached her lover with open arms, but he was quickly hustled out the door, it being reiterated there would be no communication between them. Edna "came reeling back into the courtroom. Bailiff Brown caught her and assisted her to the Judge's private office, where she remained." Rheinstrom was loaded into a waiting car and taken back to College Hill.

The Enquirer reporter did observe Rheinstrom speaking to Edna once during the proceedings. Allegedly he leaned over, and told her, "Never mind, little girl. It'll come out all right."

Meanwhile, Police Detectives Pflug and Heutftlein had been waiting outside the courtroom with a warrant for Mrs. Holland's arrest. Mrs. Holland, who had accompanied Edna to the courthouse, was seen leaving the building. Detective Heutflein observed her, and followed her out into the street, and arrested her. Mrs. Holland was taken directly to the Central Police Station. "She wept and pleaded, declaring she had never been in such a predicament before, and that it would ruin her." The newspaper stated she was a member of a prominent family. Mr. Holland had left town, but Mrs. Holland had remained behind to assist Edna in getting Rheinstrom released. The women had engaged Attorney Lykins on Saturday, the day after the first hearing, but nothing more could be done until the court convened on Monday.

Chapter Three. Enter Harry Rheinstrom

Knowing the detectives were waiting for her in the hallway, Lykins met with Edna in the judge's chambers, and arranged a bond for her release. When the detectives finally appeared, they took no overt action, and simply escorted Edna and her attorney back to the Central Station. At the station, Edna gave her name as "Edna Loftus," and stated she was 23 years of age, and had been born in England. The women's bond was set at $100 each, and this was immediately paid by William Seeds, the bondsman Lykins had engaged. "Mrs. Holland was beside herself with joy until the desk Sergeant informed her that she would have to be in Police Court [the following morning]. Then she broke down again and wept."

Mrs. Holland and Edna were escorted into the office of Police Chief Paul Milliken, where they were briefly interviewed by the Chief and Detective Chief Crawford. "The officers were rather favorably impressed by the actions of the two women." Afterwards, Edna made a brief statement to the press, saying, the whole thing was like a horrible dream to her. "I would like to dramatize it all, and I could play the part without rehearsing it." Lykins assured the reporter there would be more developments in the case of Rheinstrom, and Edna would be seeking redress for her arrest in the courts.

The attorneys for the Widow Rheinstrom alleged a woman, who remained unidentified, had called on the Widow saying she had

Chief Paul Milliken and unidentified dog (courtesy the Greater Cincinnati Police Historical Society).

overheard two women talking in a café. Allegedly these women said they were going to get a lawyer and file a writ a habeas corpus to have Rheinstrom freed. The two women supposedly said they expected to make a lot on money out of it. The caller "also advised Mrs. Rheinstrom to meet her at the Traction Building [on Monday] morning." The mystery woman was met at said place, not by the matriarch, but by an unnamed relative of the family. The mystery woman was said to have been dressed in green, and a proposition was made regarding money. The details of this proposition were not disclosed. The mystery woman then left. The relative followed her. However, when the woman realized she had a tail, she boarded a streetcar, eluding the shadower. The implication was either Edna or Mrs. Holland had tried to extort money from the Rheinstrom family.[7]

On January 5, *The Commercial Bulletin* reported that Edna had moved out of the Havlin Hotel and it was rumored she had left Cincinnati. However, Attorney Lykins explained,

> Miss Loftus left the hotel simply to avoid the annoyance and unpleasantness. The notoriety has been very distressing to her, and she felt very much humiliated, and on that account it was decided she should remove to a place where she can have some quiet and be free from disturbances. She is in the city and will remain here.... There has been no thought of her going away. [Edna said] I have no intention of leaving Cincinnati until I see Harry released and justice meted out for this outrageous business. I have friends who will see I get justice.

It was not disclosed where Edna had moved to.[8]

The following day, under the headline "Freedom Given to Miss Loftus," *The Cincinnati Enquirer* provided the details of Edna's appearance in Police Court on the charge of loitering. The courtroom was reportedly thronged with people, all hoping to get a glimpse of "the young actress who came from New York to marry Harry Rheinstrom." In fact, it was so packed in the courtroom, Edna and Mrs. Holland chose to stand in the corridor outside, near an open window "to escape the gaze of the crowd and get some fresh air."

Rufus Smith and Froome Morris, the prosecuting attorneys, made a motion to have the case postponed, as they claimed to have witnesses coming from New York and Dayton, Ohio. Police Judge August H. Bode replied, saying Judge Smith had called him Tuesday night with the same request, and it had been refused. "I must make the same refusal to you," said the Judge.

> These women were arrested on a warrant charging them with being loiterers on the streets day and night, without visible means of support, and unable to give a good account of themselves. Whatever testimony you bring from

Chapter Three. Enter Harry Rheinstrom

Dayton or New York or other cities cannot, in my opinion, have any bearing on this case. Your witnesses certainly cannot be in possession of competent testimony as to what these ladies have been doing in the past 48 hours. Proceed with the case.

At some point during the proceedings, Attorney Lykins asked, "Is this Mr. Froome Morris, the attorney for the Rheinstroms?" The Judge answered in the affirmative. Edna, with tears in her eyes, blurted out, "And you have been Harry's lawyer for so long have you not?" "Oh, yes..." began Morris. Edna's eyes flashed, as she half-whispered, "Oh yes; but you went back on him didn't you?"

The reporter observed Morris "reddened up to his ears and coughed nervously."

The first witness called by the prosecution was J.W. Werden, but he was not present in the courtroom, and could not be found outside. In frustration, Judge Bode barked to the officers of the court: "If the prosecuting witness, J.W. Werden, is not in this court, send to Rheinstrom's place of business, where he is employed, and have him come immediately. If he does not come willingly, take means to bring him here at once. I will have no trifling with this court." Judge Bode then declared a recess while the officers went to fetch Mr. Werden. About noon, after Werden was delivered, the court reconvened. Werden was put on the stand, but "declared that he knew nothing about the prisoners, other than what had been told him by attorneys Smith and Morris in addition to what he had gleaned from newspaper reading." He stated further he was only an employee of the Rheinstrom Brothers, and had no stake in their business.

The prosecution proceeded to call to the stand A. Julius Freiberg, Simon Fechheimer, and Charles J. Freidman, who claimed to be a newspaperman from New York. Their contrived testimony was a blatant attempt to besmirch Edna's character, and paint her as a gold-digging woman without morals. This strategy was overruled by the Court, who observed that the men had "no competent testimony to offer." The best they could do was prove Edna was a divorcee, which also had little relevance to the case.

In presenting the defense, Attorney Lykins simply put Edna on the stand. Her performance was first rate. "We are not loiterers," she said, with tears welling in her blue eyes. "I came to Cincinnati with Harry and Captain and Mrs. Holland and we registered at the Havlin Hotel. Harry insisted that I register as his wife and, as we were to be married, I complied. He gave me $50, and Captain and Mrs. Holland have the money." This was the extent of her testimony. The prosecution attempted to besmirch Edna's character by bringing out the fact she was previously married to Winnie O'Connor and had only been divorced six months. Judge Bode stated this was an irrelevancy.

Mrs. Holland followed Edna in the witnesses' box. She was rather reticent, saying only that she was a married woman, and dependent on her husband for financial support. She did state that she had enough money for her "immediate needs." After observing "there was not a particle of evidence to prove the assertions of the complainant," Judge Bode turned to Edna and Mrs. Holland and said simply, "A motion for dismissal is in order, and you are both free."

A photographer for *The Cincinnati Post* was able to snap two photos of Edna, which appeared on the first page of the newspaper's January 4 edition. The first photograph showed Edna and Mrs. Holland standing between two officers of the court. What is remarkable about the photo is it shows how diminutive Edna really was. Everyone is about a head taller than she is, even Mrs. Holland. Gaby Deslys had good reason to call her "petite Edna." The second photo was a portrait in which Edna is wearing a large hat with a white ostrich plume and what looks to be a fur

Miss Loftus and Mrs. Holland as They Appeared in Police Court Tuesday

The to picture shows Mrs. Holland on the left, Miss Loftus in the center and Attorney Lykins on the right, flanked by court officers.

Attorney M.C. Lykins, Edna Loftus, Mrs. Minnie Holland, and unidentified police officer in court from *The Cincinnati Post*, January 1910.

Chapter Three. Enter Harry Rheinstrom 63

coat. The reporter from *The Post* also got an exclusive statement from Edna. Under her picture was the headline "My Heart is Broken," Says Miss Loftus, "But I'll Forget."' Edna was quoted as saying:

> I still love Harry in spite of everything that has happened to crush out our romance. I believe that we will yet get each other. I will never lose hope. The only message that passed between aHrry [sic] and me as we sat in the courtroom Monday was his injunction "Keep up hope." It was sent to me silently. I saw only the motion of his lips, but I understood.
>
> I met Harry in New York seven weeks ago. It was love at first sight. I can speak for myself, and I know what Harry told me. The very night we met he whispered to me, "I love you."
>
> He said at that time that we should wait two years before we were married. I told him that suited me perfectly. Then he left me and returned to Cincinnati. Three weeks later, I received a long distance telephone message from him to meet him at Dayton.
>
> I did not wish to make the long trip, but he insisted, and I came all the way from New York, and spent Sunday in Dayton with him. I returned home the same evening to New York, and he went back home. A week later, Hary [sic] came to New York.
>
> He wanted to get married there, but I preferred to come to Cincinnati and meet his people. He seemed so much more honorable. So we came to Cincinnati, and then my troubles began.
>
> My heart is broken over the affair. It is for aHrry's [sic] as well as my own that I am determined to stay here and fight. I know he loves me. He told me that he never could be loved as I have loved him. It is no disgrace where love is concerned. Love will conquer.

The article was attributed to Edna directly, and beneath it was a facsimile of her rather loopy signature.

Outside the courtroom, Edna was asked about her life prior to coming to Cincinnati. She replied,

> I was born in England and my parents are well-to-do respectable people. My family has been connected with the stage for years and some of my relatives are high up in the profession. I would rather not mention any names, for there is no reason for dragging them into print. I was 16 years of age when I first went on the stage and played ingénue parts in London and the provinces. I learned to dance, but I do not follow that particular line, and am not a professional dancer, as has been stated. I was in England for about a year, when I went to France and remained for about three years. It was there that I learned to dance, while studying the language. Later, I took part in a number of French dramatic productions. I have been to Australia and many parts of the world. I was to have left for England to-day, but my meeting Harry Rheinstrom changed my plans. I will not leave now until I have cleared my name and seen the man I love given justice. Harry wanted to marry me in New York, but I told him that it would be more honorable to wait until I met his mother. That's why we came to Cincinnati and trouble.

Mysterious interest was taken in in our affairs by persons outside of the family and spoiled our plans. I am not a "woman with a past," and I know that no one can say a thing to stain my character, unless a conspiracy would bring up such a thing falsely.[9]

The Enquirer picked up the story again the following day, stating it was likely Rheinstrom would be freed within the next twenty-four hours, if not sooner. Apparently, some sporting men in the crowd which had gathered at the courthouse were actually taking bets on the outcome, giving five-to-three odds, "but no takers appeared." After speaking with the press the day before, Edna engaged a second attorney, C.H. Jones, and, when she and her legal team appeared before Judge O'Connell in the Probate Court in the habeas corpus proceeding, the motion was summarily withdrawn. A second writ was secured from Judge Warner of the Insolvency Court. It was further revealed Edna had retained the law firm of Littleford, Frost, & Foster, and it was under their auspices this bold move was decided upon. "The former habeas corpus proceeding had been continued by Judge O'Connell until [Monday, January 10th], in order to give the Probate Court an opportunity to complete its hearing.... This was not deemed satisfactory, and the new writ was secured."

The hearing on the new writ was scheduled for three o'clock that afternoon. When Attorney Freiberg learned of this, he hired a fast automobile to drive the sanitarium and "spirit Rheinstrom away from the place" before Deputy Sheriff Wecht could serve the papers. Unfortunately for the Rheinstrom family, their attorney's plans were for naught. Being apprised of the plans of Freiberg by Attorney Amos Foster, Deputy Wecht called the sanitarium and ordered the staff, under penalty of law, not to release their patient to anyone but him. Soon after, Wecht arrived at the facility, served the papers, secured Rheinstrom, and drove him back to the courthouse.

Edna arrived at the courthouse before Rheinstrom, in the company of Mrs. Holland, her attorneys, and a man with a cut beside his right eye. George F.E. Mulqueeny was his name, and he had, until the day before, been an attendant at College Hill Sanitarium. When Rheinstrom was admitted, Mulqueeny was assigned to watch over him, and escort him wherever he went. The two took a walk together, and when they reached the town of College Hill, Rheinstrom asked Mulqueeny if he would be allowed to telephone Edna. Mulqueeny allowed this, and "quite a little talk was had over the phone, and arrangements were made later whereby Miss Loftus and [Mrs.] Holland were whirled out to College Hill in an auto with Attorney Lykins, and there a short conference was had between the two young lovers." Mulqueeny's machinations

Chapter Three. Enter Harry Rheinstrom

Edna Loftus and George E.F. Mulqueeny from *The Commercial Tribune*, January 1910.

on behalf of Rheinstrom were discovered, and he was subsequently discharged.

Beneath a photograph of Edna and a smaller inset photo of the mustachioed Mulqueeny, *The Commercial Tribune* recounted the story of Mulqueeny's subterfuge on behalf of the couple. The newspaper described the former nurse as "a gallant and chivalrous man" and a "brave and gallant soul." After the phone call was made, it was reported an automobile arrived on the scene.

> "I want to talk with Mr. Blank," said a sweet voice from inside the tonneau, and before the astonished (Mulqueeny) knew what was talking place, the radiant sweetheart of Rheinstrom stepped from the machine, and pressed a note into his hand, asking him to deliver it to the young man." [Mulqueeny, who was interviewed for the story, said] "What could I do when a fair lady asked me to do her favor like that? I knew it meant my position to deliver the sweet missive and my peace of mind not to. I decided to let the job go plunk and save my piece of mind, so I did the fair one's bidding. I can get another position, but I would be afraid to meet my sainted ancestors with the crime of refusing the request of a distressed lady on my soul." The interviewer called Mulqueeny a "gentleman of the old school."

Edna was also interviewed by a reporter from *The Commercial Tribune* the evening before the hearing.

> "I love Harry with a pure and unselfish affection that makes me want to be more to him than anything else in this world," she said in her quaint little English accent. "I would work my hands to the bone to make him happy, and the only thing I am afraid of now is that he will cease to care for me because of all this trouble of which I have been the unwitting cause. Why, I wouldn't cause him anything to worry about for anything in the wide, wide world. I told him today that his poor old mother's heart was breaking, and that if he would agree to it, I would wait until she softened toward me, but he wouldn't hear of it for a minute." "I love mother," he said, "but she has lost me now when I need her most by turning on the woman I love."

Edna continued, saying, "I would give him up to save his poor mother, even though it would break my heart to lose him."

The reporter observed, "The continuation of the legal tangle ... has proven the old adage with respect to true love having a rough road to travel...." Little did he know how rough the road would eventually become for Edna and Rheinstrom.[10]

When the case was finally called at 3:00 p.m., Attorney Freiberg immediately asked that Rheinstrom be separated from Edna, with whom he had been talking, "declaring his fear that the young man would become excited and that he might do something." As absurd as the attorney's assertion was, it was sustained, and Deputies Wecht and Finn, as well as Lykins took places between the couple. However, during the proceedings,

Rheinstrom, Free, Embraces Girl; Are Refused a Marriage License

Edna Loftus and Harold "Harry" Rheinstrom in court from *The Cincinnati Post*, January 1910.

the deputies and the lawyer "obligingly stepped aside so that the young couple could gaze lovingly at each other and even whisper a few words."

The family attorney, Rufus Smith, began by asking for a continuance, claiming he had not had time to prepare his case and contending that the new habeas corpus proceeding was a "discourtesy to both the Probate Court and Judge O'Connell." Attorney Littleford countered, stating O'Connell had endorsed the dismissal of the case in his court, "and was glad to be rid of it." He noted the Probate Court had no right to commit a person to the custody of a relative, and only had the right to commit insane persons to Longview Hospital. The attorney further declared, when a man's liberty was at issue, there could be no "discourtesy." Littleford declared,

Whether this man consented or not to go to a sanitarium I am not prepared to say, but if he was sent to the sanitarium under a threat that he would be committed to Longview if he did not consent, then he is still under duress. For them to come before this Court and ask to hold this man until they find evidence against him is a palpable outrage, and the fact that there is great wealth at the back of this does not alter the case, nor excuse anyone. If this man is insane, he must be confined in the place which the law says he shall be sent to.

With a broad sweep of his arm toward the attorneys assembled by the family, Littleford declared, "These people have caused (Rheinstrom) to be incarcerated with a lot of crazy people on the ground that he is thought insane. If the probate court has done this, there is no law in the land to uphold it." He then went on to cite the relevant statutes. Littleford concluded by pointing out the Probate Court made no entry showing any continuance of the case.

Attorney Smith immediately asserted there was an entry. Judge Warner dispatched a clerk to retrieve it, but he returned saying no such document could be found. Smith insisted there was a continuance, that he drew it up and Judge Lueders had signed it. "Let's have it then," replied Judge Warner.

Attorney Freiberg and the Clerk of the Court left the courtroom, with the former taking the lead. "Freiberg called the Probate Deputy into Judge Lueder's private office, and when they returned, [Freiberg] had the entry." Attorney Littleford examined the document, saw it was dated January 3rd, and objected, stating this piece of evidence had been denied him. The Probate Deputy also stated he had not seen the document before. It was found to be "proper," but stated the insanity charges against Rheinstrom had not been heard in full, and until a decision could be reached, the defendant was to be placed in the charge of his mother, Mina W. Rheinstrom, "with the right to place him in the hands of some suitable persons."

Inscribed upon the document was a statement which read "the entry heretofore made on December 31, 1909, dismissing this cause, is hereby set aside, and the cause reinstated." This made it appear an entry of dismissal was made in regard to the insanity charges, but the case was reopened on Monday, when the first habeas corpus writ was secured in Judge O'Connell's court. Littleford reiterated his argument that the Probate Court did not have the right to commit a man anywhere but to the State Hospital—not to friends, or family, or relatives. Neither could an insane man choose where he was to be committed.

Attorney Smith again asked for a continuance. Attorney Littleford countered, saying the family was stalling for time in order to hunt up

Chapter Three. Enter Harry Rheinstrom

more witnesses to bolster their case. Smith denied this. "Judge Warner held that he would have jurisdiction," and that Rheinstrom "was entitled to be heard under the writ secured upon the question of the legality of his restraint...[and] upon the question of his sanity." The Judge steadfastly refused to issue a continuance, unless the request came from the defendant and his counsel. Rheinstrom, he said, was entitled to an immediate hearing upon the matter, and it was the obligation of the opposing attorneys "to have the right persons present to make up the issue, if one was contemplated."

Attorney Smith then asked for a recess to send for Dr. F.W. Langdon and John C. Sheets of the College Hill Sanitarium. Judge Warner granted this, and an automobile was dispatched. While the prosecution's witnesses were being procured, Littleford asked to speak with Rheinstrom in private, and the Judge offered them his chambers. After a time, the attorney asked for Edna and Mrs. Holland, and they were sent in to the judge's chambers. The conference lasted over an hour, reported *The Enquirer*. "Rheinstrom was quite downcast at first, saying that he had been told his mother was dying as a result of his actions. He was greatly worried over this and could not be comforted until word reached him that his mother and sister had just arrived in an automobile, and were ... in consultation with their attorneys."

When the defense was ready to return to the courtroom with their answer, the Widow Rheinstrom, again dressed in mourning with a veil,

College Hill Sanitarium, Cincinnati, Ohio.

and her daughter entered the courtroom, A moment later, Rheinstrom, Littleford, Mrs. Holland, and Edna appeared from the judge's chambers. When Rheinstrom saw his mother, "he went to her side and threw his arms about her, kissing her affectionately." The Widow Rheinstrom broke into tears, as did Edna and Mrs. Holland when they heard the old woman's sobs. Rheinstrom remained by his mother's side for a few moments, talking quietly. Then he stood, walked over, took his place at the defendant's table beside his lawyer, "and smiled affectionately at his fiancée."

Littlefield and Smith went at it a bit longer, until Judge Warner adjourned the court until ten o'clock the following morning, Littleford suggested Rheinstrom be remanded to the custody of the sheriff and returned to College Hill. The Judge agreed to this, "Rheinstrom bade his mother good-by and then returned to Miss Loftus. They went into the corridor with the deputy sheriffs and talked for some time while waiting for the auto to take them back to College Hill. Rheinstrom bade the young woman good-by, kissing her before all present," He then said to the reporters,

> I love my mother and I went to her and kissed her when I came in. She loves me too, but she is being misled. She has been told that Edna is not a good woman, and I know that she is. Freiberg told me that this was the only course that they could pursue to break it up. Well, it won't get them much, darling [to Miss Loftus], I have only about six cents to my name, but it will be all right in the end.

Crying, Edna replied directly to Rheinstrom, "I do not want your money, I only want you, and I will work for you." She then said good-bye once more as Rheinstrom was ushered out to the waiting car. After her lover was driven away, Edna and Mrs. Holland got into a cab, and they too were whisked off.[11]

"Cupid Triumphs at Last" read the headline on the tenth page of *The Cincinnati Enquirer* the following day. A little after ten o'clock Judge Warner called the courtroom to order. He then gave his ruling in the matter of the writ. He stated the law which gave the Probate Court authority to commit an insane person to the custody of family or friends did not apply in Hamilton County. Further, Judge Warner ruled the Probate Court had the authority to turn a person over to family and friends pending the outcome of an insanity hearing, but did "not permit him being deprived of his rights or restrained of his liberty." In Rheinstrom's case there was only the allegation he might be insane, but no charge he actually was. "Therefore, he could not be restrained of his liberty, as he had been." Judge Warner then summarily granted the writ, and dismissed the applicant, Harry Rheinstrom.

Chapter Three. Enter Harry Rheinstrom

The attorneys Edna had retained were said to have been jubilant, while Attorneys Freiberg and Morris were described as "crestfallen." However, Attorney Smith declared they would prosecute the error in the Circuit Court, and reminded Judge Warner Rheinstrom's case was still pending in the Probate Court, and asked Rheinstrom be turned over to the custody of the Sheriff's Office, Judge Warner retorted, "I have no authority to do that." He did, however, agree to give the family's attorneys until three o'clock to go to the Circuit Court on the alleged error and secure a stay of sentence.

The attorney, the Widow Rheinstrom, and her daughter left the courtroom to discuss what their next move should be, leaving Edna, Rheinstrom and Mrs. Holland to talk among themselves. They spoke for about an hour, and decided, since Rheinstrom had been given his freedom, he and Edna should marry at once. He then dispatched his attorneys to find out if Judge Lueders would issue a license. It was expected he would. However, Lueders "called attention to the fact there was an insanity matter against Rheinstrom still in his court and unsettled, and also an order to refuse Rheinstrom a license." Having been thwarted there, the couple decided they would go to either Covington or Newport, Kentucky, to obtain the necessary document so they could be married.

An automobile was ordered. Just as they were about to leave, Rheinstrom stepped forward to shake hands with Judge Warner and thank him. Warner took his hand, and gripping it firmly, told Rheinstrom he was obliged to remain within the jurisdiction of the Court to await word from the Circuit Court. "The spirits of the party fell to zero, and Miss Loftus began to weep." The Judge ordered Edna and Mrs. Holland to go to his office on the First National Bank Building, saying Rheinstrom would join them once the matter had been settled. Attorney Frost accompanied the women, while Attorney Lykins ordered another automobile, which would be waiting outside the courthouse when Rheinstrom was released.

Rheinstrom took the opportunity to speak with his mother and sister, who were waiting on the anteroom of the Probate Court. The newspaper stated he greeted them "affectionately," despite the circumstances, "and entered into an earnest conversation with his mother." He told her she was being badly advised.

> Please don't listen to these people. You have my interest at heart and I have yours, but my interest lays in the direction I have taken. You know that I love you, and that I always shall, and shall never blame you for this, for I know that it is not your fault. Don't let these people ill-advise you. I know exactly what I am doing, and it is for the best for me and for everybody.

His mother's answer was inaudible, said *The Enquirer*, but she "seemed happier than she had been since the proceedings here begun."[12]

What confounds is Harry Rheinstrom's seeming inability (more probably, willful ignorance) to see his mother as the prime mover in the entire affair. Further, one wonders at Mrs. Rheinstrom's motivations. Why was she so opposed to the marriage? It may well have been for religious reasons. The Talmud is explicit, stating that the institution of Jewish marriage, *kiddushin*, can only be affected between Jews, and a marriage between a Jew and a Gentile is both prohibited and does not constitute a marriage under Jewish law. Further, the paternity of offspring resulting from a Jewish man's marriage to a Gentile woman are not recognized as being Jewish. The *Torah* (Deuteronomy 7: 3–5) states that the children of such marriages will be "lost to Judaism," as the faith is passed along matrilineally (which makes much more sense than trying to trace anything paternally). For a Jew to marry a Gentile is, literally, to invoke the wrath of God.

It may also be that the Widow Rheinstrom saw Edna as an unscrupulous "golddigger," who was after the family money. Certainly, Rheinstrom and Edna's little wild time in New York City—their fabulous nights out and his extravagant gifts—did nothing to dispel this impression. The fact was, Edna had not worked in at least three years, having quit the stage when she married O'Connor. Edna did state she had come to New York with the intention of returning to the theater, and she may or may not have had a brief run at The Lyceum. However, she had not found any other engagements. Worse, she was an actress. It may be assumed that the Widow Rheinstrom shared the common sentiment about theater people, especially actresses, as being profligate, flighty, and given to excess. Had she not read the scandalous reports about Cléo de Mérode, Lillie Langtree, Evelyn Nesbit, and Edna's former friend Gaby Deslys, in the newspapers?

Further, the Widow Rheinstrom undoubtedly realized her son was already quite the playboy, and given to debauchery and dissipation. Doubtlessly, left to his own devices, and as general manager of the family business, her son could easily squander a good portion of the family fortune. She probably believed a nice, sober and demure Jewish woman, with a sense of responsibility, propriety, and familial obligation would have the effect of tempering her son's licentious proclivities. The Widow Rheinstrom certainly did not want her son to marry a divorced English actress with an alleged predilection for lobster houses, expensive clothing, costly jewelry, and high-living. If they married, Edna would surely hasten her son's squandering of the family fortune.[13]

Chapter Three. Enter Harry Rheinstrom

At noon, Attorney Foster, who had returned to the Insolvency Court, asked the Court Clerk James Casey if a stay had been issued or error of proceeding noticed. Clerk Casey answered in the negative. Foster then turned to Rheinstrom, and said, "Come on, Harry." Moments later, a procession including Attorney Foster and Lykins, Mr. Mul-Queeny, Rheinstrom, and "a corps of newspapermen," proceeded out onto the street. It was soon discovered the car which had been ordered was not there. Rheinstrom approached one of the chauffeurs who drove for the Rheinstrom family, and tried to induce him to drive them over to the bank building, "The chauffeur refused, saying his livelihood depended on him his following orders of the family."

The party then decided to walk over to the bank building, but at Ninth and Main streets they were met by the car they had ordered. They all piled in, including the newspapermen, and "the machine raced down Court Street to Walnut to the bank building." Moments after they pulled up, Attorney Frost appeared on the sidewalk with Edna and Mrs. Holland, "and they crowded into the already overcrowded machine and a hurry run was made to Covington," just over the state border in Kentucky. At the suspension bridge which spanned the Ohio River, they were stopped at the ticket taker's booth.

"What's the matter now?" asked Edna. "Are we stopped?" "No," came the reply from Foster, "but we are not yet out of the jurisdiction of the Court, and a Sheriff could stop us even now; so don't let your spirits get too gay." "What? Don't say that!" cried Edna.

The automobile started forward again, and at the point directly over the center of the river, the attorney shouted, "Now, you can cheer. We are over the line and in Kentucky." And a cheer went up from the numerous occupants in the car.

The next stop was at the Covington County Courthouse, and the Office of the Clerk of Kenton County, Kentucky, where the crowd from the car went rushing up the stairs en masse. However, when they approached County Clerk John Dillon and asked for the license, they were refused. When he was asked the reason, Dillon replied, "Attorney Freiberg telephoned to me that the family did not want it issued, and that there were Court proceedings in Cincinnati, and I would rather not issue it." Anticipating Rheinstrom's leaving the state, the family had its lawyers call all the clerks in the nearby Kentucky county, and threatened them with legal action if they issued a license to the couple. A telephone call to neighboring Newport in Campbell County confirmed this.

A quick meeting was held, and one of the newspapermen suggested they drive to the town of Independence, which he said was the real county seat of Kenton County, even though most the county business was transacted in Covington. It was then agreed that they would employ subterfuge, and put out the word the couple and their entourage were going to turn back to Ohio in an attempt to reach the town of Hamilton in Butler County. Clerk Dillon did not think the couple would find any place in Kentucky to obtain a license. "Then there appeared James Bratt, known in Covington as 'Cupid's Side Partner,' and the man who knows all the ropes that lead to the altar on the Blue Grass State." The situation was quickly explained to him, and he joined the others in the now severely over-crowded automobile.

The whole scene took on the appearance of a slapstick comedy film, with a car stuffed with "laughing and cheering passengers" racing at breakneck speed along the snow-covered Madison Pike, the horn blowing incessantly, and pedestrians and other vehicles pulling off the road to watch the auto flash past. The revelry of the occupants was short-lived. "Thirteen miles had to be covered before the goal was reached and every one became uneasy when the roadway became rougher and more uphill." It was also a concern that the subterfuge undertaken would be unsuccessful, and the Rheinstrom family would once again succeed in frustrating the marriage plans of the couple. Finally, the car pulled over at a roadhouse in Bandfordstown, where some of the passengers were let off, while the rest continued the journey. The party which was left at the roadhouse immediately called for another vehicle.

"The lightened auto negotiated the distance up the hill in half an hour and the little party entered the courthouse and leisurely lounged up to the desk. No one apparently seemed to be in a hurry." Edna was observed to be playing with a small child who was in the room, while Mrs. Holland tried to find some candy to give to the youngster. Rheinstrom and Attorney Foster approached the desk of Deputy Clerk Elmer Stanisfer, and after making some small talk about the weather, asked if he could provide the marriage license. Mr. Stanisfer said he could. Edna was called to the desk, and the process was begun. "Not once did the deputy balk, though he did look askance when Miss Loftus answered that her home is England, but she quickly corrected herself by explaining that she meant that she was born there."

Once the document had been signed and the fee paid, "three cheers were given for Elmer and his baby and a tiger for the rest of the family." About this time, the other automobile arrived, and after a brief discussion, it was decided they would drive back to Covington and be married by Judge Wheeler. On the way, the two autos stopped again at the roadhouse in Sandfordtown for sandwiches and refreshments. When Edna, Rheinstrom, and their entourage arrived at Judge Wheeler's house in

Covington, "Judge Wheeler met the party at the door, and in a moment more every one was trying to drive the chill out of his marrow in front of glowing grate fires."

The wedding itself was brief and rather informal.

> Mrs. Wheeler took charge of the women, but they wasted little time in making themselves presentable, and surrounded by the entire party, Rheinstrom and his pretty actress sweetheart joined hands while Judge Wheeler pronounced the mystic words, which were to join them together for life, and so they hoped, were to put an end to the efforts of Rheinstrom's relatives to have him incarcerated in an insane asylum.

When the ceremony was complete, a cheer went up from the onlookers. A phone call was placed to Attorney Littleford to advise him the deed was done. In turn, the attorney advised Rheinstrom not to return to Ohio until it could be determined what the next move of the family's attorneys was to be. He reminded the newlyweds that Rheinstrom's insanity hearing had been postponed until the following Monday, January 10.

Two casual wedding photos were taken after the ceremony, one of the newlyweds in front of the automobile, and one of the entire party. The couple then proceeded to a photographic studio with Mrs. Holland, where they had more formal photos taken. The wedding dinner was held at Cody's café. At the diner, Rheinstrom addressed the guests, saying,

> I do not know what I shall do first, now. I don't know if I have got a job or not. It had been arranged that the company was to be reorganized into a corporation the first of the year, and I was to have been President, but I guess that's all off now. Well, I don't care. I can get along. I am not crazy and never was, and they know it. Say, hand it to those attorneys. They are the ones who have been handing out bad advice to my mother. She would never have taken any such action against her son if she had not been badly advised. I know that, and that is why I haven't a word to say against what she did. She's not to be blamed. One thing is certain, we will stay here a while, and then we will likely go to England or France.

Edna interjected, "Yes, but we will come back here, Harry. This is yours and your mother's home, you know."

"Well, of course we will come back, but we will have to get something to go away on first, I guess that I will have to get a job somewhere. This is only the start and, if necessary, we will be married by every rite that there is in the religious world."

In the column immediately following the one containing the wild ride, *The Enquirer* reported the Widow Rheinstrom "was prostrated upon receipt of the news of her son's marriage to Edna Loftus, and denied admittance to all callers." The son-in-law, Samuel Fechheimer,

Edna and Harold Rheinstrom.

responding to a query from reporters about what the family would do next, said Harry's brother James refused to see anyone, and the entire matter had been placed in the hands of the family attorneys. When asked if Harry would be able to support Edna on his salary from the business, James said he did not believe so. "That salary has been overdrawn for some time to come and he has no connection with the firm at present." James reminded the reporter their father had left everything to their mother.

When he was pressed for a comment, Attorney Freiberg declared it was the family's intention to continue with the lunacy proceedings, and said the case was to be heard in Probate Court on Wednesday, January 14. "We did not want to protect Harry from Edna Loftus. We wanted to protect him from himself." Freiberg implied it was in agreement with the family's wishes that Rheinstrom had been sent to College Hill, "to avoid the stigma of a commitment to Longview." Freiberg stated the lunacy proceedings would continue, and said he was not certain the Widow Rheinstrom would provide any money to the couple. "That is a matter that the family have not consulted me upon." The attorney also disclosed the Rheinstrom family had cabled Paris in order to obtain "definite information" about Edna's divorce from Winnie O'Connor.

The news of the couple's elopement was disseminated across the country by the wire service, from Bangor, Maine, to Oakland, California. In fact, it was the first time Edna's name would appear in the California newspapers, including *The Oakland Tribune* and *The San Francisco Call*. In general, the tone taken in the articles were very much in Edna's favor. Just a few years later, this would not be the case.[14]

The Cincinnati Enquirer did not pick up the story again until its edition of January 10. "There was a lull in the Rheinstrom case yesterday, and both sides appear to be 'resting on their arms' awaiting the coming of Wednesday, when the hostilities will resume in the Probate Court." It was reported there had been some "caustic responses" from friends of the couple to the statements made by Frieberg and Fechheimer in the press. It was also said Rheinstrom had called his mother in an effort to effect a reconciliation, and even offered to visit his mother at home. However, when he insisted Edna accompany him, his demand was "met with disfavor." Rheinstrom became angry, and decided not to meet with his mother after all, "and all efforts at an amicable settlement were called off."

Though attorney William Littleford had sworn the couple to silence, it does not seem Edna heeded her attorney's admonition. Edna made a statement to the press, in response to brother-in-law Samuel Fechheimer's allegation that had she kept quiet about the affair, that she "might have been given a sum of money, but the family are firmly resolved now not to give up a cent." Edna was quoted as saying,

> They declare that if I had kept quiet. I might have been given a sum of money. Well, they probably wanted me to keep quiet, but they never got a chance to buy me off. I was not for sale. The idea of their saying that they "might have" given me money if I kept quiet. It generally takes two people at least to make a bargain, and I want to say that they never could have had any chance to buy me off. They never attempted to, and the only reason that I have for being sorry for that is that it prevented me having the opportunity to tell them what I think of such a proposition.
>
> I do not want their money, and do not care whether Harry has a cent of it. I have my profession as an actress, and I have earned from $350 to $500 a week on the stage. I can do it again too, and I think that Harry and I can live on that. Of course, I know that Harry is not one of the kind who would want to be dependent upon his wife, but I also know that he has ability and he can easily secure something to do that will make us both independent of his family.
>
> I should like to have Harry become reconciled to his mother. I know just how she must feel, and I feel sorry for her, but Harry will never go back to

them without me, and I will not go unless they are willing to receive me as Harry's wife, and accord me the treatment that Harry's wife is entitled to. I am not begging of them or asking anything but for my just due as Harry's wife. We love each other, and the difference in our religion is all that they can find against me. It is not only cruel, but ungentlemanly for [Fechheimer] to give out such impressions about me, and I wish to declare, most emphatically, that the Rheinstroms have not enough money to have bought me off from taking the course I did in securing the release of Harry from the sanitarium, And they have not enough money to make me leave him or induce him to leave me either.

Rheinstrom also seems to have disregarded the attorney's advice. *The Enquirer* observed he seemed to be in good spirits, although he was "worried that his mother should have all the trouble and notoriety because of his affair." When pressed, Rheinstrom continued, saying he and Edna were "happy and contented." He then proceeded to upbraid the attorneys hired by his mother, saying their actions were "un–American and unprofessional," and he believed that Freiberg and Morris had a lot of explaining to do. "The few paragraphs in this morning's *Enquirer* will not suffice. They are supposed to be working in the interest of my mother, but so far it seems to me, they have acted wholly on their own." Rheinstrom believed, or so he said, his mother had acted on the attorneys' bad advice, but would never have done so had she met Edna.

When asked if he was willing to attempt another reconciliation with his mother, Rheinstrom replied that both he and Edna were agreeable to this, "though there is much on the part of our folks that we will have to forgive." He was also adamant in his demand that Edna be recognized as his wife, and that this was non-negotiable. "Another thing is this: I want all references to Edna Loftus stopped, for there is no such person now. There is a Mrs. Rheinstrom, who is my wife, and those who refer to her in any other terms will have to settle with me."

Rheinstrom was subsequently read a statement from Fechheimer, purported to have been derived from a missive sent by Captain Holland, in which he told his wife that if she did not keep away from Edna, he would divorce her. Rheinstrom declared it to be "a lie, manufactured from the whole cloth manufactured by Mr. Fechheimer." To prove it apocryphal, Rheinstrom produced a letter from Holland to Attorney Lykins in which Holland stated he was in the hospital as the result of an accident, but that he was still willing to travel back to Cincinnati, and testify on Rheinstrom's behalf. In the letter Holland praised Edna, saying her "character is of the best, and reports spread about her [are] untrue, and without the slightest foundation." This missive was dated January 7.

When asked about his plans for the future, Rheinstrom reiterated that he hoped for a reconciliation with his mother, but he could stand on his own. "I have been a partner in the business of the Rheinstrom Bros., and I have been actively engaged in it for eight years. If my folks and I cannot come to the only terms that I'll consider ... I will make arrangements to give up my share of the business. But I have no fear of the future, for I can always make a living for my wife and myself. I have had a very good proposition made by a reliable concern, which promises as lucrative an income as the one I have had."

When interviewed by the newspaper, Rheinstrom's brother James stated the former had not seen his mother since before the wedding, but James was convinced a reconciliation between mother and son would likely occur at the hearing on Monday, Fechheimer was quoted as saying, "As far as I know, there have never been any differences between Harry and his mother, so, how could there be a reconciliation?"[15]

The following day, the newspaper stated no reconciliation was reached between the Widow Rheinstrom and her son, and that a "strenuous legal battle" was expected. The attorneys for the family were said to have been calling in medical experts, and witnesses to testify about Harry Rheinstrom's alleged erratic behaviors, while the defense team was doing the same, as well as subpoenaing the numerous reporters who had been with the couple for several days in Kentucky, and friends of Rheinstroms who were willing to testify to "the soundness of his mind." Details of what occurred in the courtroom were not published in the newspaper until Thursday.

After the court was convened by Judge Lueders, the attorneys for the Rheinstrom family asked for a continuance in the insanity hearing, and for an immediate hearing on their application to have a guardian appointed to Harry Rheinstrom. In response, the Judge stated the insanity hearing would be heard first. Attorney Miller Outcalt, who had been added to the family's retinue of lawyers, moved for a dismissal of the case, without prejudice. Attorney Littleford protested "unless an entry was made finding your Rheinstrom sane." This was refused by the Judge, who stated the complainant had a right to dismiss. Littleford then announced he would apply for a writ of mandamus, to compel Judge Lueders to complete the hearing. A continuance was granted to give Littleford time to prepare the writ. A short time later, the writ was filed with the Circuit Court, but the court had adjourned for the day, so the matter was tabled until the following morning.

During the opening salvo, Judge Smith observed the primary motivation for the hearing was to stave off the marriage between Rheinstrom and Edna, but as the marriage had taken place while the inquest was pending, now the focus was on the validity of the marriage. If Rheinstrom was found to be mentally ill, he could not legally consent to be married. Attorney Littleford objected, saying the validity of the marriage was not in question, and Judge Lueders agreed, stating it had nothing to do with the proceedings.

The reporter for *The Enquirer* noted the courtroom was very crowded, and Rheinstrom and "his pretty actress wife" were both in attendance, though Rheinstrom was seated with his attorneys throughout. The Widow Rheinstrom and her daughter, Mrs. Fechheimer, sat outside the courtroom, and never entered. He entered the courtroom through a side door and at no time did Rheinstrom see or speak to his mother.[16]

The Circuit Court refused to take up the writ of mandamus, and so the case was returned to the Probate Court to be decided by Judge Lueders. After Littleford waived his exceptions, a conference was held with the Judge, during which the latter continued the case until Tuesday, January 18, "at which time he [would] decide upon the question of permitting the dismissal of the insanity proceedings and set a date for the hearing of the entire case." The newspaper observed, "None of the principals in the now famous case were present in court." And famous it was, with the United Press dispatches continuing to be carried by newspapers across the country. Arguably, Edna was more renowned than she had been when she was appearing on the stage in Europe.

Shortly before the commencement of Rheinstrom's insanity hearing, the suit filed by the H. & S. Pogue Company against Edna and Mrs. Holland "to recover goods bought there upon Harry Rheinstrom's endorsement" was heard before Squire Myers. "No defense was made and none of the defendants appeared in Court, judgement, with one cent damages, being entered." The company recovered all of the goods in the neighborhood of $350. That same evening, *The Enquirer*, not wanting to allow a good story to die, sent a reporter to speak with Rheinstrom, and published parts of the interview on its edition of January 15th.

Rheinstrom was quoted as saying, "The attorneys representing my folks are willing to have the case marked 'dismissed' on the Court docket, but on the advice of my attorney, Judge Littleford, I shall insist upon the case being tried and my name cleared." When he was asked about the possibility of a reconciliation being affected, Rheinstrom admitted it was not likely this would happen. He continued, "They said they would cable to Europe and prove my wife is not all I think she is. Ample time has elapsed since they cabled. Why don't they show their answers?" Still defending his mother, he said he regretted she had not waited to meet Edna before pursuing this course of action. He put his

Postcard image of Edna perched on a chair (author's collection).

mother's decision down to her being influenced by "malicious and gossiping reports." Incredibly, Rheinstrom still believed he would retain his former position in the family business.[17]

Under the headline "Edna Loftus Wins." *The New York Sun* reported on Tuesday, January 18, that Rheinstrom and his mother had a reconciliation the previous afternoon, and he would be allowed to bring Edna to meet the matriarch at her home. Rheinstrom told the press his mother had contacted him "and asked for peace and that he drop the cases in court." He replied that this would only happen if he were allowed to present Edna at his mother's home, and have her recognized as being his wife. "He told [his mother] they would not remain there very long." The Widow Rheinstrom agreed to this. The newspaper also asserted Rheinstrom was to resume his former position in the family business. This report was carried by several newspapers.[18]

When the case came up in Probate Court the following day, it seemed Harry Rheinstrom had won the day. Though *The Cincinnati Enquirer* reported "he acceded readily to the proposition made as the settlements of financial matters," Fechheimer had withdrawn his application for the appointment of a guardian for Rheinstrom, and the Widow Rheinstrom withdrew her application and affidavit in the insanity case. An entry was made in the official record which read:

> And the Court, having made its entry on January 3, 1910, that there was probable ground for the charge of insanity, in the view of the filing of said affidavit and application. Now, said affidavit and application having been withdrawn, the Court, therefore, finds there is no longer ground for the charge of insanity. This proceeding is, therefore dismissed.

However, the details of the financial arrangement between Rheinstrom and the family were ordered not to be made public. Said the newspaper:

> It is understood, that Harry Rheinstrom, though he severs all connection with the liquor business his father left, will have an income very nearly the same as it was when he was managing that business for his mother, at which time he drew $7,500 a year. It is also understood that the terms of the agreement are such that Harry and his wife will go West, where he will likely embark in some business enterprise.

After his appearance in court, Rheinstrom took Edna and Mrs. Holland to a café on Vine Street, and while dining spoke to reporters. "I have had an interview with my mother since the marriage," he said, while caressing Edna's hand. "All of my business has been in Judge Littleford's hands. I cannot say just what the sum of money I received, but it is enough for us to go and settle in Los Angeles."

Edna added, idyllically, "Yes, and we are going to live among the flowers and love each other. Harry is a businessman, and when he has amassed a fortune, we are going to send after all our good Cincinnati friends and bring them out, and we'll show them a good time." Mrs. Holland declared it was her intention to return to her husband in Detroit. "I've had some fun and a lot of wonderful adventures in this town," she exclaimed.

Edna then announced. "You know, Harry has decided to join my faith, haven't you, Harry."

Rheinstrom replied, "I have," and kissed her hand. In turn. Edna kissed him back.

Mrs. Holland asked the reporter, "Did you ever in your life behold such a love?" "Nix," said the reporter, and he took his leave of the couple.

The Enquirer did note that George Mulqueeny, the attendant who had arranged for the secret meeting between Edna and Rheinstrom while the latter was confined in College Hill Sanitarium, was to accompany them on their journey into the West. "It is not known exactly what position Mulqueeny will occupy on the Los Angeles ranch, but as Mrs. Rheinstrom intends on raising flowers, the ex-attendant will probably care for them."[19]

On January 22, on the front page, beneath a photograph of Edna wearing a shirtwaist and dark skirt, *The Los Angeles Evening Express* summed up the trial and tribulations of the young couple in three short paragraphs, and ended by saying Rheinstrom had effected a deal with his family, and intended to move to that city to start a business. The next mention of the young couple in *The Cincinnati Enquirer* was two days later, after they departed for California. It was said they intended to stop in Denver, Colorado, "where they will spend a few days," and then proceed to Seattle, Washington. Mrs. Holland had joined her husband in Detroit. "She will, however, return to this city to fight her suit against the Rheinstrom family for having her arrested on a charge of loitering."[20]

Mrs. Holland sued the Rheinstroms for $50,000 in damages, naming G.W. Werden, Samuel, Harry, and Henry Fechheimer, Julius Freiberg, Fromme Morris, and Rufus Smith in her suit. She retained Attorney Lykins.[21]

Chapter Four

Into the West

Though it was not on the front page, the photograph of Edna in her shirtwaist appeared in the February 8 edition of *The Los Angeles Evening Express*, which announced her arrival in that city with Rheinstrom. "Here to make their permanent home, after weeks of harrowing afflictions and sensations, including confinement of one in an insane asylum and the other in a prison, Mr. and Mrs. Harry Rheinstrom, bride and groom, arrived in Los Angeles today." The newspaper stated the Widow Rheinstrom had given her son $5,000 in cash, and an annuity of $3.000, and "bade him go West." During a brief interview, Rheinstrom revealed he had no idea what business he would go into, and was going to take some time before deciding. As to Edna, *The Express* described her as "a typical Irish girl, with large blue eyes, brown hair, and an athletic figure. She said she had put her sorrows behind her and intended to enjoy life in Los Angeles." Little did Edna know what fate still had in store for her.

The Oakland Tribune and *The San Francisco Examiner* also noted the arrival of the couple, the latter carrying a portrait if Edna from her days on the English stage. Again she was front-page news. *The Examiner* said of her: "Mrs. Rheinstrom is best known as Edna Loftus, who gained considerable success on the stage," and further noted she was divorced from Winnie O'Connor. The story was sent out by wire across the country, and repeated with varying degrees of accuracy.[1]

More astonishing was the news disseminated by the United Press a few days later. It was reported on the 12th that Rheinstrom had "completed negotiations for the purchase of a thirty-acre ranch near the foothills" and it was Edna's intention to purchase six dozen chickens, and "make a home for Harry." With an admirable sense of determination, Edna told a reporter, "I can bake and I am proud of my puddings and jellies. I am going to prove to Harry what a devoted wife can accomplish. There is plenty of fun in going to theaters, but real happiness is at home with the man you love." Edna explained the division of labor on the farm, saying Rheinstrom was to plow the fields and do the heavy labor, while she attended to the chickens and made butter.

Eleven days later, *The San Francisco Call* printed excerpts from another interview with Edna, in which she demonstrated the same enthusiasm for her new situation. "It's the simple life for us, and it's lovely beyond compare," she declared. The newspaper stated the Rheinstrom farm was only five acres, but was "embellished by a real bungalow and well stocked with chickens, pigs, cows, and fruits, beautified by tree shaded walks and open meadows."

Publicity photograph of Edna Loftus in feathered hat (author's collection).

Edna stated they planned to raise chickens. "Oh, of course, we will raise other things too. Harry is a strong man, you know, and can plow and hoe, and we will have all that the heart could wish, and it beats the city life all to pieces."

When asked by the reporter if she could cook, Edna replied, somewhat indignantly, "Cook? Of course I can cook, and I am going to make Harry proud of his domestic wife. It's better than balls and theaters and wine suppers and all that, is the simple life. And isn't it beautiful all about the place? I'm going to prove to his mother that Harry is in good hands, and make her glad he married me, and she may yet forgive him. For, after all, a mother should be satisfied if her son is made happy." The reporter noted the ranch was "in easy reach of San Francisco." The interview appeared on the front page beneath an artist's poor rendering of Edna in a large hat and a smaller cameo of Rheinstrom. Once again, being picked up by the wire service, it was national news.

One must wonder if Edna really believed she and her husband could make a living for themselves operating a chicken ranch.[2] She must have realized they would no longer be able to live as they once had, with expense accounts, and evenings spent out on the town. Economic historian E.A. Goldenweiser estimated yearly net earnings on the typical farm in 1909–1910 was about $724—nowhere near what Rheinstrom had earned managing the family business or what Edna had earned on the stage. Did Edna truly believe both of them, having become accustomed to the high-life, would be happy living in reduced circumstances, and eking out a living on a farm? Or, perhaps, Edna thought, if she proved herself to be a good wife and, possibly, a mother, Rheinstrom would be reconciled with his family, and they could return to Cincinnati and the *beau monde*.

Also questionable was Rheinstrom's decision to turn away from what he knew best—the distilling industry—and become a farmer. Doubtlessly, there were numerous firms in California which were involved in the liquor industry, and would have welcomed an employee with Rheinstrom's knowledge of the business. To take a job in an industry he knew something about, as opposed to sinking all his capital into a small farm property, would have been the wiser choice. Maybe it was the idea of being an employee as opposed to an owner, that soured him on this taking a job in the liquor industry. Or, perhaps, he believed, in time, he would be reconciled with the family, and the farming venture would be temporary. Whatever Rheinstrom's reasoning, buying a chicken farm was not the best course of action he could have taken.[3]

Meanwhile, back in Detroit, Captain Herbert Holland was still convalescing in the Grace Hospital, where he had been nearly eight weeks following an attack of rheumatism, which had reportedly crippled him. During the final week of February, Holland was interviewed by a reporter from *The Detroit Free Press*, and the resulting article was far from complimentary. Holland, who claimed to be the "president of the Michigan & Montreal River Mining Company," said he wished he had never heard of Harry Rheinstrom and "this woman." Holland asserted he had left town after Rheinstrom was arrested, not because he was threatened with being arrested himself, but because he was ill. "Went to Louisville on business, and then had to come back to Detroit."

Holland stated he met Rheinstrom at the Belmont Hotel in New York City on December 21. "Come over and see my girl," said Rheinstrom to Holland. "Then he started telling me how much he loved her and how he'd commit suicide if he didn't marry her, I met Miss Loftus, and then went back to Detroit." Holland claimed his meeting with Edna and Rheinstrom at the Havlin Hotel was purely coincidental. "Then I had to go to Cincinnati, taking my wife with me, I stopped at the Havlin hotel, and found Harry and Edna there. Harry, on my suggestion, went to apply for a special marriage license there the next evening."

Holland said he went with Rheinstrom and, on the way, they met a banker they knew. "We were talking with him when two big deputies jumped on Harry's neck. 'You're crazy! Come along with us,' they said.

The Belmont Hotel, New York City (Library of Congress).

Harry tried to tell them he was sober, or sane, but they took him to an asylum. His mother had learned Harry was about to get married." Saying he could not do anything about Rheinstrom's predicament, Holland decided to go back to Detroit, and assumed his wife would accompany him. "She didn't, I'm sorry to say." Instead, she sympathized with Miss Loftus, and decided that she would see her through. She was arrested with Miss Loftus, and charged with loitering, but it was clearly an effort to persecute them, and they were immediately released.

The Captain acknowledged his wife was suing the Rheinstrom family and their associates for $50,000, "but if I ever get out of here, I'll do my best to stop this suit. I want to pass this affair over, and have my wife forget all about it." Holland was aware Rheinstrom was residing in California. "He's got to get along as best he can, for his mother has cut off his allowance of $75,000." He said he had not heard from Rheinstrom or Edna since they were married. "If I get out of here in two weeks, I am going back to Cincinnati on business. There's nothing that I fear as the result of Harry's troubles." It was stated that the offices of Holland's company were located in the Majestic building there in Detroit.

What seems strange is that Captain Holland was not willing to support his wife in her lawsuit, especially considering what she had been through. As evidenced by the brevity of the trial of Edna and Mrs. Holland, the fact the witnesses called were all in the employ of the Rheinstrom family, and the complaint itself was filed on by a lawyer for the family, it would seem it would be easy to prove Mrs. Holland was the victim of a conspiracy, and would be entitled to damages against her good name and character. One would think Holland would also be angry about what had occurred, and would want justice for his wife. Then again, perhaps Holland did not want investigators looking too closely at his character and his business dealings.[4]

On the 26th of February, in answer to the false arrest suit filed by Mrs. Holland, the Rheinstrom family attorneys replied, stating there was no conspiracy, and "in view of the circumstances" the arrest of Edna and Mrs. Holland was "justifiable." *The Free Press* reminded its readers that Mrs. Holland had brought the suit "after the settlement of the Rheinstrom difficulties, charging that her reputation had been damaged to the extent of $50,000. It is anticipated that some interesting testimony will be developed during the trial as the woman was intimately [illegible] with the affairs of Rheinstrom and his bride and is familiar with the inside workings of the family in its efforts to stop the marriage."[5]

There was no news of Edna and her husband, the Rheinstrom family, or the Hollands in March of 1910, but the beginning of April saw Mrs. Holland amending her petition in the Common Pleas Court to include the Widow Rheinstrom in her suit. *The Cincinnati Enquirer*, which broke the story, retold the tale of the events of January, and explained why the suit was being brought: "Mrs. Holland's attorney, M. C, Lykins, stated yesterday [April 1st] that during the taking of depositions in the case it developed that Mrs. Rheinstrom was alleged to have asked Werden to swear to the warrant, and therefore it was decided to make her a party defendant." It was also noted Edna had decided against taking any action against the family, probably because she still hoped for a reconciliation.

The Detroit Free Press, which also carried the story, said Mr. Holland was still opposed to the suit, and was trying to have it quashed. Mrs. Holland was said to be in California, visiting Edna and her husband.[6]

"From Lobster Palace to the Farm" was the headline in *The St. Louis Star Magazine Section*, and beneath it a fairly well executed portrait of Edna based on a photo from her days on the stage. Also included in the full-page exposé were some poor quality photos of Edna mowing the lawn with a push mower, plucking a chicken, on her knees scrubbing the floor with a brush, and sweeping the stairs in front of the house. The caption beneath this last photo read "She sweeps the steps—Young Mrs. Rheinstrom at real, not stage, work." There was also a photo of Rheinstrom pushing a wheelbarrow. For the photos, Edna was dressed in a simple, light-colored shirtwaist and long skirt, and her hair was pulled back in a bun.

The accompanying article is reprinted here in its entirety:

> Three thousand miles from the lobster palaces on New York's Lobster square is a little five-acre truck farm. It is in California and the nearest town that has a restaurant in it is called Boyle Heights. But even the Boyle Heights restaurant is a forty mile drive from the truck farm in question, and while it is strong on ham and eggs, the nearest it comes to lobster is in cans.
>
> The echoes of the Great White Way do not cross the desert and the only sound of revelry by night is when some hilarious cowboy, riding home from the Heights, punches the atmosphere full of holes with his Colt revolver.
>
> This is not a description of the scenery. It is interesting because it is the environment on which Harry Rheinstrom—once multi-millionaire expectant of Cincinnati, son of the widow of Brewer Rheinstrom, who is worth about $20,000,000—lives with Mrs. Rheinstrom, who was the very beautiful Edna Loftus, an English actress, and one of the fairest frequenters of the lobster palaces of New York.
>
> Young Mr. Rheinstrom loves Miss Loftus, after various vicissitudes among which was Mr. Rheinstrom's incarceration in a sanitarium and a subsequent heroic rescue by Miss Loftus, he succeeded in marrying her. After that it was farewell to lobsterhood. Mr. Rheinstrom was promptly disinherited.
>
> Now, he is making his own living by tilling the stubborn soil forty miles from Boyle Heights in California, and Mrs. Rheinstrom is doing chores, plucking chickens for Mr. Rheinstrom's supper, sweeping stairs, scrubbing floors, and generally acting out the part of a real pioneer's wife.
>
> All of which would go to show, it seems, the increasing unpopularity and the lack of stability on the once famous and profitable occupation of chorus

"Lobster Palace" article from *The St. Louis Star and Times*, April 17, 1910.

girl marriages to millionaires [sic] sons. Yet, oddly enough, too, Mr. Rheinstrom seems to thrive beyond the hardships of a pioneer's life, and Mrs. Rheinstrom is far rosier and prettier than she ever was as a stage beauty.

Lobster Square is situated in New York, in the heart of the White Light district. It is bounded on the south by Fortieth Street; its northern border line is Central Park; its western, Eighth avenue, its eastern, Fifth avenue, and it is so named because very night 10,000 pounds of lobster are consumed by the after-theater crowds. The brilliant streams of humanity which appear at the doors of the New York playhouses divide into smaller rivulets and enter the refectories where the enormous streams of lobster harmonize with their moral and mental complexion. All of this vividness had given Lobster Square its vivid name and reputation.

It was there that young Mr. Rheinstrom met Edna Loftus. She was a very famous English beauty, who was born in America. She made a success on England on that happy composition called "The Rain Dears." She was successively engaged to Jimmy Britt, the prize fighter, and Norman Dumbarton, son of Lord Dumbarton of Manchester. Somewhere between the arc of prizefighter and nobleman, Miss Loftus' true affections centered [obviously the author of the article had confused the biography of Winnie O'Connor's second wife, Neva Aymar, with that of Edna]. Coming to New York, she met the young Rheinstrom. At once she realized that he was the proper centre. It was a case of love at first sight. The lobster palaces saw them every night. In five days, he had spent $5,000, and Miss Loftus received it all on dinners and suppers, on gifts of furs and laces and jewels.

She promised to marry him. Mr. Rheinstrom's telegram to his mother out on Cincinnati notifying her of the momentous fact was greeted with much consternation. Mrs. Rheinstrom, the older, however, being a diplomat, told Harry to come on home. Miss Loftus accompanied him. As soon as the young man arrived on Cincinnati, he was placed under confinement and his mother began lunacy proceedings against him.

Miss Loftus, however, was determined that her lover should not be placed in an insane asylum. When the case was called before Judge Warner, Cincinnati Courthouse, Mr. Rheinstrom, through his little actress, was able to prove his sanity. He showed no resentment toward his mother for her action. They kissed each other in court and were very friendly. Miss Loftus, however, was not noticed by the Rheinstroms. Nevertheless, her testimony was so pertinent that the judge released Harry.

Mrs. Rheinstrom swept away from the courthouse without bidding her son good-bye. Mr. Rheinstrom and Miss Loftus swept in another direction.

He also saw his mother's chauffeur before the courthouse with the Rheinstrom auto. "Hurry us over to Covington, old chap," Rheinstrom said, "Not without Mrs., Rheinstrom's orders," said the chauffeur. Then the young man and the little actress jumped on a street car and rode across to Covington. It was the first step of his disinheritness. Refused a marriage license there, they went to Newport, and were married.

If the newly wed Rheinstroms thought there would be a reconciliation, they were very much disappointed. When old Mr. Rheinstrom died, he left all his money and property to his wife, stipulating that it was all to remain absolutely hers as long as she lived, and then it was to go to the two sons, but if she thought it wise, she could disinherit either of them and give that share to charity.

"He has said that he loves that girl better than his family, better than all the millions that would have been his," said Mrs. Rheinstrom, senior. "Therefore I shall disinherit him. I tried very hard to keep him from marrying, and he fought his way out of both insane asylum and sanitarium. Now he is enjoying his own resources and will remain there if I have anything to do with the matter. Although she may be my daughter-in-law, she will never enter my house while I am alive. As long as he has anything to do with her, he will never receive one penny from me."

"What shall we do now?" said the happy bridegroom. "Make our own living," said the bride.

Young Mr. Rheinstrom counted up his money. "There are tremendous opportunities in the West," he finally decided. "We'll go out and buy a ranch." They did. Their fortune was just enough to buy that five-acre one out near Boyle Heights. It was pretty. All California is. It gave a prospect of being made valuable. At least it was enough to keep them comfortably.

Young Mr. Rheinstrom buckled right down to work. So did Mrs. Rheinstrom. Forgotten were the lights of the stage, the triumphs, the lobster suppers. It was hard work right along, and lots of it.

For Miss Loftus, last Winter there was this daily schedule: Rise at 1:30 p.m., from 1:30 to 3:30 bathe and dress. At 3:45, meet Harry Rheinstrom and some of the boys and girls at a lobster palace: 3:45 until 6, luncheon; from 6 to 7:30, fast motor drive along the Speedway, through the Park, and along Riverside drive: 7:30, to the theater to "make-up" for the evening's performance; 11:30, to another lobster palace, where the wine flowed, the lobster reddened, and jest flew, until 3 in the morning.

But now for Mrs. Harry Rheinstrom, the rising hour is 5 on the morning. She dresses in exactly fifteen minutes, Then, she hurries outside to milk the cow. To be sure, Harry Rheinstrom is quite willing to perform that task himself, but the cow, [a] cantankerous creature, "won't stand for Harry." Then she hastens on and prepares their breakfast of boiled eggs and toast and coffee with an orange.

"Doesn't this taste better than those breakfasts for which you used to pay thirty dollars a plate at Rector's, Dear?"

Mrs. Rheinstrom, flushed from her converse with the cow at dawn, a wisp of her fair hair falling becomingly across her brow, her blue eyes gay with a wholesome joy, is an enchanting picture. So enchanting that Mr. Rheinstrom, who has given up a fortune for her sake, rises and walks around the table and kisses her on the pink point of her chin. "The Lobster Square food was punk," he avers, "and to think that this layout costs us just thirty cents."

"We'll never spend money that way again, dearest."

"No, we won't, for we won't have it, darling."

"And aren't we ever so much happier, Harry, dear?"

"We are, sweetest girl on earth."

Chapter Four. Into the West

At least, that is the way idealists put it. But Mrs. Rheinstrom gives her lord little time for reminiscence. There is much to be done. The five-acre tract must be fully cleared, for it had been neglected by its previous owner. On the lavish manner of the light-hearted Westerner, he must haul away all the debris of dead branches, of weeds, and loose timber, must heap them on a big pile at the edge of the five-acre farm and burn them. Then there is the fruit to be gathered each day from the trees and from the strawberry beds. For strawberries can be gathered eleven months of the year on Southern California. And the old farm horse must be fed and watered and curried and bedded, and some of the day's gathering of fruit must be taken to town and sold.

For her, there are the breakfast things to be cleared away, the dishes to be washed, the three rooms of their tiny cottage to be swept and dusted; yes, and scrubbed. For on the day that the writer of this tale paid a visit to the humble home of the former multi-millionaire expectant, his bride was on her unaccustomed knees, scrubbing the kitchen. Then dinner must be prepared, and dinner is at noon or a little before on the truck farm. It does not begin with cocktails and end with nuts, as did the lobster palace feasts. There is a stew because meats are so high and the Cincinnati youth's funds are so low. But it is a delicious stew, he always assures the lovely cook. And there is apple pie, better than his mother made, for Harry. Rheinstrom's mother, being a multimillionaire, only knows the kitchen as a vague, yet considerable domain, one to be avoided because it is usually the disturbance centre of the household.

Young Mrs. Rheinstrom makes apple pie three times a week for the sufficient reason "Harry likes it."

Then, in the afternoon, "Harry helps with the dinner dishes," says Mrs. Rheinstrom, with the same smile that turned the heads of the Johnnies who inhabited Lobster Square, "and then we both go out and work outdoors He does the heavier work of digging and hauling, I putter around in the garden."

At the hour at which they used to "lunch" at Lobster Square, they enjoy their simple tea, when, at six, their day of hard work is finished. Simple folk who rise at five must retire at eight to secure the nine hours' rest that laborers need. So pass their days on the five-acre truck patch on Boyle Heights [near Stephenson Avenue].

There is but one brief hour of rest. That is when, the table cleared, the dishes washed by the former actress, dried by the former multi-millionaire expectant, and placed in the rough little cupboard by both, they sit on the square little porch of their cottage and, hand in hand, watch the big, brilliant sun drop for his nightly bath into the Pacific.

Each of these hardworking young pair has made a declaration of supreme happiness to this newspaper. Undoubtedly their statements are sincere.

But so, too, are the exclamations their fate has provoked on the Great White way, which diagonally crosses the vivid square. These run something like:

"Now, Violet Montmorenci, will you tell me what you think of that?"

"Yes, Jennie Flynn—excuse me for addressing you by your real name. Miss Gwendolyn-Vanderbilt-on-the-stage—I'll tell you what I think of it. I think it's the place Sherman referred to when he talked about war. No, I ain't thinking that. I know it."

"You bet. This match an' a few others we know about is puttin' the chorus girl marryin' the millionaire on the blink."

"On the blink? I should say. Why, it's as out of fashion as the peach basket hat. It's a dead dog. That's what it is."

"Look at Queenie Sanford that married Governor Draper's son. They had to live on two dollars a day."

"And Irene Bishop, that married and was left by J. Raynor Wells. And Mae Murray had to go back to work."

"There used to be somethin' in marryin' a millionaire's son."

"'Somethin'? There was millions in it."

"Anyway, alimony."

"Even when the marriage was annulled, they paid you off. I mean his folks made a settlement."

"Now, the girl has the choice of—."

"A choice? She ain't got nothin'."

"Yes, she has. The choice between bein' kicked out and goin' to work. Gee! That's tough."

"What's the use of goin' on the stage?"

"Sure! There ain't no use."

Rage and horror are the sum of the sentiment on Lobster Square, where Edna Loftus was a favorite. The project of an indignation meeting was discussed. Many anonymous letters have been sent to the elder Mrs. Rheinstrom, so many that she can be in no doubt as to the temper of Lobster Square.

"Who'da thought his mother would be so hard?"

"Poof! A balky mother-in-law's worse than a father-in-law any day. She won't listen to reason. She hits the ceiling and has continual hysterics."

"And the two end up runnin' a truck farm in California."

"And likin' it."

Deep sighs, on chorus—"That's love."

Aside from some glaring errors perpetuated in the article [simple misspellings—"on" for "in," e.g.—have been edited], one might observe the author seems to bask on the couple's unexpected descent from living among the privileged class to toiling among the working class. He seemed to especially delight on Edna's being reduced to scrubbing floors and plucking chickens like a scullery maid. He also showed a marked disdain for "chorus girls" in general, as evidenced by his employing eye dialect to make his imagined characters sound like uneducated rubes.

Chapter Four. Into the West

This same story, with the same illustrations, was reprinted in dozens of newspapers, including *The Knoxville Sentinel* and *The San Francisco Examiner*. It even appeared in *La Correspondencia de Puerto Rico*, a month and half later. And then, the world forgot all about Mr. and Mrs. Rheinstrom out on their truck farm in California, until August.[7]

On the 9th of said month, *The Cincinnati Enquirer* reported, "Six months of simple life on a chicken ranch in Boyle Heights have proved enough for Harry A. Rheinstrom, son of a Cincinnati millionaire, and his wife, formerly Edna Loftus, actress." According to the article, they had started back to Cincinnati in the hope of effecting a reconciliation with the Widow Rheinstrom. Again, the newspapers from San Francisco to New York City jumped on the story. *The Washington Post* quipped, "Rheinstrom, who married Edna Loftus, prefers his mother's millions." Under the headline "Edna Loftus Wins Mama-In-Law Over," *The San Francisco Examiner* devoted an entire column on the front page to the story. After disposing of the truck farm, Rheinstrom and Edna had gone to Oakland, and stopped over at the Hotel Metropole. "They tell with elation that their story is having the same joyous ending as the average romance recorded in the flickering light of the moving picture machines."

The newspaper recounted the story which led to their relocation to California, and again Edna was provided with Neva Aymar's biography and romances. It was stated Edna had been appearing in the show "Rain Dears" when she met Rheinstrom. "She created an impression that he was not stingy about demonstrating ... her furs, her jewels and her striking gowns began to make even the glittering habitués of the lobster palaces gape."

The reporter, who was likely the same who had interviewed them in Boyle Heights, spoke to the couple's time at that place, noting, "The pair did all their own work, Mrs. Rheinstrom milking cows after getting up in the morning and returning in time to get breakfast ready, Rheinstrom worked like a regular rancher in the fields and began to pride himself on the quality of the cantaloupes, the lettuce and the eggs and butter he took to market." Rheinstrom began to write his mother about his adventures and successes as "a real California rancher." He exclaimed "he could plow and hoe ... and his wife was one of the best cooks in the country, could wash dishes, and was a model housekeeper."

Allegedly, the Widow Rheinstrom, who "had never occasion to be troubled about details of cooking or dishwashing," began to take an interest in her son's enterprise, and "began to think that she might have formed mistaken impressions about actresses as wives." The matriarch decided to relent, and "tentative offers were made to the young Rheinstrom to return home." Edna was quoted as saying, "I hate to leave [the ranch]. I never knew such happiness on Broadway." Edna also took credit for the reconciliation. "I knew I could prove to Mrs. Rheinstrom that Harry was in good hands. I knew I could make her glad that he married me, for I realize that a mother could not help being contented if she knew her son was happy in his marriage."

The article, which was accompanied by a large oval publicity photo of Edna from *The Catch of the Season* and a smaller photo of Harry below this, was run on the August 12. It was said, after selling the ranch, the couple went to Los Angeles, and then to Berkeley to visit friends. They were reported to be boarding an eastbound train the following day.[8]

Edna also was interviewed by *The Oakland Tribune*, and said, philosophically, "Of course, I have no ill feeling toward Mrs. Rheinstrom. We do not blame Harry's mother. Everyone has a right to his or her own opinion, and if Harry's mother had a few notions of her own, it is not for us to criticize." This newspaper lauded Edna, saying "she made good her vow that she would win over her husband's prejudiced mother."

The St. Louis Star and Times told a slightly less romanticized tale of their time on the farm. According to that newspaper, the couple had staged the interview and the photographs that were disseminated earlier in the year, "to prove to Mamma Rheinstrom they were carrying out their part of the bargain." Allegedly, the Widow Rheinstrom had promised her son an income of $8,000 a year if they gave up their lavish

Publicity photograph of Edna Loftus in *The Catch of the Season* (author's collection).

lifestyle for a simpler existence in the country. After she saw the article in April, "they received congratulatory letters from the rich widow, and were told to (keep it) up." "But this they failed to do, and they finally decided to brave the wrath of Mrs. Rheinstrom and beg her to take them away from the simple life." This seems the most likely scenario, and subsequent events proved this to be the case.[9]

On the 9th of August, *The Commercial Tribune* reported Rheinstrom and Edna would be returning to Cincinnati "to effect a reconciliation with Mother Mina Rheinstrom and her $6,000,000." The newspaper said, after seven short months of "honeymoon bliss," the couple had become "disgusted with life on a chicken ranch." When asked about his older brother's eminent return, James Rheinstrom refused to discuss the matter, saying he had no knowledge of his brother's movements, "and had no desire to know." Brother-in-law Samuel Fechheimer also refused to speak with the press, though he did say "that scant welcome would be accorded to the headstrong young man by his relatives, and there would be considerable opposition to any reconciliation." One may well imagine circumstances had greatly improved for both these men with Harry Rheinstrom out of the picture.

The newspaper recounted the story of the court case, Rheinstrom's brief incarceration, and his subsequent marriage to Edna. On discussing their attempt at ranching, the author of the article was exceedingly unkind to Edna, and seemed to blame her for the failure of the enterprise. "The dispatches from the West say that the little actress' luxury-loving soul cast frequent longing looks toward Mamma Rheinstrom's millions in Cincinnati until she finally persuaded her husband to take the trip to this city to see whether the family could not be persuaded." As has been and will be seen, such reproaches of Edna in the press were commonplace. Rarely was Rheinstrom censured for his role in their misfortune.

As if to further advance his implication that Edna was nothing more than a gold-digging opportunist, the article's author added the following anecdote:

> One of the interesting features of the courtship was Miss Loftus' testimony at the lunacy trial, in which she admitted that during the entire six weeks of their acquaintanceship, from the first night when he met her in a Broadway café, Harry Rheinstrom had paid all her expenses, which she said amounted to about $400 a week. She admitted also at the time that he had purchased all of the handsome clothing which she was wearing, as well as the $400 diamond ring which she proudly displayed on all occasions.

The newspaper said it was expected the couple would be arriving in Cincinnati that evening or the following day, August 10. However, they were headed for disappointment, as the Widow Rheinstrom and the rest of the family were reported to be summering in Charlevoix, Michigan. When Edna and Rheinstrom did arrive in the city, supposed the newspaper, they will "find that they must travel further and find the mother in Michigan or sit on the front steps in Cincinnati and await her return."[10]

"Reconciliation? No! No!" read the headline in *The San Francisco Examiner* of August 20. "Harry Rheinstrom and his wife, formerly Edna Loftus, are to return to Cincinnati, but not to effect a reconciliation with Emma [sic] Rheinstrom, the widow of the late Abraham Rheinstrom, millionaire distillery owner." What prompted this change of heart was not disclosed by the newspaper, but Edna came away furious. When interviewed, she was no longer philosophical, but full of animosity. Snapping her fingers, Edna declared, "I will not speak to Mrs. Rheinstrom. If she came to me on her knees, I would not speak to her. I won't meet any of them. Do you think I want anything to do with people who have treated us the way they have? My family is just as good as theirs—every bit. They called me a dance hall singer. They tried to have me arrested as a vagrant. They tried to buy me off. Do you think I want to have anything to do with those kind of people? No! A thousand times—no!"

Though Rheinstrom was not interviewed by the newspaper, it was obvious he too was incensed, as he declared it was his intention to return to Cincinnati in direct competition with Rheinstrom Brothers. "It will be as President Harry Rheinstrom of the Golden West Wine Company of San Francisco and Oakland. And he will have 125,000 gallons of good California wine to dispose of, and he will laugh at the Rheinstrom Bros. and proceed to sell his wine." Purportedly, the Widow Rheinstrom had written her son in California, saying, "I am glad you are happy, Harry. I know you will do well on whatever line of work you take up. Enclosed, find a check." Harry received two checks a month, each for $100, from an annuity left him by his father.

It was also stated, on another missive, the Widow Rheinstrom had "expressed a fear that [Rheinstrom] might some day enter into competition with Rheinstrom Brothers, the largest makers of cordials in the world. Her fear was that he might use the Rheinstrom secret of making cordials." Was it his mother's anxiety which spurred Rheinstrom into returning to working in the industry he knew so well? Indeed, while managing his father's company, Rheinstrom had created a new process for making the distilled liquors which Rheinstrom Brothers sold. "It had pleased his father and the son obtained the sole right of title to the production." When questioned about her husband's intention to go into competition with Rheinstrom Brothers using this technology, Edna reportedly said, "And why not? The secret is his; he invented the process."

The Examiner noted the couple had moved into the Luxor Apartments, located in Oakland, at 1207 Grove Street, but planned to return to Cincinnati very soon. Heightening the sense of drama, in the best tradition of yellow journalism, the newspaper concluded the story with a cliffhanger,

> Young Rheinstrom has entered the lists against Rheinstrom Brothers. He has become associated with a California concern, true a wine concern, but Rheinstrom is a good salesman, and besides he has a "secret." Will Mrs. Rheinstrom of Cincinnati interfere with her son's homecoming? And will Edna Loftus turn up her haughty English nose at the mother-in-law, as she says she will, and ignore her and the rest of the family. Will she?[11]

For a brief time, it seemed as though Harry Rheinstrom had found his resolve, and was going to take a stand against is bigoted and domineering mother. However, this was not to be. In the end, Rheinstrom was not as strong of will as he would have liked people believe he was.

Rheinstrom and Edna never made it back to Cincinnati. After leaving Los Angeles, they had traveled up to Berkeley, but with their money nearly gone, they moved on to the Metropole Hotel in Oakland. They soon quit the hotel and settled in a small apartment house at 1207

Hotel Metropole, Oakland, California.

Grove Street in that town. Rheinstrom began looking for work. The deal with the wine concern must have fallen through, leaving the couple in dire straits. "Rheinstrom has for two weeks been reduced to borrowing money from chance acquaintances, and his clothes have become shabbier each day," reported *The San Francisco Call*. Then, on September 21, Rheinstrom was arrested after a fight with a police officer and a fireman near the corner of Fifteenth Street and San Pablo Avenue in Oakland. Rheinstrom reported *The San Francisco Examiner*, "was taken to the city prison, where he [was] held on suspicion of insanity."

Reportedly, Rheinstrom had been acting strangely for a few days prior. Out of concern for her husband, Edna called Dr. Guy H. Lilliancrantz. After examining Rheinstrom, the doctor stated he "must have immediate medical treatment and sent for an ambulance to take him to Fabiola Hospital." Immediately after the Lilliancrantz left the house, Rheinstrom jumped out of bed, dressed himself in a sweater and trousers, telling Edna someone was trying to poison him. Edna tried to restrain him, but he pushed past her, and ran out of the house. When he reached the fire station on Fifteenth Street, Rheinstrom dashed inside and, finding Fireman Hughes, started shouting that he need protection from the imagined poisoners. He also raved about an explosion.

Hughes took hold of Rheinstrom's arm, and attempted to calm him, but Rheinstrom broke away, and ran to San Pablo Avenue. There, he met up with Officer Ahren, and accosted him, repeating the story he had told Hughes. "Rheinstrom suddenly became violent. Ahern grappled with him. Hughes ran to the patrolman's assistance, and after a struggle, which taxed the combined efforts of both men, Rheinstrom was finally taken to the police station." At the station, Rheinstrom again stated he was being followed by men who wanted to poison him, and demanded police protection. Finally, he was taken to the Oakland Receiving Hospital, and locked into a padded cell. A sanity hearing was scheduled for the following day.

The Examiner put the story of Rheinstrom's arrest and incarceration on page one, beneath a montage of Edna and her husband. *The San Francisco Call* also reported the story on the first page, calling Rheinstrom "a dangerous madman," "a lunatic," and "a violent maniac." It was also stated, due to his delusional state, he had not eaten in several days. As it was picked up immediately by the wire service, this latest chapter in the ongoing drama became national news.[12]

"No complaint of insanity has as yet been sworn to against Harry Rheinstrom," reported *The Call* the following day. It was stated his condition was "slightly improved," but he was still exhibiting strange behaviors and persisting in his delusions. *The Examiner* reported the authorities were awaiting a telegram or other communication from the Widow Rheinstrom before they proceeded to press charges. Later in the day, it was reported Samuel Fechheimer, Rheinstrom's brother-in-law, had been dispatched by the family to deal with the situation. Meanwhile, Edna, who was said to have "sustained a slight collapse" after being notified about the arrest of her husband, remained in their residence on Grove Street.[13]

Peter Jorgenson, who was said to be "connected with the [Rheinstrom] family in a business way," told *The Oakland Tribune* on the 24th he had received a communication from the Widow Rheinstrom in which she stated she would "not come to the aid of [her son] as long as he maintained his present mode of living, and that her objection to his wife was inalterable." However, Mrs. Rheinstrom also said, if the authorities found her son was insane, and they attempted to put him under restraint, she would do all she could on his behalf.[14]

Meanwhile, Edna remained at their house on Grove Street. *The San Francisco Call* reported she was under a physician's care, and was unable to leave her room. "She has been suffering from nervous prostration since her husband became demented two days ago." It was said she had wanted to visit Rheinstrom at the hospital, but the doctor forbade her to do so.

The newspaper stated Rheinstrom's condition had not changed, but that he was not violent. The previous day, it was reported in *The Examiner* the young man had been manacled when he was placed in the cell. "No complaint has been sworn against him accusing him of insanity," said *The Call*. "It is believed that his mother's refusal to recognize his wife unbalanced his mind." *The Examiner* had put his condition down to "financial troubles," and his inability to find employment.[15]

Beside a large photo of Edna dressed in a touring costume, as though she was about to take a drive in an automobile, and a smaller photo of Rheinstrom on the farm, *The Examiner* reported the Widow Rheinstrom had ordered her son to be placed in a public asylum. Mrs. Rheinstrom had telegraphed these instructions to Mr. Jorgenson, who, in turn telephoned her ultimatum to the hospital. It was reiterated she would not help her son in any way "unless he discarded his actress wife." Mrs. Rheinstrom's only concession was that she would pay her son's expenses if he was sent to the asylum.

Edna was said to have visited the hospital the day before, in the company of Dr. Lilliancrantz, and had told a reporter she intended to have her husband taken to a private sanitarium. Lilliancrantz was to swear out a complaint the following day, Monday, September 26. "Then

[Rheinstrom] will be arraigned and given an examination in the Superior Court by a lunacy commission." The reporter also had the opportunity to speak with Rheinstrom, who was said to be spending his time reading magazines in his cell. Rheinstrom believed his system was filled with lithium bromide, which was commonly used as a sedative in that era. "That is why I didn't eat for a couple of days," said Rheinstrom. "I wanted to get some of that bromide dope out of my system. They thought I was crazy though."

Reporters also talked to the couple's neighbors at the Luxor Apartments, who commented on "the inability of Rheinstrom and his wife to readjust themselves to their reduced circumstances." Allegedly, every time Rheinstrom received one of his $100 annuity checks, he would turn it over to Edna, and the two of them would splurge for a few days, dining out and living it up. "During the remaining portion of the month, they borrowed money and even clothing from their friends." The newspaper proceeded to recount, briefly, the story of Rheinstrom's first arrest in Cincinnati, the elopement to Covington, and their attempt to make a living on the truck farm in Boyle Heights.

The Examiner then provided a brief, not quite factual, account of Edna's life prior to meeting up with Rheinstrom:

> Edna Loftus is the daughter of Mr. and Mrs. John Loftus of Manchester, England. She is the granddaughter of the famous Manchester gun-maker of that name. She is also the divorced wife of Winnie O'Connor, the jockey.... A daughter was born to Mr. and Mrs. O'Connor, and the child is now with Edna Loftus' mother in Lancashire. The O'Connor's were divorced a year ago last August in Paris. The young woman made her professional debut in "Sergeant Breu" [sic] at The Strand Theater, London. Later, she played successfully in "Madame Lengerie," as the Lancashire Lass, in "The Folie [sic] Marigny" and "Les Ambaseuders [sic]."

That same day, *The Oakland Tribune* reported Edna had moved Rheinstrom to a private sanatorium, near Livermore, a small town southeast of Oakland (in fact, the Lowell Sanatorium, where Rheinstrom was taken, was located at 3251 Fruitvale Avenue in Oakland). The reporter for *The Tribune* was much more sympathetic to the couple, and critical of the actions of the Rheinstrom family.

> The gauntlet of maternal affection was thrown down to the youth through practical strangers. He was given the alternative of disavowing his love for the woman he chose to be his wife or clinging to her almost without any consideration from his mother or his brothers, whose displeasure he provoked when he married the stage singer.

The newspaper quoted directly from the "haughty and unrelenting" letter sent to Jorgenson:

"I refuse to interfere while Harry is married. You may have him committed to an asylum, and I will see that good care is taken of him while there. Let his wife give assistance as I have no more interest in the matter. You can notify him through the hospital authorities of what I say."

Conversely, *The Examiner* reported Dr. Lilliancrantz had also received a cable from Mrs. Rheinstrom "instructing him to be guided in the case by the orders of the actress wife."

The annuity checks were to be used to pay for his stay in the sanatorium. "He was left $1,000 per month by his father, [but] the amount has been cut down since he married the woman who is now his sole caretaker." When the reporter spoke with Edna, she said she was unsure of what her plans for the future were, and was presently only concerned about getting her husband transferred to the new facility. "If you'll be good until I return," Edna told Rheinstrom, "I'll bring your best clothes soon, and take you away to a pretty home not far away." The reporter observed, "Even in his ravings, it is evident that Rheinstrom is a man of culture, and in all his petty disturbances, he seems never to divert from the precepts which he was taught at the same home which now refuses he and his bride shelter."[16]

What occurred next is unclear, and all the accounts are at odds. *The San Francisco Examiner* reported, after he was taken to the Lowell Sanatorium by his wife and Alameda County Sheriff Frank T. Barnet, and given a room, Rheinstrom begged Edna not to leave him. "Edna, don't try to leave me here alone, for if you do I will follow you. I'll not stay here alone." Edna did her best to soothe and pacify him, and soon Rheinstrom fell asleep. Edna then left the

Postcard image of Edna Loftus with a small unidentified dog (author's collection).

facility, and returned home. Then, about one o'clock in the morning, Rheinstrom awoke. He asked the attending nurse where Edna was, and the nurse explained she had gone back to Oakland. Rheinstrom then asked for a glass of water.

When the nurse left the room to fulfill the patient's request, Rheinstrom, who was dressed only in pajamas, "leaped from the bed, fled down the stairway to the front hall, burst open the door leading to the front yard, vaulted nimbly over the high fence and fled into the darkness." Almost immediately, the police were called, and a search began for the errant young man. Up to this point, the various accounts are in agreement.

The Examiner stated Rheinstrom was taken in by H. Hermanson, who lived at 543 Olive Street. Hermanson quickly realized his guest was not in his right mind, but as Rheinstrom was not violent, he did not think it necessary to call the police. It wasn't until 3:30 in the afternoon that Hermanson called Edna, who in turn called the sanatorium and the police. Edna then went over to the Hermanson home, taking with her some of her husband's clothing. After getting Rheinstrom dressed, Edna was alleged to have "started away with him." Then the police showed up, and Rheinstrom grabbed his wife by the arm, and dragging her along, ran up Redwood Road. He continued to flee until Edna became exhausted and fell. The officers then caught up with Rheinstrom, and after "a hard fight," were able to handcuff him, and return him to the sanatorium.

Once he was safely back at the facility, the reporters interviewed Dr. Lowell, Dr. Lilliancrantz, and Edna. The former believed Rheinstrom's condition was the result of "a prolonged debauch or extended use of drugs of some kind." The latter claimed Rheinstrom's mental illness was "due to excessive use of cigarettes." Edna firmly denied Rheinstrom was a drug addict. She remained optimistic, saying, "I don't know whether Harry's mother will help him or not, but if she doesn't, he shall have the best attendance I can get. I will go to work and will earn the money necessary to pay for his treatment until he is well again. I know he will get well soon, and we will be happy again."

As noted, the accounts were in agreement about how Rheinstrom escaped, but *The San Francisco Call* stated he had wandered from house to house, seeking shelter, and "he was caught at nightfall … in the foothills near Allendale, fully clad … and accompanied by his wife." The newspaper further stated Rheinstrom and Edna had planned the escape. When the police found him, he "was walking quietly with his bride, holding the woman's arm." However, when he saw the police, his demeanor changed, and he began "raving," and fighting, "and for 15 minutes his captors rolled on the dust with him." *The Call* reported Rheinstrom was then packed into an automobile, taken back to the sanatorium. "There the prisoner was strapped hand and foot, and ... two attendants sat with him in the room, behind nailed windows and locked doors."

The Evening Times-Star, the Alameda newspaper, reported that after he escaped, Rheinstrom eluded police until late in the afternoon. It was then a policeman in an automobile spotted him "hiding in a ravine in the rolling country in the Allendale district." *The Times-Star* also said Rheinstrom had randomly rung doorbells and knocked on doors, frightening the residents, by his "unseemly appearance." He was denied entry at several homes before he "secured admission at some house in the hills, where he secured additional clothing, and refreshments." He stayed there for some time, but finally stated he wanted some fresh air, stepped outside, and vanished.

This author is of the opinion the first of these accounts is closest to being factual. The question remains where Edna was taking Rheinstrom when they left the Hermanson home. Amusingly, and probably much to the continuing embarrassment of the Rheinstrom family, the news of Rheinstrom's incarceration in the sanatorium and subsequent escape were carried the following day in *The Cincinnati Enquirer*.[17]

Dr. Frank S. Lowell, the head of the Lowell Sanatorium, was interviewed by *The San Francisco Examiner* the day after Rheinstrom's escape.

> "Harry Rheinstrom will probably recover his sanity," said the physician, "although it will be a month or more before this can be definitely stated and before we can restore him to his normal condition of body and mind, can be sure of the causes for his recent nervous breakdown, or that he can ultimately be cured."

Lowell went on to say, since Rheinstrom's return, he had been extremely nervous, but showed no inclination toward violence. At times, the young man was completely lucid and at other times he babbled "in a most erratic manner." He was still restrained, as he often spoke of going away, and insisted he was being held illegally.

"He is in the condition of one who has indulged in a prolonged debauch of some kind that has left him a neurotic. It will take some time to restore his nervous and physical health. When that has been accomplished, we can make a reasonable diagnosis of his mental condition and predict the outcome." The doctor added he intended to write the Widow Rheinstrom in Cincinnati and acquaint them with his patient's condition. Edna, who had been at Rheinstrom's side constantly since he was returned, did not believe the family would do anything for their relation, especially not financially. It was said Edna alone was able to quiet him when he became agitated.

"Harry's mother and other members of the family are opposed to me because I am a gentile and he is a Jew, and not because they have any other objection to me. They want to get rid of me, but I love Harry and I will not leave him no matter what they might offer me in money." Edna reiterated it was her intention to seek out gainful employment to defray the cost of his treatment at the sanatorium. She did not indicate if she would return to the stage—which would have been her best, most lucrative option—or work in another field. Unfortunately, her options, like most women of that era, were rather limited.[18]

There was no further news about Edna or Rheinstrom until October 16, when *The Oakland Tribune* announced Edna would be returning to the stage. "Accepting the challenge of Mrs. Rheinstrom of Cincinnati, Edna Loftus, the English musical comedy actress, has obtained employment for the purpose of meeting the expenses of her husband." The newspaper did not elaborate further, but *The San Francisco Examiner* did. Edna was said to have signed a contract with a downtown café for a nightly concert each evening for six weeks, starting October 22. *The Examiner* did not give the name of the café, but said Edna would be supported in her act by Miss Allies Clark, Miss Hazel Spinelli, and Miss Frances Howard. The newspaper also ran a photo of Edna, who was quoted as saying,

> I suppose Harry's family will have a fit when they learn I am going to sing in a café. Well, I don't think it any disgrace to work for a living, and that is my way of earning a living. If his mother will send me $10,000, I'll give up the contract I have signed, but in the meantime, Harry and I must have money to live. After I close my engagement at the café, I am going on the Orpheum circuit. If Harry's family won't support him, I will have to, in view of the fact he is not well. His mother says she will take him back if he returns without me, but, of course, we won't separate. They send his expenses while he is at the sanatorium, but what he gets doesn't support me.

Under the headline "Edna Loftus Goes to Work," *The Commercial Tribune*, which had inferred Edna was little more than an over-priced prostitute just two months prior, showed some sympathy for the couple's plight. "Rheinstrom is in a sanitarium near by (San Francisco), where he is said to be a physical wreck. Mrs. Rheinstrom said that it would be necessary for her to go to work to support herself, and has returned to the stage, her former occupation. Relatives of young Rheinstrom are in this state, but refuse to help his wife."[19]

The day after this announcement was made, there was yet another dramatic turn in Edna's story. *The Oakland Tribune* reported, "Pretty

Edna Loftus, petite and fascinating, not quite as beautiful as when she left the gay whirl of the New York chorus ... but fascinating withal, and winsome, was locked in the city prison this morning, charged with defrauding an automobile driver." Edna, who had moved back into the Hotel Metropole, had gone into the city of San Francisco to finalize arrangements for her engagement. Afterwards, she called for a taxi driver. When it arrived, she instructed the driver, J.V. McClausland, to wait outside for her. He did, but Edna never came out. Two hours later, McClausland went inside and demanded a payment of $3.60 from Edna. Derisively, the embittered columnist wrote,

> For a moment last night, Edna Loftus forgot her new life. She followed her natural inclinations. She was a chorus girl once more, and the belle of them all. She was to be admired, petted, spoiled. She was to pass through, if only as a looker on, the gay night life of the western metropolis. She did. She drank from the cup of pleasure, she came, she saw, and she certainly conquered, but the end was far too prosaic to suit her cultivated sense of the Proprieties. It was a café that was the scene of the finale.

When Edna refused to pay the driver, the police were called. The responding officers, identified as Sergeant Fraher and Policeman Welch, arrested her, and took her to jail. "There was a short trip to the booking sergeant, a few questions asked and answered, and with a gay toss of her head and a smile which was meant to express the scorn she felt for the prison policemen in particular, but all the guardians of the peace in general, the former chorus girl was bailed out." It was not disclosed by whom. Later that morning, she appeared in police court, but her case was continued to the following day. "Meanwhile, the public is soon to see her once more before the footlights. Harry is sick, and these heroes of a romantic love affair must have a place to sleep and something to eat."[20]

More details about the incident were revealed in *The San Francisco Chronicle*. Edna had "fluttered moth-like around the gleaming lights of the Tenderloin early yesterday morning, and was arrested at 5 o'clock in the Mirror saloon at 145 Eddy street." McCausland stated Edna had telephoned for a cab from the Mirror at 2:30 in the morning. He found Edna in the saloon, in the company of Mrs. W.H. Deming, and told her the automobile was at the curb. "She waved her hand somewhat imperiously and ordered him to wait outside." After waiting in the cold for two hours, McCausland went back in and demanded payment. Edna refused to pay him, and the police were called. Edna was taken to jail, where she languished for four hours before being bailed out by Attorney Cadwallader with a bond of $20. When she appeared before Police Court Judge Charles T. Conlan, the magistrate thought she seemed "slightly confused," so he ordered the case held over.[21]

Postcard image of Edna Loftus with a ribbon (author's collection).

Chapter Four. Into the West 109

Was Edna's "confusion" due to imbibing alcohol and/or drugs? The editor of the *San Jose Mercury News*, Everis A. Hayes, made mention of Edna's arrest in a column in the newspaper's October 19 edition. Hayes was complaining about the newspapers in larger cities, and their predilection for the sensational and mixing facts with fiction. Wrote Hayes:

> True, we like a sensation and read it with avidity whether it be truth or fiction. If Edna Loftus, the actress, is taken from a saloon to jail because she refused to pay her chauffer, most of us rise to the fly and swallow it as though it were the most important thing in the world. It is the appetite of the times, this craving for the unusual or abnormal.... We know the newspaper man is playing with our perverted tastes, dangling the same old fly before us; yet we rise to it each time as though it was the freshest bait in the basket.

Of course, Hayes was doing exactly what he derided his contemporaries for doing—selling sensational and lurid stories to his readers, but doing so under the guise of an editorial. Worse, Hayes, simply by mentioning the incident, only added to Edna's growing notoriety.[22]

San Francisco's Tenderloin District is a 31 square block area bounded by McAllister, Polk, Geary, and Mason Streets. As Tenderloin

Tenderloin District, San Francisco, California, ca. 1910 (San Francisco History Center, San Francisco Public Library).

historian Randy Shaw observed, the legend that has grown up around the district that it was "a vice-dominated neighborhood akin to the Barbary Coast" is just that—a legend. Certainly, the area had its fair share of low-rent saloons, gambling dens, and brothels, but it was also home to numerous upscale restaurants, theaters, and hotels.

After the earthquake and devastating fires of 1906, the mayor of San Francisco, Patrick Henry "P. H." McCarthy, declared the new San Francisco would be the "Paris of America." Shaw stated the Tenderloin "outdid all other neighborhoods in fulfilling this vision."

Among the notable businesses which opened in the area were The Odeon, Blanco's Café, The Poodle Dog, The Cadillac Hotel, The Panama Café, and The Black Cat Cabaret. Mason Street, which formed the eastern border of the district, was re-christened "The White Way" on account of the myriad of electric lights which illuminated the thoroughfare at night. However, the Tenderloin did not replace the Barbary Coast, which prior to 1913 had been the city's premier red light district. In contrast, the Tenderloin was largely a residential neighborhood. What made it unique, says Shaw, was the lack of single family homes. The area "was overwhelmingly comprised of studio and one bedroom apartments as well single room occupancy hotels," and most its residents were middle and working class adults without children.

As the majority of these dwellings had neither kitchen facilities nor private baths, residents, both male and female, were obliged to frequent the cafes and bathhouses in the district. "With thousands of Tenderloin single adults living alone in single rooms or small apartments, the cafes, restaurants, saloons, and other entertainment venues had a ready-made customer base." Being that many of the residents of the district were young males, dance halls and brothels flourished as well. Until the second decade of the 1900s, when a very vocal minority of religious reformers and self-appointed moralists began a campaign to end vice in the district, prostitution was quasi-legal, and was generally accepted as "a necessary evil" (deemed "necessary" because it served the sexual desires of the patriarchal hierarchy). Historian Jacqueline Baker Barnhart observed, "When (the middle class Victorians) mentioned prostitution, it was to condemn it, but they seldom used their influence to force the police or legislators to put an end to it."

However, the majority of the young, unmarried women living in the Tenderloin were not prostitutes. Many were shop-girls, domestics, and factory workers. For these women, the district offered them real freedom. These women lived in the same buildings as men, regularly went to the cafes and clubs without chaperones, and drank liquor, fraternized and flirted, and danced well into the night. Such open displays of female autonomy and independence drew the ire of the reformers. "(N)ewly independent, wage-earning women represented such a departure from the middle class values of the past," said Shaw, "that their dancing in public and openly expressing their sexuality were seen as symbols of 'moral decay.'" The moralists decried women's independence as a threat to the traditional domestic roles allotted women within the patriarchal social construct as wives and mothers.

Shaw asserts the Tenderloin district was never really as vice-ridden and corrupt as these sanctimonious moral reformers and the period newspapers led the public to believe it was. Certainly, it was home to gambling halls, bordellos, saloons, and opium dens, and the police and city officials regularly accepted bribes from the owners of these establishments to turn a blind eye to the illicit activities going on within, However, as Shaw noted, none of these businesses were actually engaged in illegal trades. Shaw postulated the reformers had a "much broader agenda than shuttering bordellos and clamping down on prostitution." They were seeking to curtail the freedoms young women living in the district were enjoying, and force them to return to traditional Victorian-era gender roles.[23]

A reporter from *The Chronicle* sought out Moses "Morris" Meyerfeld, Jr., the president of the Orpheum circuit, to verify Edna's story about working there. Meyerfeld said he had interviewed Edna, and she had brought him photographs and press notices from her days on the English stage. "She wanted to make an appointment to show me what she could do in the way of a vaudeville act, but I heard from those who know her that she would not be likely to be a valuable addition to the Orpheum circuit, so I gave her no encouragement. She has received no offer from us and will receive none, although she is a very attractive-looking young person."

Doubtlessly, Meyerfeld had heard of the Rheinstrom affair and Edna's run-ins with the law, as these had been widely publicized. He may well have even known the Rheinstrom family, as he had formerly been in the liquor distribution business. Was Meyerfeld's decision not to employ Edna based on a lack of talent, or did Meyerfeld, who like the Rheinstroms was Jewish, decide to side with the family—"those who know her"—against Edna based on the fact she was a Gentile? Doubtlessly, having Edna Loftus, who had garnered so much publicity nationwide since the affair with Rheinstrom began, would have been quite the draw on the Orpheum circuit, which makes Meyerfeld's decision not to sign Edna to a contract seem all the more curious.

After her ordeal, actress Evelyn Nesbit observed, "Notoriety had made it next to impossible for me to earn a living like other people."[24]

The United Press picked up the story of Edna's arrest, and over the next couple of days it was disseminated by the newspapers across the country. On page one, above a photograph of Edna and Rheinstrom, probably taken at the time of their marriage, *The Commercial Tribune* trumpeted "Rheinstroms Under Arrest." The article below the photo was brief, making mention of Rheinstrom's being detained by the police as a "fugitive from justice" on the complaint of Dr. Lowell. Additionally, there was a charge of disturbing the peace pending against him in Oakland. "Lately, however, [Rheinstrom] has been confined in a sanitarium at Livermore. He escaped from that institution and was arrested [in San Francisco]." Edna's arrest on the charge of defrauding a chauffeur was summed up in a sentence by the newspaper.[25]

Publicity photograph of Miss Evelyn Nesbit (author's collection).

More embarrassing still for Edna was the revelation which appeared in *The Chronicle* the following day. When she returned to court, Edna was standing near the door in the courtroom when the bailiff called for "Mollie Wilson." Edna "looked about curiously, waiting for someone to reply. Then it dawned on her that Wilson was the name she had given at the City Prison on Monday morning ... she gave a little start and answered, 'Here!'" Why Edna was even called is unknown, as a few minutes prior, Mr. McClausland had told Judge Conlan the matter had been settled and he did not want to prosecute.

Judge Conlan asked, "Where were you paid?" The cab driver replied, "At Staak's. I was told to come there and she paid the bill." At this, Judge Conlan retorted, "It strikes me that the police courts are being made collection agencies. You had no right to receive the money! I will have this investigated, and if possible I will punish you for this."

Edna, dressed in "a blue suit of girlish cut, with a dainty lace collar which showed her throat to excellent advantage," then took the stand. She told Judge Conlan, "I told him to take me home and I would pay him, but instead he took me to jail. I would have paid him. He also lied when he said I wanted him to take me to the beach. Why, I *nevah* heard of the place" (Again, we see the use of the dialect being used by the author in mockery of Edna's accent.) Attorney Cadwallader, who had paid Edna's bond, represented her in court. He stated he could supply "reputable witnesses" who would testify to the fact that Edna was perfectly able to pay the fare, and had no intention of defrauding Mr. McClausland. The case was continued until the following day by order of the court.

The Chronicle also reported, after hearing of Edna's arrest, that the Widow Rheinstrom had sent a telegram to her son in the sanatorium in which "she expressed her sincere sympathy to her son in the trouble that had been forced upon him." It was said to be evident from the tone of the cable that the Widow was still insistent that Rheinstrom divorce his wife, and stated all support, even his annuity would be cut off come January. When asked about Edna's arrest, Rheinstrom said he deeply regretted the incident, but remained loyal to his wife. "He does not know what the plans or intentions of Edna Loftus may be, but [was] confident she [would] return to him at the sanatorium and stay by his side till he is in the best physical and mental condition." The newspaper said those who are closest to Rheinstrom were "deeply interested as to what will be the result as regards Edna Loftus," and were speculating about whether she would remain with him or return to the stage.[26]

Edna was supposed to return to court on the 20th, but she did not. When asked where his client was, Attorney Cadwallader admitted he did not know. A bench warrant was then issued for her arrest. When Edna did return to Police Court on October 21, "looking pretty as usual, but exceedingly fragile withal, and with an element that appeared much like repentance in her countenance," more drama unfolded. When the bailiff read the bench warrant to her, instructing that she be taken into custody, Edna fainted away. "She put both hands to her head and would have fallen had not the officer held her." *The Oakland Tribune* insisted Edna's faint was not merely stagecraft, as evidenced by the fact it took four women fifteen minutes to revive her. Edna was removed to the judge's chambers, "where Mrs. Ella S. Tuttle, her mother Mrs. Seaton, and her sister Mrs. Foley, having in their charge Effie Wilson, the girl murderer ... set to the task to revive Edna, which they did with considerable difficulty."

Judge Conlan, who was too sick to take his seat upon the bench, was immediately contacted by telephone. He was apprised of Edna's condition "and the fact she had been placed under arrest [and] dismissed the charge against her."[27]

The very next day, the newspapers across the country reported Rheinstrom had once again escaped from the Lowell Sanatorium. Dr. Lowell told the police Rheinstrom had stolen some of his clothing and then fled Oakland, making it across the bay and into San Francisco. Dr. Lowell followed Rheinstrom into the city. On Polk Street, the doctor pointed Rheinstrom out to a policeman, and the young man was arrested, and taken to jail. Rheinstrom was charged with being a fugitive from justice. Dr. Lowell stated he made the charge against his patient "on the order of Rheinstrom's mother [and] that incompetency proceedings may be begun against the young man." *The San Francisco Examiner*, which broke the story in the Bay Area, also recapped Edna's brush with the law, saying Judge Conlan had dismissed the case against her because he believed Edna "had suffered enough."[28]

Though he was reportedly strapped to a bed at the Receiving Hospital to prevent him attacking the attendants or once again attempting to escape, *The Oakland Tribune* reported Rheinstrom "exhibited sufficient lucidity ... to declare that he will make a hard fight in the superior court to prevent his commitment to a state insane asylum." Judge William H. Waste had scheduled Rheinstrom's hearing before the lunacy commission for Monday, October 24. Rheinstrom stated he had engaged an attorney and would demand a jury trial.

After Rheinstrom's latest arrest, Dr. Lowell asked the San Francisco authorities to hold him until charges could be brought against him in Alameda County. Dr. Lowell then returned to Oakland, where he filed a complaint with the district attorney, and a warrant was given over to Deputy Sheriff Emlay, "warden for the insane," which he served later that evening. Deputy Emlay returned to Oakland, and Rheinstrom was lodged in a "strong room" at the Receiving Hospital. Dr. Lowell confessed it was no longer possible to hold Rheinstrom at his sanatorium.

It was not believed that Edna's legal troubles were the catalyst for Rheinstrom's latest escape, as he had not seen her recently. "All that Deputy Sheriff Emlay could get out of Rheinstrom during the trip back to Oakland ... was that he had a 'hot time last night in San Francisco dodging the tall buildings." However, Dr. Lowell maintained "the influence of Edna Loftus over her husband has been, and was, even at the present time, very bad." Even though Edna was previously said to have a calming influence on her husband, Dr. Lowell had several times refused to let her see Rheinstrom. After her arrest, Edna had not been to visit

Rheinstrom at all. "Her present whereabouts are unknown," said the newspaper. However, when asked if he wanted to see Edna, Rheinstrom replied, "You bet I do, but she will be here in due time."

Dr. Lowell did reveal that upon telling Rheinstrom he had received a letter at the sanatorium from the Widow Rheinstrom in which she wrote "if he returned home with Dr. Lowell, she would forgive everything and provide for him," Rheinstrom said he would accept the offer. However, an hour later, Rheinstrom declared he had changed his mind, and would not give up Edna.

The 22nd was also to be the day Edna started her six-week engagement at the café as a chanteuse. It is not known if this occurred, as it was not advertised or reported in the local newspapers. Considering all that had happened with Edna and her husband, the owner may well have decided to cancel the engagement.[29]

On the 23rd, *The San Francisco Call* reported Edna had not been to visit Rheinstrom at the Receiving Hospital. Worse yet, on the 24th, it was reported Edna had been hospitalized after drinking herself into a stupor. Few details were provided by *The Call*, which said Edna, "when she was unable to care for herself," had been rescued at about four o'clock in the morning by a benevolent taxi driver. The taxi driver took her to the Park Emergency Hospital. "Edna is of athletic build, and although she disturbed the serenity of the hospital, she was placed on the operating table by Steward William Maloney and her stomach was pumped out. It was found she had almost incapacitated herself by imbibing too much liquor." Edna was then placed on a cot until ten o'clock, when she was transferred to the German hospital.[30]

"Tired in mind and body, nerves completely shattered from over-indulgence in intoxicating liquors, penniless, and sick at heart ... Edna Loftus is under observation at the German hospital," reported *The Oakland Tribune*, later in the day. Dr. Walter D. Harder confided that Edna, "while in an advanced stage of intoxication," had fallen out of a taxicab and sustained a severe injury to her head. Though she was reportedly better than when she had been brought in, she was still not well, and she believed that she was being kept from seeing her husband. At some point Edna declared "as long as she [was] separated from him, she doesn't care what happens to her." The newspaper alleged, on Saturday night, that Edna had been seen in the company of another man, and it was this man, not the taxi driver, who had brought her to Park Emergency Hospital. When asked about Rheinstrom, Edna cried, "I want to know his exact condition. I want him to love me again. I want to be near him."[31]

"Edna Loftus Near Delirium Tremens" announced *The Sacramento Daily Union* on the front page of its edition of October 24. The newspaper reported she had become "hysterical" at a San Francisco beach roadhouse earlier that very morning, and "was rushed to the Park hospital in a taxicab," arriving about 4:00 a.m. It was Steward Malone who stated she was on the verge of delirium tremens. He ordered that Edna be put to bed and administered medication to help her to sleep. *The Daily Union* ended the article saying Edna was at the German hospital and "resting easily." It was expected she would be released within 48 hours if not sooner.[32]

The Ohio newspaper *The Alliance Daily Review*, proved to be a little more sympathetic than most the other newspapers. Under the headline "Two People are Unfortunate," *The Daily Review* reported Rheinstrom "was strapped to a cot in the Oakland receiving hospital" after having been judged insane, while Edna "became so hysterical at a beach road house ... she was rushed to the Park Hospital in a taxicab." There was no mention in *The Daily Review* or any other newspaper of Edna's falling out of the taxi or being injured as had been reported by *The Oakland Tribune*. *The Alliance* went on to say Edna had been diagnosed by the steward as being "on the verge of delirium tremens" and was summarily medicated and was put to bed.

The man with whom Edna had been keeping company was identified by *The San Francisco Chronicle* as Arthur Steele. It was further stated that Edna had been found "in an Ocean Beach roadhouse in an unconscious condition," before being was taken to the Park Hospital in the taxi. Dr. Harder, the physician at the hospital, stated Edna was suffering from "alcoholism." After she had started feeling better, she was moved to the German Hospital "where secrecy was kept."[33]

"Asylum for Rheinstrom: Edna Loftus is Blamed!" screamed the headline on page one of *The San Francisco Examiner* on October 25, 1910. Beneath a large picture of Edna in profile, the newspaper reported that after having heard the testimony and weighed the evidence, the Judge had Rheinstrom committed to the Stockton Insane Asylum.

> Without exception, the witnesses attributed the young fellow's condition to a great extent to the society of his wife. All of them advocated his immediate separation from her, and the recital of her confinement in a San Francisco hospital on the verge of delirium tremens undoubtedly entered into the consideration of the case by the examining physicians.

The physicians were not in complete agreement. It was reported that Dr. Lowell and one Dr. William W. Tedford "contributed to the excitement of the hearing by hurling charges at each other." Tedford declared that Lowell wanted Rheinstrom committed so he might realize a fee for his treatment. Lowell retorted, alleging Tedford was not actually a physician. This same insult was hurled back at Lowell by Tedford.

Chapter Four. Into the West

Insane Asylum of California at Stockton.

Finally, Judge Waste pointed out that Lowell had verily forfeited any chance he may have had to collect a fee when he swore out the complaint against Rheinstrom. "Tedford explained he was an old friend of Rheinstrom, and announced the young fellow was being persecuted and that his rights were being taken away from him." He continued with this harangue, until Judge Waste threatened to charge him with contempt of court.

Peter Jorgensen appeared on behalf of the Rheinstrom family, and "shed considerable light upon the origins of the young fellow's troubles." After the death of his father, Rheinstrom had been put in charge of the company, but within a few months had severely jeopardized the financial stability of the company by his extravagant expenditures. Rheinstrom was constantly traveling between Cincinnati, Chicago, and New York, and had wanted to buy a Pullman train car to put the company offices in. His meeting Edna in New York, and his spending of thousands of dollars on her in a matter of days, were not seen as a symptom of his own profligate and imprudent habits; these were blamed on Edna. She was painted as a shameless golddigger, who had attached herself like a leech to Rheinstrom in the hope of bilking him all she could. Jorgensen then recounted the tale of Rheinstrom's first arrest, the elopement, the truck farm, and his unsuccessful attempts to "enter into various business enterprises about the bay."

Jorgensen stated he had been in daily communication with the Rheinstrom family throughout, and it was their desire to have Rheinstrom committed to a state institution. Dr. Lowell declared the young man would benefit greatly from being separated from Edna. He also spoke to the grandiose plans which Rheinstrom had shared with him, including establishing businesses to complete with steel magnate Charles M. Schwab and oil baron John D. Rockefeller, and building an exclusive sanitarium for Emperor Kaiser William and Theodore Roosevelt. Warden Emlay testified about various other delusions, though Rheinstrom insisted he had been joking with the man.

"I admit that I sometimes have trances." said Rheinstrom in his own defense. "They are only temporary, however. I am high-strung and maybe it is natural. I love my wife, and I would marry her all over again. Maybe that is insanity also." Doctors Todd and Dodsworth, after examining Rheinstrom, declared he was suffering from "hallucinal [sic] insanity," and recommended his commitment to the state asylum.[34]

The report carried by *The San Francisco Call* read as indictment of Edna, with nothing in the way of reference to Rheinstrom's delusions. "The story of Edna Loftus' control over the youthful brewer was told today by Peter Jorgensen.... From the time she met Rheinstrom, said Jorgensen, she became the master of his destiny." After Abraham Rheinstrom's death in 1909, almost a year before he met Edna, Harry Rheinstrom had taken over management of the brewery, as "it was thought that Harry Rheinstrom would display the same commercial genius." By Jorgensen's own account, as recorded in *The Examiner*, young Rheinstrom had not displayed such acumen, but had begun acting the part of a high-roller. *The Call* summarily ignored this portion of the testimony, and, like Rheinstrom's family' laid the blame for his downfall before Edna's "scintillating slippers."

After meeting Edna in New York, "Cincinnati held no charms for him. He made frequent trips to the great metropolis.... He abandoned his business. He was caught in the maelstrom and borne down on an eddying torrent. His family sent him to an Ohio sanatorium. Finally, Edna herself tore him from his surroundings, took him to Kentucky, and there they were married." The rest of the half column article continued on in this same vein, with Edna being cast as the femme fatale who destroyed the life of young Rheinstrom in a quest for fame and riches.[35]

"Two crises in the tempestuous careers of Harry Rheinstrom and his wife, Edna Loftus of the London music halls, Lobster square, New York, and our own Great White Way occurred at almost the same time yesterday," reported *The San Francisco Chronicle*. Rheinstrom was adjudged insane, and was committed to the Stockton Insane Asylum, while Edna "was evicted from her little white bed at the German Hospital and left there without dress or hat at 3 o'clock in the afternoon." The newspaper stated Edna had been admitted suffering from alcohol poisoning, "induced by unrestrained indulgence in champagne too liberally provided by admirers gathered by the wayside."

It was said Edna had hoped to remain at the German Hospital for a week or so, until she had recovered from "the effects of her exuberant enjoyment of the night life." However, Edna only had 25¢ to her name, and no one among her friends stepped up to help her to pay the cost of her stay at the hospital. This being the case, the hospital staff informed Edna that she had "recovered sufficiently to fare forth," and told her she needed to vacate the premises by three o'clock that afternoon. "Vigorous use of the telephone brought no responsive friends," so, at the appointed time, Edna dressed herself in pumps and a veil, and covered her silk petticoat with a long plush coat. It was said her dress and hat had been lost during her "meteoric dash" along the Great White Way.

Edna departed with a man who was not identified, and who came only to escort her, not to pay her bill. A while later a young man showed up with a big bouquet, and asked to see Edna. When told she had left with another, the youth was crestfallen. He threw the flowers on the ground "and departed in moody disappointment." Needless to say, Edna was not present at the examination, but allegedly called the receiving hospital to see if she could get possession of the $100 check which Rheinstrom had in his possession when he was arrested on Saturday, "but she made no inquiries at all as to the fate of her husband."[36]

The editor of *The Morning Union*, a sanctimonious man named William F. Prisk, penned a decidedly spiteful editorial about the Rheinstrom affair in the October 29 edition of said newspaper. After entreating his readers to "set ... to thinking over the carelessness of society," he set his sights on Rheinstrom, saying he was "nearly an imbecile and has always been a degenerate. And yet he was allowed to marry and with his wife journey throughout the country giving despicable and revolting exhibition of depravity in life." Prisk was no kinder to Edna, saying she "was entirely lacking in womanly qualities" and stating her "penchant for indulging in liquor," which left her mind "besotted."

Prisk briefly recapped the events of the past few weeks of the couple's lives, and then launched into a Pecksniffian diatribe. "This is a couple which should be suppressed. It is exhibit one of the degenerate tendency of society and should teach a lesson, but it might also cause a malign influence to be exerted over the minds of some of the young, who are not as yet trained in the discerning discrimination between what is and what is not right."[37]

Chapter Five

Spiraling Downward

After his incarceration in the Stockton Asylum, the public lost interest in Harry Rheinstrom. On the 30th of October 1910, *The New York Tribune* published what could well have been an obituary for the unfortunate young man, saying, "The career of Harry Rheinstrom, son of the millionaire Cincinnati brewer, came to an end ... last week, when he was adjudged insane and placed in an Oakland sanatorium." The newspaper stated he had been an "active businessman," until he met and became infatuated with Edna. "He lavished large sums on her, and when his mother tried to separate the pair, he married her." This resulted in his being cut off financially, which led to his drinking heavily, "and soon he became a wreck." The newspaper told of the circumstances of his arrest and, in closing, said Rheinstrom "has been put in a place where he can do no more harm."[1]

On the other hand, Edna continued to be fodder for the press. Despite having lost her husband to mental illness, there was little sympathy shown her by the newspapers. *The Lincoln Star* quipped, "Anyhow, Edna Loftus is luckier than most actresses who bag millionaire husbands. Hers doesn't waste money in divorce courts, but has his fun racing through California highways in his nightgowns and goes to the asylum like a good fellow."[2]

San Francisco police officer Thomas Kelley was alerted to a woman screaming "Burglars! Burglars!" on November 13, and rushed to 1780 O'Farrell Street. When Kelley arrived on the scene, he found Edna, who in "excited tones" told the officer a tall, dark man, dressed in a black suit, had attempted to crawl in her window. Kelley searched the premises and the neighborhood, but found no one fitting this description. Edna, who had been screaming in terror—"a somewhat new thing for her"—was finally calmed, and persuaded to re-enter the house. A later report stated the man had only peered through the window while Edna was retiring. This "Peeping Tom" was said to be wearing a brown suit, a soft light hat, and a red necktie. He was also clean-shaven. *The Oakland*

Chapter Five. Spiraling Downward

Tribune, which first reported story, said, "The bewitching actress of other days, whose trials and tribulations have been made public property, seems to be getting in the public eye of late."[3]

Four days later, Edna was featured again in that newspaper. This time she was in court and attempting to challenge Peter Jorgenson's suit for guardianship of Rheinstrom before Superior Court Judge Frank H. Dunne. During his testimony, Jorgenson alleged the couple had frequently engaged in "sprees, drinking bouts, and escapades" in the Tenderloin district.

> With her big blue eyes flashing and her general appearance indicative of prosperity, Edna Loftus was on hand to push her claim and was prepared to object to any aspersions cast on "Dear Harry,'" and to hiss, "That's a lie!" when accused by a witness of accompanying her husband on a series of debauches after the receipt of an allowance from mamma-in-law.

Jorgenson, who was a retired confectioner, claimed the Widow Rheinstrom had asked him to look after her son, because of his connection to the family and its business, and this was his reason for applying for the guardianship. In her petition for guardianship of Rheinstrom, Edna asserted she was Rheinstrom's lawful wife, and the application submitted by Jorgenson was part of a larger conspiracy to keep her and her husband apart. In question were the $100 annuity checks, which would continue to be sent to Rheinstrom until the first of the year, and who would control these funds.

Postcard image of Edna Loftus in her stockings (author's collection).

Obviously, Edna, who had no other income to speak of, needed these checks to survive.

Edna's having control of these funds was one of the main reasons Jorgenson objected to Edna's appointment. "I understand that since the couple left Cincinnati, when they would receive a check twice a month, they would go on a debauch for two or three days, and then Harry would go around without any clothes," said Jorgenson from the stand. "That's a lie!" cried Edna, half rising from her seat. Though Judge Dunne did not hear the interruption, the bailiff was obliged to warn Edna if there was another such outburst, she would be removed from the courtroom.

Jorgenson continued, saying he had been informed, whenever they had received one of these checks, that Edna and Rheinstrom were in the habit of going on sprees and visiting Mason Street resorts, on the eastern edge of the Tenderloin. The implication was that if Edna was in control of the money, she would continue going on sprees. Edna's attorney, Robert T. Devlin, countered, stating Edna did not really need the money. When Devlin observed that Edna "could make more money on the stage than most lawyers do ... the court suggested that it might be a good thing for her to do, and leave Harry alone for a while." Edna should have known in that moment the odds of her being appointed as Rheinstrom's guardian were very poor indeed.

Devlin then changed tactics, arguing Jorgenson, who readily admitted it was his intention to separate Rheinstrom and Edna, would do just this if he were appointed as guardian, necessarily made him the wrong person for the job. Devlin said he would not object to a third party—a disinterested party—being appointed to the guardianship. At one point in the proceedings, the court asked Jorgenson directly if he were prejudiced against Edna. "Well, naturally, a little," was Jorgenson's response. Still, Jorgenson swore he would not become part of the conspiracy against Edna, though, in fact, as an agent for Widow Rheinstrom, he already was.

To further show that Jorgenson's machinations on behalf of the Widow Rheinstrom were not in the best interest of the couple, who remained very close and very much in love, Devlin produced a letter, written by Rheinstrom, and addressed to Edna. The missive began, "Dearest thing on earth, my little wife." In the letter, which was summarily read into evidence, Rheinstrom asked Edna to continue to be patient and assured her everything would work out well in the end. It concluded, "Dearest love and truest affection for you, also a soul kiss, Your loving husband, Hal."

The story of Edna's submitting a writ of habeas corpus to have

Chapter Five. Spiraling Downward

her husband freed from the College Hill Sanitarium was also entered into evidence. Edna tried through affidavits and through her attorney to prove her husband was not insane, and that his commitment to the Stockton Asylum was part of an ongoing conspiracy to separate them from one another. "She declared that her husband did not need a guardian, but that if the court decided he did, she was the rightful person." Despite her efforts, the following day, *The San Francisco Examiner* announced. "Edna Loftus Loses Guardianship Fight." However, Devlin, by the force of his arguments against Jorgenson, as being prejudiced and in league with the Widow Rheinstrom, inclined the Judge to admonish the candy-maker. Jorgenson was told "to be careful and do nothing to antagonize the wife." Still, in the end, Judge Dunne appointed Jorgenson to be Rheinstrom's guardian.

Notably, both *The Oakland Tribune* and *The San Francisco Examiner* commented on Edna's ensemble, the former observing Edna had "a general appearance indicative of prosperity" and the latter stating she was "dressed in that latest fashion." As Edna was neither working regularly nor receiving any financial support, how was she able to afford stylish clothing she attended court in? The answer to this question would not be forthcoming until January of the following year.[4]

The sanctimonious editor of *The Morning Union*, Mr. Prisk, weighed in on the decision, with his usual lack of wit. He noted a guardian had been chosen for Rheinstrom, "who had the fortune and misfortune to have a married an actress. She objected to the guardianship matter. She should be supported in her objection by all citizens, for she is a spender, and the money, representing the fortune of her husband, would soon be put back into circulation, if she has her way." Instead, said Prisk, the money would be hoarded by the family "for the use of the incompetent [Rheinstrom] ... or spent slowly in his care." Prisk reasoned it would be better to have Rheinstrom confined to a public asylum [as he was], "with just enough to pay for his actual needs, and the rest of the money in the channels of business, doing its work, and benefiting those who are chasing after the mighty dollar."[5]

The decision of Judge Dunne left Edna in dire straits. For the next three weeks, she tried to find a position or an engagement, but was disappointed at every turn. She was residing temporarily with a woman named Mrs. Dixie Montgomery at 1780 O'Farrell Street, in what is today the Fillmore District of San Francisco.

> Disheartened and discouraged by constant struggles and buffeting with which she has been contending, and brooding over her husband's absence, and the fact the guardianship of Rheinstrom was taken from her by the courts when he was sent to the Stockton asylum, she went to Golden Gate park and threw herself

in the cold, shallow water of Spreckels Lake. The water was not as deep as she thought and, as she plunged in, she screamed for help, all idea of suicide gone.

A passing motorist heard her anguished cry. He stopped his vehicle, and ran into the lake, and "dragged the unhappy but repentant Edna to shore." It is not known if Edna asked to be taken there, but her unidentified rescuer drove the would-be Ophelia to Cairn's Roadhouse to recuperate. *The Oakland Tribune* indicated Edna had been living there, and not at the address given by *The Evening Mail*. It was a full week before the news of Edna's suicide attempt leaked out, and was being generally disseminated in the newspapers across the country. By that time, Edna was reported to be seriously ill. The nature of her illness was not disclosed.[6]

"Who saved the actress' life could not be learned," said *The San Francisco Chronicle*, "but that he is a man of wealth and social position and, is taking more than a passing interest in the young woman, whose recent escapades are still fresh in the public mind, is vouchsafed by a number of her friends." The newspaper also corrected the prior news about Edna's living arrangements. Indeed, she had been residing with Mrs. Dixie Montgomery on O'Farrell Street, but Mrs. Montgomery had to give up those apartments, and Edna had moved in with Mrs. Willie Britt at 46 Portola Street. However, after the suicide attempt, Edna had been taken to the Cairn's Hotel, which was at the northwest corner of 36th and Fulton in the then sparsely settled Richmond District, where Mrs. Britt and Mrs. Shaw were caring for her.

"It is hinted that her rescue, romantic, though not entirely thrilling, may culminate in more than friendly relations with the heroic automobilist. However, Mrs. Rheinstrom appears to care more for her husband than many suppose." Edna was interviewed by the newspaper, but was rather reticent, saying only, "Do not believe everything you hear. I have been very sick, and may be obliged to go to a hospital to recover." The article was accompanied by the profile photo of Edna the newspaper had used in prior editions. Once again, Edna's name was splashed across newspaper throughout the country. Some reported the incident with embellishments. Few were sympathetic to her plight.[7]

The Mrs. Essie Shaw, who was mentioned as being of aid to Edna after her suicide attempt, had her own moment in the press in January of 1911. Previously, Mrs. Shaw was Mrs. Dixie Montgomery, but after obtaining a divorce from her second husband, she began using her previous married name. Mrs. Shaw had recently come into an inheritance of $35,000 in timberlands, and wanted to gloat to *The San Francisco Chronicle* about her good fortune, and how she had kicked Mr. Montgomery to the curb.

Chapter Five. Spiraling Downward

Journalist Helen Dare was only too happy to provide her with a forum to vent her spleen. "When he wouldn't work and he wouldn't pay bills, out he went...," said Mrs. Shaw. "And I want my husband— er—Mr. Montgomery to know that I've come into an inheritance. I know just how sore that'll make him feel." Mrs. Shaw also said she "got wrong with the public by trying to do a charitable act by befriending that Edna Loftus. I took her in when she needed help, and all the thanks I got for it was being mixed up with her in the papers until..."— the journalist indicated Mrs. Shaw did not finish her sentence, but simply "shrugged her plump shoulders," leaving Dare "to conjecture the awful result." Encouraged further by Helen Dare's attentions, Mrs. Shaw continued her rant for another few paragraphs, but did not mention Edna again.[8]

Two days later, on January 11, it was finally revealed how Edna had been able to appear so prosperous at Rheinstrom's guardianship hearing. After leaving the German Hospital without either dress or hat, her attorneys, Cadwallader and Jackson, went to meet with her. They found "Edna was not sufficiently well-garbed to allow for her appearance on a street car." The attorneys packed her into a taxicab, and took her to the White House, a clothing store for women. They paid $110 for "proper clothing" so "that the public gaze might not fall upon her." *The Oakland Tribune* reported that Attorney Jackson had appeared in court and asked that Peter Jorgenson, Rheinstrom's guardian, be made to reimburse them.[9]

Said Jackson, "Mr. Cadwallader and myself were compelled to pay $25 deposit to allow Mrs. Rheinstrom credit in order that she might secure clothing which was absolutely necessary. She was not fit to appear on the street, or in a car, and we had to smuggle her down to the White House in a taxicab." *The Sacramento Bee* insisted the former actress was "in rags." The judge in the case advised Mr. Jackson to arrange a meeting with Jorgenson "and see if arrangements to satisfy the credit could not be made without recourse to a Court order." As there was no further news about this matter in the newspapers, it may be assumed the attorneys received from Rheinstrom's guardian what they had asked for.[10]

After this, there was no mention of Edna in the newspapers for nearly two months. Then, in March, under the headline, "Arise Showgirls! Join that Look Before You Leap Club," *The San Francisco Examiner* spoke jestingly about some of the actresses and singers who had wed millionaire's sons only to have the family cut the couple off. Among those mentioned were Dessa Gibson, Mae Murray, Edna Goodrich, Bessie Van Ness, and, of course Edna. It was stated these women were starting the "Chorus Ladies' Anti-Millionaires' Sons Amalgamated Union." The story of each of the actresses was told in turn.

> Edna Loftus, the English music hall beauty, listening to the love-song of young Harry Rheinstrom, son of the late millionaire distiller of Cincinnati, and who was dependent on the well-lined purse on Millionaire Mamma. Mamma was so fiercely opposed to theatrical association, and Harry was so helpless as a wage-earning proposition, that young Mrs. Rheinstrom was obliged to return to her stage work to support both.

Mae Murray, who would become a noted silent film actress, had a similar tale. After she married William M. Schwenker, Jr., "the son of a millionaire dealer in brewers' supplies," in September of 1908, Schwenker's father immediately cut him off financially. Mae soon found herself in a $7-a-week room, cooking over a gas stove. They divorced less than two years later.

The full-page spread, which featured a photo of Edna mowing the lawn, was all very tongue-in-cheek. However, for Edna, her marriage to Rheinstrom seemed to have permanently derailed her stage career, left her destitute, and without a safety net of any kind. She had neither friends nor family in the United States, and, generally, the press had been jeeringly antagonistic towards her. She was blamed for Rheinstrom's descent into madness, mocked for standing up the taxi driver, derided for her inability to be appointed her husband's guardian, and ridiculed for attempting to end her life. The newspapers further implied she had become an alcoholic and was working as a prostitute.[11]

Later in March, *The San Francisco Chronicle* revealed Edna had left the City by the Bay for the City of Angels, and implied she had returned to the stage to earn a living. She had not. It was also asserted she was considering bringing an action of divorce. "We never wanted Harry to marry her, and I can only hope that she does get a divorce, because then he can get out of the sanatorium into which she was the cause of his going," said the Widow Rheinstrom, in response to the rumor. The newspaper then went on to recount the couple's adventures during the previous year. Speaking to her life after Rheinstrom was committed, *The Chronicle* said,

> Edna Loftus, deprived of her income, found life in the great city not all flowers and sunshine. She was arrested for refusing to pay an automobile bill and the chauffeur testified that she had used the automobile to visit a number of all-night resorts. She soon became a familiar face in the resorts in the red light district.

Dr. Lowell finally tipped his hand, showing he too was a pawn of the Rheinstrom matriarch. In a statement made to the press, he declared

Chapter Five. Spiraling Downward

the marriage of Rheinstrom and Edna was not legal. He argued that when Rheinstrom had been declared legally incompetent by the court in January of 1910, he could not legally marry, "as no marriage with an insane person was binding." Lowell said any attempt of Edna's to realize material gain from a divorce would prove to be in vain if the family cared to raise the point. "He also said Rheinstrom was still suffering from the influence of Edna Loftus, who ... was an exciting cause superimposed on a weak mentality."

It is unknown where it started, but the rumor of Edna's desire to divorce Rheinstrom was carried by several newspapers over the next few days. Upon hearing it, Peter Jorgenson felt compelled to make a statement on the family's behalf, saying Edna was "doomed to disappointment" if she hoped to profit from the divorce proceedings. Still, Jorgenson was doubtful the rumor was true.

> I have not heard from [the Widow Rheinstrom] in three months. She always refused to free Harry, and there can be nothing in the rumor that after a divorce, Mrs. Rheinstrom senior will be able to have her son released. The man is insane. Dr. Young at the State asylum said there is absolutely no doubt of that. He will not be allowed at large.[12]

Four days later, on March 26, it was reported that Jorgenson had also been named as Rheinstrom's guardian in Hamilton County, Ohio, by a probate judge there. Cincinnati was, of course, the county seat. Basically, the Widow Rheinstrom was laying the foundation to have her son moved out of the Stockton Asylum, and far away from Edna. "His mother wishes to place him under the care of several physicians," said *The San Francisco Examiner*.[13]

A report from Los Angeles that Edna had found employment somehow reached *The Sandusky Register*, a small newspaper that served the town of the same name in northern Ohio. "Edna Loftus went to work today, having given up all hope of assistance from her husband, Harry Rheinstrom.... When she married him, she was hailed as an actress of parts. Today, the best job she could get was with the moving picture show of Santa Monica Canyon. She went to work with bogus cowboys and Indians, and says she will make her living and enough to keep Harry when he is released from the asylum." The article ended stating Edna "was very much subdued." At the time, the burgeoning motion picture industry was considered inferior to all forms of live theater.

Where this story originated from is unknown, as there was no mention of Edna's being employed with a motion picture company in any of the California newspapers of the time. In fact, both Edna and her husband were absent from the newspapers across the country throughout the summer and into early fall. Then, in late October, Edna got herself into trouble again, allegedly after drinking far too much, and the police had to be called. Subdued she was not.[14]

Edna had been living "quietly" in a hotel in San Jose since leaving San Francisco after her suicide attempt. On Monday the 23rd, in the company of attorney Ralph W. Rose of San Francisco, whom she had engaged as her counsel, she left San Jose, for the city. According to *The Oakland Tribune*, Edna was making the trip to be present at the final settlement with the Rheinstrom family. "For many months, negotiations have been pending between the members of the Rheinstrom family in Cincinnati and the attorneys for Miss Loftus with a view to her consenting to a divorce for a financial consideration." In expectation of a lucrative settlement, Attorney Rose and his partner, G.R. Bartlett had been furnishing Edna with money to tide her over. Rose stated this support, in addition to legal fees, had cost them nearly $6,000. The trip from San Jose to San Francisco they undertook cost them $600.

Further, the attorney said the terms which Edna agreed to in the settlement "represented a substantial amount of money," but he was not at liberty to say how much. Undisclosed sources put the amount at either $25,000 or $50,000, in addition to the attorneys' costs. "While neither of these amounts may be correct, the fact remains that there is to be a settlement and Miss Loftus will get a large sum."

Purportedly, problems arose immediately after Edna and Mr. Rose left San Jose, when Edna began drinking. By the time they reached Oakland, "she was considerably under the influence of liquor." The newspaper said Rose, who had formerly been the world champion hammer thrower, attempted to "keep her from making a show of herself," but to no avail. When the attorney tried to put her on board a Southern & Pacific train at the depot located on Seventh Street, "She went to pieces." With a shriek, Edna kicked out both her heels, and fell into the street in a heap. She then proceeded to struggle and thrash about. Unable to deal with her, Rose called for a police officer.

When the officer arrived, the two men bundled Edna up, and carried her into a nearby candy store, followed by a crowd of onlookers. The officer hurriedly called for a police ambulance. When it arrived, Edna was put inside the conveyance, and taken to the Receiving Hospital. It was reported she fought "like a tigress" the entire way. Once they arrived, Edna was put to bed in a cell. She calmed down somewhat, and finally drifted off to sleep. "The record at the institution shows that, upon admission, she was suffering from hysteria, incident to an attack of alcoholism." *The Tribune* put Edna's behaviors down to "the prospect of her coming into a substantial amount of money from the Rheinstrom

Chapter Five. Spiraling Downward 129

family."[15] This begs the question, why would she be acting so combative when she should have been elated at the prospect?

The following morning, about eleven o'clock on the morning of the 24th, Attorney Rose picked Edna up at the hospital in an automobile, and "whisked her away to the ferry." *The San Francisco Call*, which reported on her release, also suggested Edna's actions were due to her "elation" at the prospect of a lucrative financial settlement. "Her enthusiasm was followed by depression today, and she displayed no emotion when her cell door was open."[16]

The incident was reported differently in *The San Francisco Chronicle*, and made no mention of drunkenness on Edna's part:

> While attorney Rose was taking her from [San Jose] to the supposed conference in San Francisco ... the young woman collapsed. Rose had difficulty in quieting her until Oakland was reached. For some unexplained reason a stop was made here, and when the two attempted to board a train at Seventh Street and Broadway, Mrs. Rheinstrom fell. Rose went to her assistance, and it was then she became hysterical. A policeman then took a hand and she was taken to the Receiving Hospital in the police patrol. She was hysterical during the ride, but was quieted at the hospital.

When interviewed, Rose remained reticent, divulging no information about the settlement "but remarks heard about the hospital placed the figure which the elder Mrs. Rheinstrom is willing to pay to secure her son's uncontested freedom at $25,000."[17]

Back in Cincinnati, *The Commercial Tribune* took up the subject of the settlement, and interviewed the Rheinstrom family's attorney, Julius Freiberg. The attorney flatly denied there were any negotiations between the family and Edna. "This report, Mr. Freiberg stated, possibly grew out of the fact that Edna Loftus Rheinstrom had secured the services of some enterprising attorney and was making an effort to resurrect the unpleasant marriage of the two parties concerned." The newspaper reminded its readers that Harry Rheinstrom was confined in an asylum "at some point in California." It also reported that Edna, "while meeting an engagement in Oakland, Cal., recently, having as its purpose a final financial settlement with members or representatives of the Rheinstrom family, became hysterical and was taken to the hospital." Surprisingly, this was all reported in a rather impartial manner.[18]

"There is no settlement and will be none, because the family has no interest in the matter now," declared Freiberg, the son-in-law of the Widow Rheinstrom, to both *The Los Angeles Times* and *The San Francisco Chronicle*. He further stated there had been no meeting between representatives of the Rheinstrom family and Edna, and no agreement reached with Edna. If this was in fact the case, why then were Edna and her lawyer traveling to San Francisco? Though there is no evidence for it, it is possible Jorgenson had either taken the initiative, or at the direct behest of the Widow Rheinstrom, without the knowledge of the family, arranged a meeting with Edna and her counsel to see if she could or would be bought off. Of course, this is conjecture, and it is impossible to say with certainty.[19]

Miss Sue Young was a showgirl, known for starring in *Kiss Waltz*, who was said to have married Julian Dillon, the son of John Dillon, a New York department store millionaire. When the patriarch found out his son had married a showgirl, he had the young man taken into custody, and sent to "a resort." Miss Young claimed she never married the young Mr. Dillon, and wrote a lengthy article in which she described "the decadence of a once lucrative profession, and sound[ed] a warning to her sisters that things [had] changed." During the month of November 1911, this article appeared in a number of newspapers, including *The Chicago Examiner* and *The San Francisco Examiner*."

Miss Young, in her exposé, made mention of Mae Murray, Bessie Van Ness, and Edna, among others. Of Edna she wrote:

> Look at Edna Loftus! One of the prettiest girls to ever walk Broadway. She got engaged to Harry Rheinstrom, son of an awfully rich Cincinnati distiller, and his ma got scared because he'd spent $10,000 in presents on Edna, though she was a millionairess herself, and chased him off to a sanitarium. Fine for these millionaires, isn't it? Making out their own brain and blood are crazy. Wonder if the doctors ever find out the boys inherited it from pop? Then Edna got him loose and they tried the simple life and making their own was independently on a chicken farm in California. Mamma Rheinstrom got Harry away and it was the sanitarium again for him.

Included in the article were quotes attributed to some of the actresses and dancers previously mentioned, including Edna. Miss Young quoted Edna as saying,

> I've finished. I've engaged a lawyer to get a divorce for me. I'm going to get out of trouble by a jump through the divorce hoop. Harry's mother heard he liked me and had him sent to a sanitarium. I got him out. We were married and tried chicken ranching. We couldn't make it a go. I went back to the music hall stage to support Harry and me. She sent him back to the asylum. I'm through. Millions are stronger than maids, especially merry, merry maids.

The authenticity of this quote is questionable, though the sentiment is no doubt accurate.[20]

Even before this mention in Miss Young's editorial, Edna had disappeared from the newspaper columns. After the incident in October, which landed her in the Receiving Hospital, nothing more was heard of her. November, December, January and February passed without any mention of her at all. Then, in March, Edna was involved in a very strange accident, which would have severe repercussions. *The Evening Times Star* made a joke of it, saying Edna, who was "quite nervous," consulted Dr. Donald Stone, "and got the cold water cure." They went for a drive, and she fell in a creek. "Now, she's more nervous."[21]

In fact, most the newspapers who reported on the accident, lampooned it in some manner. *The Santa Cruz Evening News* quipped, "Cold water, either via a shower or tub bath, is supposed to be beneficial for one suffering from nervousness. Definite data on the efficacy of the cure can now be furnished by Edna Loftus." According to the newspaper, Edna had sought out Dr. Waid J. Stone for treatment for "nervousness." While he was attending her, he received a telephone call from a patient in another part of the valley (Edna was at this time residing in San Rafael, north of San Francisco). As it was said to be urgent, Dr. Stone offered to take Edna as far as the train station so she could return home.

The automobile was driven by a chauffeur named Mr. H. Gerdies. "The little party bowled along the moonlit road, and had almost reached their destination, when an oncoming machine caused the chauffeur to turn too far to one side and the machine toppled over, precipitating the occupants into a muddy rain torrent which ran parallel to the road." Gerdies quickly pulled Edna from the water, and then the two of them attended the doctor, who

Postcard image of Edna Loftus posed on a column (author's collection).

was "floundering about in the creek." The automobile was righted, and the three of them continued on to the station, wet and muddy, but unhurt.[22]

Dr. Stone recalled the events differently. The cause of the accident was the same, but the vehicle did not turn over. Rather, it ran off the road into the creek below. "A few minutes later found Dr. Stone, thoroughly drenched, administering first aid to his fair companion and the chauffeur." *The San Francisco Chronicle*, which reported Dr. Stone's story, also took a swipe at Edna, saying the last time she "figured in a water escapade was in 1910, when an automobilist fished her out of Spreckels lake. At that time, she was quite worried over domestic unhappiness." The newspaper also noted Dr. Stone had formerly been the chief physician at San Quentin prison, and was being sued for divorce by his wife.

The accident seemed of little importance, and was reported in only a handful of newspapers around the country. However, it was only a prologue to a larger, more sensational story, in which Edna would play a leading role.[23]

The former "reigning queen of the London music halls" was named in the divorce suit which was subsequently filed by Mrs. Pauline Stone, the wife of Dr. Stone, as the cause of her "mental anguish." *The Oakland Tribune* stated Edna was "freely mentioned" in Mrs. Stone's suit against her husband. "The particular mental anguish was suffered by Mrs. Stone when she learned that her husband and Miss Loftus had been thrown out of the doctor's automobile into a mud puddle near San Rafael on the night of March 8." The doctor insisted he was simply rushing Edna to the station to catch a train after she paid him "a professional visit." He denied any impropriety. Mrs. Stone was not inclined to believe her husband's tale, and subsequently asked for a divorce.

It should be recalled, when the accident occurred, it was reported that Dr. Stone was already being sued for divorce by his wife. It must be assumed Mrs. Stone seized on the opportunity to amend her suit, using Edna to strengthen her case. Obviously, whether it was true or not that Edna was having an affair with her husband, it did not matter to Mrs. Stone. Nor did the fact that such an allegation would have the effect of further and irreparably damaging Edna's already tarnished reputation. Additionally, it should be observed that the newspapers never rebuked Dr. Stone for having a sexual relationship with a patient which, even in that era, was considered a breach of ethics.[24]

On the front page, above the previously used profile portrait of Edna, *The San Francisco Examiner* exclaimed, "More Woe for Stage Beauty; Auto Mishap, Correspondent." Beneath the photo, the headline read, "Tumble of Edna Loftus Rheinstrom and Dr. Stone into Stream Basis for Divorce." The newspaper added little in the way of new

Chapter Five. Spiraling Downward 133

information to the story, but took Edna to task, saying she had been little seen since the mishap, and had not visited Rheinstrom in the sanatorium in months. The newspaper did not speak to the fact her husband's guardian, Peter Jorgenson and family had been stonewalling Edna at every turn. It was also stated that Edna said she intended to sue for divorce from Rheinstrom, but that no papers had been filed.

"The automobile incident, which now seems destined for elucidation in court, became the theme for much gossip in society circles in San Francisco and Marin county." It was also reported, after the mishap, the party had returned to San Rafael to obtain dry clothing. It was then Edna discovered she had lost a diamond pendant when the accident occurred. It was found the following day and returned to her. It is somewhat surprising, considering her fiscal circumstances, that Edna still had anything of value to her name.

Some biographical information on Dr. Stone was provided in the article. As stated previously, Stone had been the resident physician at the San Quentin penitentiary, but had resigned in November of 1911 after a "misunderstanding" with Acting Warden Reynolds about the treatment of certain inmates. No further details were given, but the doctor told Reynolds being the prison physician "wasn't worth anything." Stone then went into private practice. He and his wife continued to live in a bungalow near the prison until January of 1912, when they separated. "Dr. Stone is the son of Dr. James S. Stone of 1276 Jones Street. Mrs. Stone is a member of a pioneer family."[25]

"She is simply tired of living with me," Dr. Stone told a reporter from *The San Francisco Call*, after the divorce story broke.

> Why she left months before the auto ride with the former actress. I have appealed to her time and again to return to me, but she always refused. I even went so far as to furnish a home here, thinking perhaps she might change her mind, but no, the joy ride she accused me of taking with the former actress happened March 8, but it was anything but a joy ride. Can not a physician, responding to an urgent sick call, hire an automobile? Can not he escort a patient to the railroad station without being accused of taking joy rides? My wife informed me by letter that she intended to sue me for divorce, but as yet she has not done so. Until recently, I did not know that Mrs. Rheinstrom was the cause. When she files the divorce complaint I will show that she left me long before the so called joy ride and refused to return.

In the divorce complaint. Mrs. Stone had accused her husband of "lavishly entertaining" Edna.

The newspaper also corrected the previous reports about the accident, stating that in order to avoid the oncoming vehicle, Mr. Gerdies had swerved off the road, over the embankment, and the automobile toppled into the ditch. After the occupants got to safety, it was obvious the machine was going to need to be towed out, so they ordered another. They returned to the city, where Edna got some dry clothing. She was then taken to the train station, and caught the last train to San Francisco. Doctor Stone continued his journey to Ross to see his other patient.[26]

Hot on the heels of this story was yet another which involved Edna. She once again been arrested and brought before the Police Court Judge on charges of defrauding a taxi driver. "She is fond of motoring," said *The Los Angeles Times*, "but ... she is not enamored with paying for it." A complaint was filed by J.W. Gilbert against Edna stating she had not paid for his services. How much Edna allegedly defrauded the driver for was not stated in the complaint. Though *The San Francisco Examiner*, *The San Francisco Call*, and *The San Francisco Chronicle* all picked up the story, none of these reported the outcome of the hearing.[27]

On the 16th of May 1912, Mrs. Pauline Placidia Rodriguez Stone, "local society matron and daughter of a pioneer family," filed her divorce suit with the county clerk against Dr. Waid J. Stone. "Extreme cruelty of a varied nature is charged," reported *The Oakland Tribune*, "but the incident involving pretty Edna Loftus Rheinstrom, the chorus girl, when she was thrown from the physician's automobile at San Rafael is the chief incident in the complaint." The newspaper went on to say the smart set of San Francisco society was "shocked and stunned by the story" of the accident when it appeared in March. Though Dr. Stone continued to deny an inappropriate relationship with Edna, Mrs. Stone accused her "of being the other woman in the case."

The Stones had been married in November of 1905, and though the accident was "the crowning fact," Mrs. Stone said for two years prior she had been treated "in an inhuman manner." Among the charges she raised against her husband was that he frequently locked her out of her own home while he "associated intimately with other women in a manner as to humiliate the plaintiff and inflict upon her grievous mental suffering." She also complained her husband swore too much.

The newspaper then proceeded to provide a history of Edna's life since she had come to the United States. *The Tribune* made mention of a rumor which had been circulating that Rheinstrom had taken his leave of the Stockton asylum and returned home to his mother. The newspaper ended the article stating, erroneously, "Edna Loftus has been a familiar figure on the streets of the city and has obtained employment several times in the cafes."[28]

The other newspapers added little to the story which appeared on the front page of *The Tribune* the day before, though *The San Francisco*

Chapter Five. Spiraling Downward

Chronicle did identify Mrs. Stone's attorneys by name, and said she would return to being Pauline Placidia Rodriguez once more. Also, the former Mrs. Stone stated on the night of the accident, "a house party was on the tapis" [under consideration] and, through no fault off her own, Edna had been invited. Mrs. Stone "declares that she did not 'connive' at the other's presence. Mrs. Rheinstrom was there simply because she was there." Mrs. Stone was adamant that the doctor was not treating Edna for any malady, but was "entertaining her" at their San Rafael home.[29]

According to *The San Francisco Call*, though Edna was named as a co-respondent in the suit, "no allegation of misconduct is made." Mrs. Stone only said the accident had resulted in "undue publicity and notoriety" which caused her to be humiliated. The newspaper also reported Dr. Stone still maintained his innocence, but would not contest the suit. The physician was quoted as saying, "If it was the last act of my life, I would not contest Mrs. Stone's wishes. I have appealed to her to return to me, but she would not. Now that she wants a divorce, I will let her have her ways again, although I still love her and will hope that she will reconsider this action." The newspaper went on to provide some more biographical information about the doctor, stating he graduated from the University of California, and was a member of the Kappa Alpha fraternity.[30]

June of 1912 passed without any mention of Edna in the local newspapers or elsewhere.

Toward the end of July, Edna was back in the newspapers, in connection with the Stone divorce case. *The Oakland Tribune* reported, on the 24th, Mrs. Stone had been granted "an interlocutory degree of divorce" that very afternoon by Superior Court Judge John James Van Nostrand.

> Despite the fact in her divorce complaint Mrs. Stone had set forth her spouse had been in company with Edna Loftis-Rheinstrom, the wife of the scion of a wealthy Eastern brewer, on an occasion when the woman was pitched out of an automobile into a creek, this incident was not mentioned in testimony.

Mrs. Stone's main complaint, which was corroborated by her father, was that Dr. Stone had frequently put her out of her own home.[31]

Beneath a rather flattering photo of Pauline Placida Rodriguez, formerly Mrs. Stone, *The San Francisco Examiner* reported on the divorce case, and revealed Dr. Stone, true to his word, had not challenged the suit. In fact, he had not even shown up in court, and Mrs. Stone won the case by default. The newspaper elaborated on the testimony given by Mrs. Stone. She alleged her husband had "cursed her and called her vile names; struck her on many occasions and put her out of the house many times." It was said the property settlement was affected out of court, and it was rumored "a large sum" was paid to ensure Mrs. Stone would leave Edna's name out of her testimony.

It is possible Mrs. Stone was provided an incentive not to mention Edna's name, but who would have done this and why? Certainly, Edna did not have the means. Dr. Stone did have the means, but why would he do such a thing? It was not as though he was going to save face if the "joy ride" testimony was introduced. The doctor was already being accused of being mentally and physically abusive, so it would not serve one way or another for him to do so. It could be Dr. Stone was trying to protect Edna, and keeping her name from being dragged through the mud once more. This seems the most likely scenario, but this assumes there was such a clause in the "settlement" with Mrs. Stone, which there is no proof of, and may well have been an invention of the author of the article.[32]

Even if such a settlement was made, it did not matter, as the press corps rehashed the story of the accident, and reiterated that Edna had been named in the suit, even though her name had not been brought up in court. Whether she actually had an affair with Dr. Stone or not, Edna had been branded as "the other woman" in the eyes of the public. The woman who had destroyed the home and happiness of Mrs. Stone. By way example, though the local newspapers were adamant in their reports to the contrary, *The Los Angeles Times* insisted Edna *had* been named by Mrs. Stone in court, being called the "soul mate" of Dr. Stone. *The Times* further asserted several newspaper accounts of the March 8 accident had been read into the court record, and Mrs. Stone had spoken to the humiliation they had caused her.[33]

Even though this was a complete fabrication on the part of the Los Angeles newspaper, it was the story which was carried by the wire services and disseminated across the United States. The accompanying headline for several of these reports read "More Notoriety for Edna." Back in Cincinnati, *The Commercial Tribune* picked up the story. "Edna Loftus Rheinstrom, the former English actress ... today added another chapter to her American career." The newspaper said Mrs. Stone was said to have identified Edna as Dr. Stone's "soul mate." The tale of the auto mishap which landed Edna in the creek was recounted. "Upon this and other testimony, Mrs. Stone was granted a divorce." Doubtlessly, the Widow Rheinstrom and her family took a certain delight in the news, though they were probably not pleased that Edna was still employing the Rheinstrom name.

The newspaper also reiterated the story of the wedding, and in doing so, took a couple of cheap shots at Edna. It was said "the Loftus woman made inquiries as to Harry's income and prospects and was seemingly satisfied after her investigation that she would not have to keep up stunts on the stage any longer." Further, it was alleged, "Rheinstrom's coin gave out" and Edna and Mrs. Holland were forced to move to another, smaller hotel. "They were marked women on the street, as both were well dressed and bore the unmistakable air of the stage." The reporter also invented a little dialogue which purportedly took place during the post-wedding dinner at the Vine Street cafe:

> **EDNA (HOLDING HARRY'S HAND):** "We are going West, are we not, Harry? And, in the morning, while the dew is on the grass and the birds are singing, we will get up at our ranch and we'll plow. Won't we Harry?"
> **RHEINSTROM:** "We will indeed!"
> **MRS. HOLLAND:** "When that pipe has gone out, I'll give you another match, Edna."

After this, *The Commercial Tribune* would only feature Edna one more time within its pages—at the event of her death.[34] Her increased "notoriety" in the press, though undeserved, brought Edna Loftus a backlash which was both swift and severe. On the 4th of August, less than two weeks after the conclusion of the Stone divorce case, newspapers across the country carried the story of her expulsion from the town of San Rafael. In response to the "numerous complaints of alleged disorderly conduct" by residents of the Luke Hotel, which had been filed with his department, City Marshal Edward C. Daly went to see Edna. He was armed with an order for her to leave town. The notice was served at 6:00 p.m. and gave her one hour to pack her belongings and depart. By 7:30 p.m., she was gone, having boarded a train for San Francisco.

It was purported that Edna, who had been living in the town about four months, had engaged in "a series of joy rides and other touches of the high life involving a number of young men." These accusations against Edna were all filed after the accident she was involved in with Dr. Stone. *The San Francisco Call*, which was among the first to report Edna's eviction from San Rafael, recounted the story of Edna's marriage to Winnie O'Connor, their divorce, her subsequent marriage to Rheinstrom, and his incarceration in the Stockton asylum.[35]

The same day, *The Pensacola Journal* reported Harry Rheinstrom was to sue Edna for divorce on account of the "wild night ride with Dr. Waid J. Stone which cost Dr. Stone his wife." The Florida newspaper repeated the aspersion that Mrs. Stone had testified to the fact Edna and the doctor were "soul mates" during her divorce proceedings, and "had shown newspaper articles recounting the auto ride." To add insult to injury, it was stated "several other escapades have added to her romance." Where this story originated is unknown, but it was unlikely Rheinstrom, who was still incarcerated in an asylum, was talking to lawyers about divorce suits.

It was the former story which was most widely disseminated with varying degrees of accuracy, but in all of them mentioned either "her numerous escapades" or her "disorderly conduct"—both being veiled references to prostitution—as the reason why Edna was run out of town. But was this really the reason? Or was Edna's expulsion due to the machinations of the former Mrs. Stone. Alas, it cannot be definitively proved either way. Edna could very well have finally had to resort to some form of prostitution in order to support herself. Then again, according to the newspaper reports, Mrs. Stone was a rather affluent and influential woman in San Rafael. She certainly had reason to want Edna removed, as Edna would have been a constant source of embarrassment to her. Further, the former Mrs. Stone possessed the political and social pull to make it happen. At this remove, it is impossible to say with any certainty.[36]

The year 1912 ended without any further news about Edna in the local or national newspapers. What she was doing from the time she departed San Rafael until the end of the year remains unknown.

Chapter Six

Dissipation and Death

"Edna Loftus Once More in Public Light" read the headline which appeared in *The Oakland Tribune* on the 24th of February 1913, and, once again, the reason was not a favorable one. The incident was classified as another of Edna's "escapades" by the East Bay newspaper, which interviewed Captain John L. Mooney to obtain details about the crime. The officer stated Curtis Hayden, who claimed to be the son of the president of the wholesale hardware firm of Dunham, Carrigan, & Hayden, had gone to visit Edna at the Pacific State Hotel in the company of two friends. The two friends of Hayden's, who were not identified by the name, had a quarrel while in Edna's rooms. Irene and Patrick Kelleher, who occupied the rooms next door, upon hearing the argument, went to the door, and then invited Hayden and Edna back to their place to distance the two belligerents.

Edna and Hayden visited with the Kellehers for a while. Finally, Hayden decided to return to Edna's rooms to retrieve his belongings, which he had left behind. He quickly discovered his gold watch was missing, "and immediately a second disturbance arose." Hearing the angry, raised voices, the hotel's proprietor telephoned the police. The responding officer, J.J. Casey took Edna, the Kelleners, and Hayden into custody, and they were transported to police headquarters. Edna was questioned about the theft, and then released. "After ... she was given her liberty, she expressed her disgust with the police and their methods of dealing with members of the fair sex, and declared that she was going to shake the dust of San Francisco from her feet."

Hayden, who stated he lived in Oakland, said his only interest was in the recovery of his watch.[1]

Though they did not quote her directly, *The San Francisco Call* also reported that Edna was desirous of leaving the City by the Bay. "[She] declares that whenever she steps into the street she meets trouble, usually in the form of a policeman." The newspaper stated Edna had gained her freedom with a show of tears, and Hayden had declined to press charges against her or the Kelleners. The other two men had left the hotel before the police had arrived on the scene. *The San Francisco Examiner* did quote Edna as saying. "I can't turn around here but what I get into print." All three newspapers used the incident to bring up Edna's history with Rheinstrom, her suicide attempt, and her being named in the Stone divorce case.[2]

Several of the other California newspapers which reported the incident, including *The Daily Telegram* (Long Beach), *The Evening Times-Star* (Alameda), and *The Los Angeles Times*, insinuated Edna had been responsible for the theft of the timepiece, and had only been released because Hayden refused to pursue the matter. *The Times* also quoted Edna: "This is the limit! This town is full of rollers and I am through with San Francisco forever. Honolulu will be my next stopping place and I will take the first boat that clears for the islands." She concluded her diatribe, saying "They don't know how to treat a lady in this town!" The following day, *The San Francisco Chronicle* replied sarcastically to her charge, saying. "Edna Loftus ... says she doesn't like San Francisco and is going to leave. What's your hurry? Here's your suitcase."[3]

A month later, it seemed as if Edna was to get her wish, and would be able to take her leave of San Francisco, but not quite as she had expected. *The San Francisco Call*, in breaking the story of Edna's arrest by the United States Marshal's office, wrote:

> It's a far cry from the dressing room of a London music hall star, acclaimed by thousands, to the San Francisco prison cell, as a keeper of a house of prostitution, charged with being an undesirable alien. Yet these points are only the beginning and, perhaps, the end of the primrose path trod the last four years by Edna Loftus O'Connor Rheinstrom.

An order was issued by Captain Frank H. Ainsworth, and the warrants served on the evening of April 9 by Deputy U.S. Marshal J.A. Robinson on "the woman in the house at 756 Commercial Street, in which she recently obtained a half interest." The woman in question was Edna Loftus, and she was being charged by the Bureau of Immigration with being an undesirable alien.

Captain Ainsworth stated Edna had been arrested after a two-week investigation based on "information conveyed in an anonymous fashion." The unidentified source alleged that Edna's marriage to Rheinstrom had been illegal, as she had never obtained a divorce from Winnie O'Connor. "If this is true," said the newspaper, she is not a citizen of the United States and never has been, despite her marriage with the young Rheinstrom." Though it cannot be proved, deductive reasoning would point to the fact that the anonymous tip the authorities had received

Postcard image of Edna Loftus in a white gown (author's collection).

Edna Loftus' former residence at 756 Commercial Street, San Francisco (photograph by the author).

Chapter Six. Dissipation and Death 143

was provided by agents of the Rheinstrom family, who were still interested in nullifying Edna's marriage to Harry. If Edna had still legally been married to O'Connor, her marriage to Rheinstrom would have been bigamy, and could be annulled. Obviously. The agents for the family, if this is who was behind the action, had not properly investigated the case, as O'Connor had divorced Edna in 1909.[4]

On March 15, Inspector John A. Robinson sent a missive to Samuel W. Backus, the Commissioner of Immigration at Angel Island, which read:

> Pursuant to your instructions, I have conducted an investigation a to one—Edna O'Connor, alias Edna Loftus O'Connor, alias Edna Rhinestrom [sic], prostitute, who is located at #756 Commercial Street, San Francisco, and have to report as follows:
>
> This woman is 25 years of age, and claims to have been born in England, arriving on the United States four years ago at the port of New York, ex SS "La Provence," about September 1909; she further claims to have arrived at the time mentioned with her husband, an Englishman, she using the name of Mrs. Edna O'Connor, his name being Wingfield [sic] O'Connor. She says her occupation previous to her arrival on the United States was that of actress, and she formerly resided on Liverpool, England. She further claims that a short time after her arrival, her husband—Wingfield [sic] O'Connor—whom she married in England, returned to England; that she never secured a divorce from him, and she does not know whether he ever applied for a divorce from her or not.

Samuel W. Backus, Commissioner of Immigration.

Three years ago, she married a man named Harry Rhinestrom [sic] at Independence, Kentucky, but she states that she does not know his present whereabouts, and does not know whether he ever secured a divorce from her, but believes she is still married to him. He is a citizen of the United States.

I am informed that her alleged husband—Harry Rhinestrom—who is the son of a wealthy Eastern brewer, is, at present, confined at Napa State Hospital for the Insane, at Napa California.

I am further informed that there is some question as to whether this woman has been on the United States three years, as since her arrival on the United States she has made several trips between the United States and England.

It would seem Inspector Robinson did speak directly with Edna during some point in the initial investigation, but either misunderstood what she told him, or purposefully misconstrued her answers. He must have also spoken with some others, possibly agents of the Rheinstrom family, who supplied the inspector with patently false information, like asserting Edna had sojourned to England and back several times.

On March 25, H. Etsell, the Acting Commissioner, applied to the Secretary of Labor and Commerce (of which The Bureau of Immigration was a subordinate agency) for a warrant for the arrest of "Mrs. Winfield O'Connor, alias Mrs. Edna O'Connor, alias Mrs. Edna Loftus O'Connor, alias Edna Loftus, alias Mrs. Edna Rhinestrom [sic]," saying "The above named alien is a prostitute in San Francisco, California." The Acting Secretary of Commerce, Charles P. Neill, responded on April 4 with a warrant for Edna's arrest. The warrant stated, "from evidence submitted," that Edna had been "found in the United States, in violation of the Act of Congress approved February 20, 1907, amended by the Act approved March 26, 1910," more specifically, "That said alien is a prostitute and has been found practicing prostitution subsequent to her entry in the United States."

Commissioner Neill commanded Edna be taken into custody, and granted a hearing, "to enable her to show why she should not be deported in conformity with the law." In an addendum, it was stipulated, "Pending disposition of her case, the alien may be released from custody upon furnishing satisfactory bond in the sum of $1000." Needless to say, this was well beyond the means of a woman like Edna who was eking out a living selling her body.[5]

What was newsworthy, at least to the press, was Edna's new "business venture." *The Call* stated it had "astonished even the most blasé of tenderloin habitués, used, as they are to sudden falls from what liberal society is pleased to term the path of righteousness." It was her part interest in the brothel which resulted in Edna's being charged as an "undesirable alien." Though prostitution was still legal in California

Chapter Six. Dissipation and Death   145

at the time, the reformers and moralists had been pushing legislators to criminalize it. Just two days before Edna's arrest, under pressure from these groups, Governor Hiram Johnson had signed into law the Red Light Abatement Act, which stated "every building or place used for the purpose of prostitution, and every building or place in or upon which acts of prostitution, are held or occur, is a nuisance which should be enjoined, abated, and prevented, and for which damages may be recovered."

Edna, who had lately been employing the alias "Ethel O'Connor," was now in the position of having to show cause why she should not be deported. The newspaper cautioned, "If she defeats the government immigration officials, she may have to face another federal charge of an even more serious nature," but did not elaborate further.[6]

The Oakland Tribune put the story of Edna's arrest on page one beneath an old publicity photo of her from when she was starring in *The Catch of the Season*. It stated Edna was being held at Angel Island, and sanctimoniously declared "she has not been comporting herself with proper regard for the morals of the community since she has been in San Francisco." After, referring to Edna as a "popular English soubrette," *The San Francisco Chronicle* reported that her case had been transmitted to the Secretary of Labor, William Bauchop Wilson, in Washington,

William Bauchop Wilson, U.S. Secretary of Labor (Library of Congress, Bain News Service Collection).

D.C., with a recommendation she be deported. It was said the immigration officials were awaiting his decision. The newspaper then proceeded to speak to Edna's numerous "escapades." Regarding her arrest in the Hayden case, the newspaper uncharacteristically gave Edna the benefit of the doubt, saying "it was the general belief that two strange men who had been with the party earlier in the night were the culprits."[7]

The facility at Angel Island, in the San Francisco Bay, was built as a quarantine station in 1890, for the purpose of screening Asian immigrants for bubonic plague. The U.S. designated the entire island a military installation in 1850, later christening it as Fort McDowell. Construction of the Angel Island Immigration Station began in 1905, but it was not put into operation until five years later. Nicknamed "China Cove," the primary function of the facility was controlling Chinese immigration into the United States in accordance with the Chinese Exclusion Act signed into law in 1882. The facility had a dedicated detention/dormitory building where persons were supposed to be incarcerated pending investigation by the U.S. authorities. However, as historians Erika Lee and Judy Yung noted, the different ethnicities were actually housed in different locations. "Occidentals" were generally housed in the administration building, while "Orientals" were housed in the detention barracks, a two story building set on the hillside above the

Angel Island Immigration Station Administration Building.

administration building. Edna, being of Western European extraction, would have been housed in the Administration Building.[8]

Within days of her arrest, Edna had a hearing before Captain Ainsworth. After Edna was sworn in, Ainsworth asked her a series of questions, and Stenographer M.A. Howarth recorded the answers. The transcript of the hearing is reproduced here:

Q: *What is your name?*
A: Loftus, O'Connor, Rhinestrom [*sic*]

Q: *What was your maiden name?*
A: Edna Loftus.

Q: *How old are you?*
A: Twenty-five.

Q: *What is your occupation?*
A: Well, I was always married until lately.

Q: *And now are you a sporting woman?*
A: Not exactly.

Q: *Are you not registered at the clinic?*
A: Well, I was running a house and I had to go down there—they said everybody in the place had to register.

Q: *When did you first come to the United States?*
A: 1908, on the *La Provence*, a French boat, arriving in New York in August or September.

Q: *Under what name?*
A: Mrs. O'Connor

Q: *Are you married to Mr. O'Connor?*
A: Yes.

Q: *What is his full name?*
A: Winfield.

Q: *When were you married to him?*
A: In 1906, I think.

Q: *What were you doing previous to your marriage?*
A: Singing.

Q: *How long had you been singing?*
A: Two years.

Q: *Did you start life as a singer at the age of sixteen?*
A: Yes.

Q: *With whom did you live previous to your marriage?*
A: My mother.

Q: *In Liverpool?*
A: In Liverpool, London, and France.

Q: *What was your husband's [Winfield O'Connor] occupation?*
A: Jockey.

Q: *Where was he born?*
A: Brooklyn, New York.

Q: *Where did you meet him?*
A: In France.

Q: *Where was the marriage consummated?*
A: In France—Chantilly.

Q: *Have you any evidence of that marriage in the way of a license or certificate?*
A: He divorced me after I came over here.

Q: *Have you any evidence of that divorce?*
A: I have no papers.

Q: *Where was the divorce obtained?*
A: Chantilly.

Q: *When was the divorce obtained?*
A: It must have been about two months after I got here.

Q: *The first time?*
A: Yes.

Q: *That would be December, 1908?*
A: Yes, I think it was just before Christmas.

Q: *Did he apply for the divorce?*
A: Yes.

Q: *Did you oppose the divorce?*
A: No, I never bothered.

Q: *What were the grounds for the divorce?*
A: Desertion.

Q: *Was he in the United States at that time?*
A: No, I came over here by myself—he was riding in France.

Q: *How long has he lived in France?*
A: Ten years.

Chapter Six. Dissipation and Death

Q: *Has he been to the United States since?*
A: Yes, twice.

Q: *Do you know whether he is a citizen of France or the United States?*
A: United States.

Q: *What evidence have you that he was born in the United States?*
A: His birth certificate, I have seen it.

Q: *Do you know if he has any relatives in the United States?*
A: His mother lives in Bay Ridge, Brooklyn, New York,–279–75th Street.

Q: *After O'Connor was divorced from you in December, 1908, what did you do then for a living?*
A: I got married.

Q: *When did you get married?*
A: A couple of months after.

Q: *That would be in the spring of 1909?*
A: In January.

Q: *To whom were you married?*
A: Mr. Rhinestrom [sic].

Q: *What is his first name?*
A: Harry.

Q: *Where was he born?*
A: Cincinnati, Ohio.

Q: *Where is he now?*
A: In San Francisco.

Q: *Are you still married to him?*
A: Yes, sir.

Q: *Are you living with him now as his wife?*
A: I have not been living with him for over a year.

Q: *Do I understand you to say that you are separated from him?*
A: Not on his part or my part, but his mother.

Q: *You are separated by reason of mutual consent?*
A: Yes.

Q: *Have you ever been divorced from him?*
A: No.

Q: *Has he ever been divorced from you?*
A: No.

Q: Are you aware that it is a criminal offense for him to allow you to be in a house of ill fame?
A: He don't know anything about it.

Q: You say he is in San Francisco?
A: Yes, but he is with a guardian.

Q: Who had the guardian appointed for him?
A: His mother.

Q: You mean by that, that he is not mentally responsible?
A: They said he was not, but he seems to be.

Q: Still, as your husband, he is responsible in a measure for your acts. In this respect, how is it that he does not know your present occupation?
A: I have not seen him for over a year.

Q: Has he contributed anything to your support?
A: No.

Q: How long since he supported you?
A: Up to last year.

Q: Have you any certificate of marriage or license showing your marriage to him?
A: In Independence, Kentucky.

Q: Is that where you were married?
A: Yes.

Q: Were you married before a civil or religious authority?
A: Justice of the Peace.

Q: What was his name?
A: Warner.

Q: Do you know his initials?
A: I was trying to think of them yesterday.

Q: Who were the witnesses to this marriage?
A: About eight reporters.

Q: You stated your first trip here was in 1908, have you been to Europe since?
A: Yes, I went back with my first husband after we had been here several months.

Q: When did you come in the last time?
A: Just a few months after.

Chapter Six. Dissipation and Death

[Note: The witness now corrects her former statement and states that she was married to Rhinestrom [*sic*] in 1910, a little over three years ago.]

Q: *Then how long had you been in the United States on the second trip before you married Rhinestrom?*
A: About two or three months.

Q: *Well, I have a record here showing that you came to the United States on the SS* La Touraine, *August 30, 1909, under the name Mrs. Winfield O'Connor, is that correct?*
A: Yes.

Q: *Then, at that time, you stated you had been in New York in 1905.*
A: No, I never stated that.

Q: *That is what the record shows.*
A: It is a mistake.

Q: *Then, when you came to the United States in August 1909, were you divorced from O'Connor?*
A: He got a divorce after I left.

Q: *When did you leave him—just before you came to New York the second time?*
A: Yes.

Q: *You gave your destination when you came the second time to Mrs. O'Connor in New York?*
A: I intended coming to her, but I did not.

Q: *When you arrived in New York in August, 1909, where did you go?*
A: I went to visit some people I knew and lived with them.

Q: *And did you follow your occupation as a singer?*
A: No. I intended to, but I met Mr. Rhinestrom [*sic*] and married him.

Q: *Do you know whether any steps toward a legal separation have been taken by your husband, Mr. Rhinestrom [sic].*
A: I do not think so. I have talked to my attorneys about getting a divorce, but they say he cannot get a divorce for he is incompetent.

Q: *Has he been declared incompetent by the court?*
A: Yes, but he is alright now.

Q: *Who are your attorneys?*
A: Mr. Ralph Rose and Mr. Robert T. Devlin.

Ainsworth concluded the questioning, saying, "Well, I will now advise you that you have been arrested under the authority of Departmental Warrant No. 53575/236, issued April 3/ 13, by the Acting Secretary of Labor, charging you with being an alien on the United States on violation of law. You may have opportunity to inspect the record and to show cause why you should not be deported to England. You may also employ counsel and make such a defense as you and your counsel deem proper. You may be released from custody on furnishing a bond on the sum of $1,000, pending the determination of your case.

Q: Have you any further comment or statement to make at this time?
  A: No.

One might wonder why Edna chose to fight the deportation instead of just yielding, and let the Immigration officials send her back to England. Probably, it was the fact she was now of the demimonde—officially branded a prostitute—which was a stigma she could not live down. Worse, the press had made it public knowledge that Edna was a "fallen woman." She likely felt too ashamed of what she had been obliged to do to survive, to return to England and to her family, and especially to her daughter. Even if Edna had attempted to return to her middle-class roots, it is doubtful society would have allowed her to. Those doors were now closed to her.[9]

The Sacramento Star of April 17 featured a photo of Edna as well, but it was more recent. She was sitting and looking somewhat downcast, her eyes cast towards the floor. She was dressed in what looked to be a checkered jacket and skirt, with a light-colored shirtwaist beneath. She was wearing gloves, and her hands were folded in her lap. The newspaper also carried an interview with Edna (less formal than that which Ainsworth subjected her to). The interviewer stated she was twenty-five, and though English, "there is just the suggestion of French accent to her speech." The interview took place in a visitor's dock at the Angel Island immigration station. This is what she had to say:

> Only yesterday I was a star; today, I—oh well, why worry about things we cannot help? Fate plays funny tricks with all of us.
> I left Sacred Heart Convent in France before I was 17. At 18, I was a star. I never played small parts; I never "suped." I made a hit right from the start.
> And who do you suppose I worked with at the Gaiety in Paris? Gaby Deslys! I taught her to speak English on the stage. We were chums. Today, she is a star. And look at me! Five years ago, if anyone had told me I would be sitting in a detention dock with Japanese, Chinese, French, Germans, and Russians of the lower class. I would have called him crazy.
> Before I was 19. I was married. Gaby told me not to do it, but I wouldn't

Chapter Six. Dissipation and Death

listen to her. She said: "You are foolish to marry. You are young and you have a wonderful chance." She was right. She is famous, and I—well—

Gaby called me "ma petite Edna." It was her pet name for me. I can hear her now laughing in her cheery way, chiding, mocking playfully at those about her as she "made up" for her act.

My first husband was Winfield O'Connor, the famous jockey. My life with him was happy until the other woman came. She was my dearest friend. I took her to my house to live, to be my companion, my comrade, my pal and she stole my husband.

This was the beginning of my troubles. Since then it has been out of the frying pan into the fire. Slowly, I have been slipping, sliding down, down, and now this is the end. When I get out of this, I am going to change my name and go away to the country, where I hope I never see a man.

Publicity photograph of Miss Gaby Deslys (author's collection).

I arrived here in America in 1908 and started rehearsing a play in New York, but I never showed in that play for I met Harry Rheinstrom. Son of a Cincinnati millionaire brewer. We met at a party. It was case of love at first sight.

His folks did everything in their power to prevent the wedding, but despite their interference, we were married in Harry's home town and came to the Pacific Coast to live. We settled on a little ranch outside of Los Angeles, and were blissfully happy for six months. We raised chickens and kept a horse and a cow, and lived in the cheerfulness of a home.

Then Mrs. Rheinstrom swooped down and carried Harry off to a sanatorium, declaring him insane. She couldn't bear to see us happy. Do you think that was fair to me?

When Harry was taken away, I was left penniless. I arrived in San Francisco disheartened, discouraged, without means and without friends. What was I to do? To whom could I turn? The outlook was so black that it appeared hopeless. There was one way I could have made money—yes, plenty of money, but it wasn't in me to lead a life of shame—not then. I saw only one way out—suicide.

When they fished me out of the lake, I was more dead than alive and my only regret is that they didn't let me finish it.

From then on, my troubles came thick and fast. I was certainly born under an unlucky star. Circumstances were against me. Now, I am supposed to be bad. People read the stuff the newspapers print about me and it's hard to get along. I never willfully did anything wrong in my life. When you are in trouble, it is surprising how few friends you have in what the world calls "society." It seems if you want people to stand by you, you have to go to the "underworld."

The interviewer made no comment and made no judgment, just simply let Edna tell her story. Though her tale was at times self-serving, as when Edna neglects to mention she and Rheinstrom could not make the truck farm turn a profit, and they deserted it for the city, her assertion that she never willfully did anyone wrong seems a genuine statement of truth. It could be argued, what had led her to this point was due to her poor choices in men. Edna probably would have done well to have heeded Gaby Deslys' advice, but then who heeds advice when they are young and think they are in love?[10]

Modern readers will doubtlessly recognize the classist, if vaguely racist, statement Edna made concerning "Japanese, Chinese, French, Germans, and Russians of the lower class." As noted earlier, as a person of western European descent, Edna was housed in the Administration Building, separate from persons from Japan, China, and other countries to the East, as well as Latinos and Eastern Europeans. Historians Lee and Yung observed, "Maintaining racial segregation was a consistent goal over the years" at Angel Island. However, they also stated, "despite the government's intent to keep the different groups separated, the close quarters and forced confinement meant Chinese, New Zealanders, Italians, and others often bumped against each other."[11]

In his book *It's Your Misfortune and None of My Own*, historian Richard White posited, "Virtually all nineteenth-century white Americans were racially prejudiced—that is, they thought non-whites were inferior to whites." Western Europeans, who were brought up in a culture steeped in ideas of a natural aristocracy and noblesse, were also decidedly classist. For Edna, who was brought up in a white, Anglo-Saxon, Christian, middle-class environment and taught white, Angle-Saxon, Christian, middle-class values, not to believe she was of a

Chapter Six. Dissipation and Death

superior caste would have been remarkable. Ironically, as a known prostitute, Edna had descended to the lowest rank in the social order which had spawned her. She was a "fallen woman" and past either redemption or salvation. She would never again be accepted as a member of the middle class again.[12]

The interview with Edna, and photograph, were reprinted in several newspapers across the country, including *The Seattle Star*, *The Fort Wayne Sentinel*, and *The Brooklyn Citizen*. The quote from Edna in this last-named newspaper was recorded differently. The last paragraph read: "From then on my troubles came thick and fast. They cannot deport me. I will be out of here even before you publish this. I am an American citizen and, as such, am entitled to protection from the government."

And another paragraph was added: "If I ever marry again, it will be somebody humble and obscure—just a plain man. I long for a simple little home in the country, where I can do the housework and make a husband happy."[13]

The Fort Wayne Sentinel also recorded the quote differently. After Edna spoke of Mrs. Rheinstrom swooping down," she said: "If Mrs. Rheinstrom had given me a fair chance and I had failed, she would be justified in breaking Harry and me up. But she hasn't done that! She vowed from the very first that she would never quit until she had succeeded in deporting me. That is why I am here today."

Also, another paragraph was added before the last ones printed in *The Brooklyn Citizen*, in which Edna said: "How I long for my little girl. She is six years old now and I haven't seen her for nearly five years. If I had baby with me, I am sure things would never have happened as they have."[14]

Of course, the story was salacious and sensational—an actress, who once had the world at her feet, reduced to working as a common prostitute in the Tenderloin District of San Francisco. And how many readers must have gloated at the tale of Edna's misfortune? It could be read as a cautionary tale by the sanctimonious reformers who were convinced the world was going to hell in a handbasket, or as a comeuppance tale for a patriarchal culture, which asserted a woman's role in society should be confined to the domestic sphere. This was a perfect tale for the age of yellow journalism.

For the next month, Edna languished at Angel Island while investigators tried to determine if she was a citizen of the United States, and if she was actually divorced from Winnie O'Connor. Finding evidence of her marriage to Rheinstrom was not difficult. A marriage license and certificate of marriage were readily available from Kenton County, Kentucky, and John B. Dillon, the Clerk of the Court, provided these to the investigators.

The Bureau of Vital Statistics in Cincinnati, Ohio, provided a notarized copy of Harry Rheinstrom's birth certificate proving he was born in the United States and was a citizen thereof. Along with this, William Littleford, the attorney, sent a signed and notarized affidavit stating Rheinstrom was "a native born citizen of the United States."

More difficult was proving O'Connor had divorced Edna. It is not known if the Immigration Inspectors attempted to contact O'Connor, or made application to the courts in Chantilly for documentation. The only documentation in Edna's case file is a telegraph from William Williams, Commissioner. It reads:

EDNA LOFTUS, ONCE THEATRICAL STAR, NOW CALLED "UNDESIRABLE ALIEN."

Edna Loftus in custody of immigration officials, from *The Sacramento Star* of April 1913.

> Immigration Service.
> Report mailed case Mrs. Winfield O'Connor. Mrs. O'Connor and son believe Edna Loftus divorced by son and brother, Winfield, respectively in France, 1909. They learned from the newspapers she later married Rheinstrom, born U.S., at one time in asylum. Winfield O'Connor, her former husband, native this country, prominent jockey.

No supporting documentation was provided. Apparently, this was enough as, on May 7, 1913, Acting Commissioner Edsell sent the following missive to the Captain Ainsworth at Angel Island:

> I have the honor to transmit herewith the record in the case of Mrs. Winfield O'Connor, alias Mrs. Edna O'Connor, alias Mrs. Edna Loftus, alias Edna Loftus, alias Mrs. Edna Rhinestron [sic], who was arrested by virtue of authority contained in Departmental Warrant No. 53575/236 dated April 3, 1913.
> This is the case of a prostitute, who has gained considerable notoriety. Although the verification of landing stated that she was a native of England, she appears to be now the wife of a citizen of the United States. She had

been married to one Winfield O'Connor, and the mother and brother of said Winfield O'Connor believe that a divorce was secured in France in 1909. Both husbands are no doubt citizens of the United States.

It is recommended that the warrant be cancelled, and pending your decision, I have taken the liberty to release the detained on her own recognizance, and trust that this will be met with your approval, for she has been in custody nearly a month.[15]

Whereas news of her possible deportation made headlines across the country, and resulted in lengthy columns and photographs, the dismissal of the charges against Edna was worthy of only a few paragraphs, sans photos. On May 8, *The Long Beach Daily Telegram* devoted two short paragraphs on its first page to the story, saying Edna had escaped deportation "by a mere shave," and that she "had enough of the west" and planned to return to England. *The Pomona Progress* ran the same short notice. *The Oakland Tribune* gave Edna three paragraphs on page two, stating she "had been released by the immigration authorities on her own recognizance" as her "status of wife of Rheinstrom" and been officially established. The newspaper stated she had been incarcerated for a month at the facility on Angel Island.[16]

On May 9, *The San Francisco Call* expounded upon these reports slightly, stating Edna had been arrested for violating the "white slave act" and was to be deported for doing so. However, "a decision was received at Angel Island from the head of the [immigration] department in Washington, D.C. yesterday restoring her to freedom on the ground she is an American citizen and not subject to deportation as an alien." There was no mention of her divorce from O'Connor or any other facts pertinent to her case. Who had lodged the complaint against her was also not revealed either. Oddly, *The Call* contradicted *The Tribune*, saying Edna had been free on bond since her arrest.[17]

The Sacramento Bee, on reporting on the Immigration Department's decision not to deport Edna, quipped, "Edna is angered at the action taken against her and says she will return to London voluntarily. Her vindictive spirit leads her to taking a revenge which will be most acceptable to the American people."[18]

A rather amusing anecdote was added to Edna's story by a man who identified himself only as "Carl," from Winnebago, Nebraska. Hearing of Edna's troubles with the immigration authorities, Carl wrote to Arthur G. Fisk, Postmaster of San Francisco, saying:

Dear Sir,

Kindly have this fall into the hands of Edna Loftus. Poor, unfortunate lady, my heart sobs for her. I am most tender-hearted and would make her life oh, so happy. I know all the particulars of her past, and that shall be forgotten. I can act some myself. I don't want to give you my right name now, but you tell Miss Loftus to send a letter addressed to Carl, Lock Box 102, Winnebago, and then she can come on and marry me, or I might strike out for 'Frisco.

Enclosed in the letter were four cents in stamps. *The San Francisco Examiner*, which reported the story, stated Postmaster Fisk took no action in the matter, stating Miss Loftus could see the letter at the post office. It is not known if she ever did.[19]

After the news she would not be deported died down. Edna disappeared from the newspapers again for several months. It may be assumed that she returned to the brothel located at 756 Commercial Street, near Chinatown, which she had part ownership of [the building is still standing today]. In late September of 1913, Edna again made the news. *The Long Beach Daily Telegram* was among the first to carry the story, which was spread far and wide on the United Press wire service.

If it was the Rheinstrom family behind the effort to deport Edna [which is the most likely scenario as they had the most to gain], their plan had unintended consequences.

> It was the calling into question of the validity of Mrs. Rheinstrom's divorce from Jockey Winnie O'Connor, previous to her marriage to Rheinstrom, which would have invalidated her later marriage and left her still an Englishwoman, that detained Mrs. Rheinstrom at Angel Island. Now, she carries with her the government's recognition of her divorce and the legality of her marriage to the millionaire brewer.

Armed with this, it was Edna's intention to file a suit against the Rheinstrom family for support. She told reporters,

> I am going to Cincinnati to sue for maintenance from Harry. When they took him from me in Los Angeles it ended the happiest period of my life. I do not believe he was insane, as his mother represented, and certainly he is not now, for he is at the head of his father's business. He still writes to me, and he will not divorce me, despite the pressure brought to bear on him, for he still loves me. And I will not divorce him. I know he is willing to give me money, if he were not prevented. I intend to leave for Cincinnati this week—in fact, as soon as get a telegram from the east that I am waiting for. When I arrive there, I will buy whatever I need and charge it to Harry. I am not going back on the stage. I am going to win this suit.[20]

The San Francisco Examiner quoted Edna as saying,

> I shall begin my suit as soon as I reach Cincinnati. I have engaged Attorney William Crittendon here and three other lawyers in Cincinnati. I am going to fight in the courts and out of them. Harry has never supported me and has refused to divorce me, and now I am going to get separate maintenance.

Chapter Six. Dissipation and Death

I will not divorce him and I know he fails to support me only because of the interference of his family.

"What if they contest the suit?" asked a reporter. Edna, her "childish blue eyes [becoming] quite cold" and her dimples suddenly disappearing, replied,

> I am going to fight. There was never a wife in the world who has been treated as I have been. I have been forced down—down. I have had no money except what my friends have given me. My detention at Angel Island they were responsible for. Now, I am going to fight. Not only in the courts, but out of them. Under the law of the state, a husband must support his wife—buy her necessities. My husband had never supported me. For the first time, I am going to make him. I am going to buy everything I need when I reach them—and charge the bills to Harry. Remember, I have friends there who will take my part. I cannot go on living in this hand-to-mouth fashion. I am going back to the stage, but I am going to win this suit.[21]

The story also appeared in *The Cincinnati Enquirer* under the headline "Here's Edna Again." In response to the news, Harry Rheinstrom, who was again employed in the family business, declined comment, except to deny he corresponded with Edna, and "intimated that there was no truth in the story that she was coming to Cincinnati, and that there would be no welcome for her ... if she did come."

In May of 1912, *The Oakland Tribune* reported Rheinstrom had been released from Stockton into his mother's care. However, several other California newspapers, including *The San Francisco Examiner*, stated he was still incarcerated in Stockton at that time. It remains unknown when he was sent back to Cincinnati, and when he was deemed fit enough mentally to resume his former position with Rheinstrom Brothers.

Then, there was no more news of Edna for another four months. It is doubtful, despite all her bravado, that Edna traveled to Cincinnati, or filed suit there against the Rheinstrom family. If she had, it certainly would have been a major news story, and would have been picked up by the press. Being that it was not, and that there are no extant court records indicating there was any legal action undertaken against the Rheinstroms by Edna, it may be assumed her attorney (assuming she still retained one) told her she really had no case against either Rheinstrom or the family. Possibly, she was dissuaded from following through with her plans for other reasons. It could well have been she simply did not have the means to undertake the journey back east or to employ the necessary legal representation.[22]

There are several later newspaper articles extant which allege Rheinstrom divorced Edna after his release from Stockton. However, there is also no record of anyone by the name of Rheinstrom obtaining a divorce between 1909 and 1916 in either the Common Pleas Court, which handled divorce cases prior to 1914, or the Insolvency Court, which handled divorce cases after 1914. It is quite likely the Rheinstrom family, through some source, possibly Jorgenson, discovered Edna had contracted tuberculosis. Rather than risk the scandal of a divorce case, and the possibility a judge might find in Edna's favor, and award her alimony or some other form of monetary settlement, it was simpler to let the disease take its course, and await her inevitable death. It is not as though the Widow Rheinstrom would be above such unscrupulous machinations.[23]

There was a brief notice which appeared in *The Sacramento Bee* in February of 1914 regarding Peter Jorgenson, Rheinstrom's court-appointed guardian. It was stated Jorgenson had filed his final report with Judge Frank Dunne, stating he had expended $340 and been compensated in the same amount. Jorgenson was then discharged as Rheinstrom's guardian. The newspaper also reported Rheinstrom had "recently" been released from the Stockton Asylum and was residing with his mother in Cincinnati. *The San Francisco Examiner* also made mention of this development, and added, "Edna Loftus has been a prominent figure in the night life of this city since her husband was committed two years ago and was a co-respondent in the divorce of Mrs. Wade [*sic*] Stone, wife of the former San Quentin physician."[24] And "This is the last echo of the romance of Rheinstrom and Edna Loftus, music hall artist, whose marriage was annulled," stated *The San Bernardino Daily Sun*.[25]

It also marked the disappearance of Edna and Rheinstrom from the pages of the country's newspapers for over six months. The next news of Edna was in October when she was once again being arrested, this time on a charge of vagrancy, i.e., prostitution. On the evening of the 17th of said month, the police raided the Art Hotel, located at 833 Kearny Street, on the outskirts of the Tenderloin District, and arrested four women. "The detectives were suprised [*sic*] to recognize, beneath the paint and powder, the fair Edna Loftus, who at one time had all London at her feet." *The Oakland Tribune* lamented Edna's fate, saying, "In three years, during which the fair Edna has run the gamut of nearly every human experience, she passed one social step after another in the thorny path, and would never be recognized today for the prize beauty of the prosperous days gone by."

The newspaper briefly recounted the story of her doomed marriage to Rheinstrom, stating, "She accepted, with good grace, the role of housewife and swept and scrubbed and starved, it may be, for the sake of her love for the man of her choice." Though there had been rumors about

Chapter Six. Dissipation and Death 161

Kearny Street, San Francisco, California (San Francisco History Center, San Francisco Public Library).

the couple's debauches in San Francisco, the newspaper insisted it was not until Rheinstrom was committed to the asylum, that Edna "sought the solace in the region of the bright lights. Since then, her career has been a checkered one." Almost as an afterthought, *The Tribune* noted, the Thursday before the raid, October 15, Edna had attempted suicide once more, by cutting into her wrist with a safety razor, in her rooms at the Art Hotel. She had been taken to the Harbor Hospital for treatment. Upon being admitted, Edna gave an assumed name, and was not recognized.

Subsequent to their arrest, Edna and the others were bailed out by the proprietor of the hotel. They were scheduled to appear in police court on Monday, October 19. *The Sacramento Bee* was the only other newspaper to take notice of the arrest. Neither newspaper bothered to report the outcome of Edna's hearing.[26]

On the morning of November 9, *The Tribune* reported Edna herself called the police:

> Mrs. Rheinstrom, who was at one time a favorite in the London music halls and a dashing Gaiety Girl in the New York musical shows, has recently

been running a hotel, on Kearny street, known as The Art. Recently she was arrested in a raid on the place. This morning, she complained that she had entrusted $105 to her night clerk, whose name she gave as Edward Bell, and that the man had disappeared with the money.

Edna Loftus' name would never appear in print again while she was alive.[27] It is not known when Edna contracted tuberculosis. Judging by the description given of her in the newspapers in October of 1914, there is a good chance she already had the disease at that time. During the nineteenth and early twentieth centuries, tuberculosis, a.k.a. the white death, or consumption, was the leading cause of death in the United States, and one of the most dreaded diseases in the world. It is estimated, in the late 1800s/early 1900s, in the United States, 450 people a day were dying from the disease. Typically, tuberculosis attacked the lungs. Symptoms included difficulty breathing, extreme fatigue, night sweats, and a slow wasting away. The victim would also cough up blood or white phlegm, hence the name the "white plague." There was no cure for the disease in Edna's time. Victims were simply sent away to sanitariums or tuberculosis wards in hospitals to die.[28]

Then 1914 closed out, and 1915 passed without news of Edna in any newspapers. The next notice of her was on the 16th of June 1916, when *The San Francisco Examiner* announced her death, under the headline, "Edna Loftus Dies, Friendless, Alone." The article was brief, saying Edna, who was "the keeper of the Art Hotel," had succumbed to tuberculosis at the

Postcard image of Edna Loftus in furs (author's collection).

Chapter Six. Dissipation and Death 163

Tuberculosis Ward No 1, San Francisco City Hospital (author's collection).

City and County Hospital in San Francisco, and she was to be buried in the potter's field, if her husband's family did not claim the body.[29]

"The last chapter in Edna Loftus' story is like that of a homely novel that is read for the moral contained," observed *The Oakland Tribune*, wryly. "The body of the girl who heeded not, so long as the money and beauty lasted will be buried in the potter's field unless her former husband's family claims it." The newspaper blamed Edna for the failure of the truck ranch venture, saying she yearned for "lobster places and the flowing champagne to which she was accustom." It went on to imply Edna received her just desserts at the hand of providence: "Then fate, in earnest, began to take from under her, one by one, the steps of the ladder on which she climber to position. Desperately, she tried to keep from slipping, but surely, sometimes slowly, and often long spaces at a time, she went down." The newspaper's condescending, faux-obituary ended thus—"At the time of her death, Miss

Loftus was the keeper of the Art Hotel, 833 Kearny Street, a pathetic figure pointed out as a bit of a curiosity because she once had been famous on two continents."

Again, a number of the newspapers, in reporting on her death, stated she was divorced from Rheinstrom, though, as noted earlier, there is no record of a divorce suit ever being filed by her husband. In fact, Edna seems to have still been Mrs. Rheinstrom at the time of her death.[30]

The Cincinnati Enquirer was among those newspapers who stated Edna was the "divorced wife of Harry A. Rheinstrom." The newspaper told the story of their relationship in some detail, and stated, in 1914, after returning to Cincinnati Rheinstrom had filed suit against Edna and was divorced. As to Edna, it was said she "figured in a number of sensational episodes," and her suicide attempt in the lake and the automobile accident with Dr. Stone were made mention of. "She became interested in boarding houses (a period euphemism for a brothel) until ill health forced her to give it up for a cot in the charity ward." *The Enquirer* reporter further, a few friends of "the once beautiful showgirl" on hearing of her death, and that her remains were bound for the potter's field, pooled their resources, and purchased a funeral and a grave for her at Cypress Lawn Cemetery in Colma.[31]

Who was it that saved Edna from an anonymous grave in the potter's field? The name of her rescuer was withheld from the press, probably because her benefactor was a notorious individual. Lee Earl was listed by J.S. Godeau Funeral Home as being the person who paid for her burial. Earl resided at 731 Commercial Street, a brothel owned by Jerome Bassity, and located not far from the one where Edna worked. According to the record, Mr. Earl bought Edna a $25 casket, and paid another 55 dollars in additional costs, including the hearse. There was no headstone placed on the grave, and it remained unmarked for over a century. There was a funeral service for Edna held on June 16, at 41 Van Ness Avenue. It is unknown if this was the site of a chapel. Today, the space is occupied by a high rise.[32]

Again, Edna was national news, if only for a few days. Some of the newspapers were generous in reporting her demise, mentioning her marriage to Rheinstrom, but elaborating no further, and saying that she had been taken to the hospital several days before her death. Others delved into her past, and spoke to her "earning a precarious living in the poor section" of San Francisco. *The Cosshooton Morning Tribune* put it most succinctly, saying, "Edna Loftus, one time musical comedy queen, was save from burial in the potter's field by the charity of friends. A good sermon could be preached on that fact."[33]

Chapter Six. Dissipation and Death

The author at the grave of Edna Loftus at Cypress Lawn, Colma, California (photograph by the author).

Postcard image of Edna Loftus in a yellow gown (author's collection).

Chapter Six. Dissipation and Death 167

* * *

And the rest of the cast of this tragedy?

Harry Rheinstrom died two years after Edna, on October 14, 1918. *The Cincinnati Enquirer* stated he was working in a government shipyard in Philadelphia, and there was an accident. No further details were given, but the story of his relationship to Edna was recounted. *The Los Angeles Times* reported Rheinstrom had succumbed to injuries sustained in an automobile accident. This newspaper also spoke to his life as Edna's husband (though the article had more space devoted to Edna's career than his). Rheinstrom's death certificate indicated he fractured his ribs when he fell from a girder at the shipyard, and subsequently developed pneumonia, which killed him, Harry Rheinstrom was 34 years of age at the time of his death.[34]

Edna's first husband, Winfield S. "Winnie" O'Connor, died in 1947. Ben Gould, who stated he was a friend to O'Connor, wrote his obituary for *The Brooklyn Daily Eagle*. Said Gould, "On Saturday, March 8th, 1947, O'Connor was buried in the Cypress Hill Cemetery in Brooklyn. Thus ended one of the most remarkable careers of any athlete born and bred in this boro [sic]." The author went on to talk about the jockey's career at some length, speaking to his winning record and well as his numerous broken bones (it was alleged he broke his collar bone twelve times). His marriage to Neva Aymar was mentioned, but not his marriage to Edna or the daughter he fathered by her.

Winnie O'Connor had served as an ambulance driver in the First World War. In 1923, he rode his last race, and retired to become a trainer. He was not particularly successful in this venture. O'Connor ended his career as a bartender in a racing themed bar on Broadway, telling

Portrait of Winfield S. "Winnie" O'Connor.

stories about his glory days. He dictated his memoirs to Earl Chapin May, and these were published under the title *Jockeys, Crooks and Kings* in 1930. Seventeen years later, on March 6, at the age of 63, O'Connor died of a heart attack in the home of a friend. The inscription on his headstone read "One of America's Great Jockeys." In 1956, he was posthumously inducted into the National Museum of Racing Hall of Fame.[35]

Neva Aymar, who became Mrs. Winnie O'Connor, died on February 1, 1932, at the age of 43, in Jamaica, Queens, New York. Like Edna, she was a victim of pulmonary tuberculosis, which she contracted during the First World War, while serving with the Red Cross. She was 43. Her remains were interred in the Maple Oak Cemetery. It was stated Mrs. O'Connor quit the stage after her marriage in 1909. There was no mention in the obituary of Edna, or the divorce. It was said "less than a score of relatives" attended the funeral service for Neva Aymar O'Connor.[36]

Gaby Deslys, Edna's friend during her early days in the theater in Paris, had a long, lucrative career on the stage. By the second decade of the 20th century, she was making $4,000 a week as a performer and dancer. Deslys starred in five silent films and recorded two songs, "Tout en Rose" and "Philomene," which are still available. Deslys had a scandalous affair with King Manuel II of Spain, which ended when he was deposed in 1910. Unfortunately, in December 1919, Deslys contracted a severe throat infection during the Spanish flu pandemic. She was operated on multiple times in an effort to eradicate the infection, on two occasions without the use of an anesthetic. Surgeons were inhibited by Deslys' demand that they must not scar her neck. She died in Paris on February

Publicity photograph of Miss Gaby Deslys (author's collection).

11, 1920, but was buried in the Cimetière Saint-Pierre in Marseille. In her will, Deslys left her villa on the Marseilles Corniche Road, and her other properties in Marseille, valued at 12 million francs, to the poor of Marseille.[37]

On April 16, 1926, Dr. Waid James Stone died in San Francisco after an illness of two years. Stone, his wife, Mrs. Hannah Elizabeth Stone née Weaver, and his sister, Bertha, had traveled to University of California Hospital from Healdsburg to seek treatment for the physician. It was decided that an operation was his only hope of recovery. Dr. Stone died at nine o'clock on the operating table. Officially, Dr. Stone's death was caused by cirrhosis of the liver,

Postcard image of Edna Loftus from Dover Street Studios, London (author's collection).

hemorrhage, and post-operative shock. In its obituary, *The Santa Rosa Republican* stated the doctor had served as a surgeon during the First World War, and was a member of several fraternal organizations; the newspaper refrained from mentioning either his first wife, their divorce or Edna.[38]

Pauline Placida Rodrigue, the former Mrs. Waid Stone, died on the 20th of January 1959, in San Francisco at the age of 76. She was interred in the Holy Cross Catholic Cemetery in Colma, just down the road from Cypress Lawn, where Edna was buried. She was given no obituary in the newspapers. In fact, after her divorce from Dr. Stone she slipped back into obscurity.[39]

Mrs. Minna W. Rheinstrom, who through her bigotry and class prejudice became Edna's nemesis, died October 2, 1937, at her home at the age of 76. *The Cincinnati Enquirer* gave her a brief, paragraph-length obituary, stating she was born in New York City, was the widow of Abraham Rheinstrom, had been president of the Ruth Lodge, and on the board of directors of the Child Guidance Home. "Mrs. Rheinstrom leaves two daughters, Mrs. S.H. Fechheiner and Mrs. Louis J. Kopald, and a son, James A. Rheinstrom." Her mortal remains were cremated.[40]

Chapter Notes

Prologue

1. Sara Delamont and Lorna Duffin, eds., *The Nineteenth-Century Woman: Her Cultural and Physical World* (London: Billing & Sons, 1978), 16.
2. Tracy Davis, "Actresses and Prostitutes in Victorian London," *Theater Research International* 13, no. 3 (1988): 221–234.
3. James Douglas Morrison, *The Lords and the New Creatures* (New York: Simon & Schuster, 1969).
4. Evelyn Nesbit, *Prodigal Days: The Untold Story* (New York: Julian Messner), 191.
5. Sally Mitchell, *Daily Life in Victorian England* (Westport: Greenwood Press, 1996), 20–21.
6. Lisa Picard, "The Victorian Middle Classes," *Victorian Britain*, 14 October 2009, The British Library, retrieved 13 January 2022, https://www.bl.uk/victorian-britain/articles/the-victorian-middle-classes.
7. Sid Schwarz, "Me and Jewish Supremacy," *The Times of Israel*, 11 February 2021, retrieved 13 January 2022, https://blogs.timesofisrael.com/me-and-jewish-supremacy.

Chapter One

1. "Freedom," *The Cincinnati Enquirer*, 6 January 1910, 14.
2. "From Lobster Palace to the Farm," *The St. Louis Star Magazine Section*, 17 April 1910, 25.
3. "H.A. Rheinstrom Has a Guardian," *The San Francisco Chronicle*, 23 November 1910, 8; "Edna Loftus Freed from Cell," *The San Francisco Call*, 25 October 1911, 8; "Deaf to Plea," *The Los Angeles Times*, 23 November 1910, 1; "Golden Vision," *The Oakland Tribune*, 24 October 1911, 7.
4. "Rough Voyage for Liner," *The Evening Star*, 30 November 1907, 2; "Mother Orders Rheinstrom in Public Asylum," *The San Francisco Examiner*, 25 September 1910, 29.
5. "Edna Loftus," *The Sacramento Star*, 17 April 1913, 3.
6. Paul Howarth, "Sergeant Brue: A Musical Farce," *British Musical Theatre*, 10 March 2017, retrieved 12 February 2022, https://gsarchive.net/british/sgtbrue/index.html; "At the Play," *The London Opinion*, 25 June 1904, retrieved 12 February 2022, https://www.madameulalie.org/ldnopinion/At_the_Play2.html.
7. Mrs. O'Connor, lines 12 and 13, p. 14. SS *La Provence* sailing from Havre, 23 November 1907, Passenger Lists of Vessels Arriving in New York, New York, 1897–1957, microfilm publication T715, 8892 rolls, NAI: 300346, Records of the Immigration and Naturalization Service, National Archives, Washington, D.C.; "Edna Loftus," *The Sacramento Star*, 17 April 1913, 3; James Gardiner, *Gaby Deslys: A Fatal Attraction* (London: Sidgwick & Jackson, 1986), 18–24.
8. Jessica Howe, Presentation Binder on Edna Loftus for David Grassé, 2022, provided by Legacy Tree, Inc, author's collection. Aside from searching the available online databases from the United Kingdom and employing Legacy Tree genealogists to undertake further research in both the UK and France,

this author also contacted the Society of the Sacred Heart in search of school records for "Edna Loftus." This group had no record of an Edna Loftus being a pupil in their databases. Further, this author searched for any record of a "Eileen O'Connor (or Loftus)," the child Edna had by husband Winnie O'Connor, whom she allegedly left with her mother in Lancashire before traveling to New York in 1908. This search was also in vain.

9. "Rough Voyage for Liner," *The Evening Star*, 30 November 1907, 2.

10. Hearing in the case of Mrs. Winfield O'Connor, immigration file for Mrs. Edna Rhinestrom [sic], RG 85, Entry 9, File No. 53575/236, Records of the Immigration and Naturalization Service, Archives File, National Archives, Civil Reference RG 35, National Archives Building, Washington, D.C.

Chapter Two

1. Jacky Bratton, "The Music Hall," *The Cambridge Companion to Victorian and Edwardian Theater* (Cambridge: Cambridge University Press, 2004), 164–182.

2. Steven Gerrard, "The Great British Music Hall: Its Importance to British Culture and the Trivial," *Culture Unbound: Journal of Current Cultural Research* 5 (2013): 487–515.

3. Kurt Ganzl, 1 January 2020; "Ivan Caryll & the Heyday of the Gaiety Musical Comedy," *The Encyclopedia of Musical Theatre*, http://operetta-research-center.org/ivan-caryll-principal-composer-conductor-heyday-gaiety-musical-comedy/, accessed 10 May 2022; Elizabeth Marchalonis, "The Shop Girl: A Unique Early Theatre Item in the University of Arizona Special Collections Main Library Archive," *The American Vaudeville Museum and UA Collection*, 2021, https://vaudeville.sites.arizona.edu/node/62, accessed 10 May 2022.

4. Michael Newbury, "Polite Gaiety: Cultural Hierarchy and Musical Comedy, 1893–1904," *The Journal of the Gilded Age and Progressive Era* 4, no. 4 (2005): 381–407, http://www.jstor.org/stable/25144313, accessed 10 May 2022; Alan Dale, "Has Musical Comedy Become Our National Drama," *The San Francisco Examiner*, 31 May 1903, 29.

5. "Refuses to Pay Her Chauffer," *The San Francisco Chronicle*, 18 October 1910, 4; "At the Play," *The London Opinion*, 25 June 1904, retrieved 8 June 2022, https://www.madameulalie.org/ldnopinion/At_the_Play2.html; "Theatrical Items," *The Globe*, 11 July 1904, 4.

6. "The Show Girl Must Obey," *The Sun* (New York), 5 April 1903, 30.

7. "Edna Loftus in Catch of the Season," *The Tatler*, 14 February 1906, front cover; "Vaudeville Theater," *The Morning Post*, 10 September 1904, 7.

8. "The Catch of the Season," *The Play: An Illustrated Monthly* 1, no. 6 (n.d.), https://books.google.com, accessed 27 February 2022; "Drama of the Day," *The Daily Telegraph*, 12 May 1904, 10;

9. "Theater Attractions in London," *The Folkestone Express, Sandgate, Shorncliffe, and Hythe Advertiser*, 3 January 1906, 5; "Answers to Correspondents," *The Referee*, 3 June 1906, 7.

10. "Gossip from the Gay City," *The Referee*, 29 April 1906, 2.

11. "A Beauty in 'The New Aladdin,'" *The Tatler*, 3 October 1906, 3.

12. "Gaiety Burlesque," *The Manchester Courier and Lancashire General Advertiser*, 1 October 1906, 7; James Gardiner, *Gaby Deslys: A Fatal Attraction* (London: Sidgwick & Jackson, 1986), 18–24; "Edna Loftus," *The Sacramento Star*, 17 April 1913, 3;

13. "Miss Edna Loftus," *The Sporting Life*, 6 October 1906, 7; "Miss Edna Loftus" and "Paris has," *Lloyd's Weekly Newspaper*, 7 October 1906, 10.

14. "London Theatres," *The Stage*, 4 October 1906, 14. Though longer, Lily Elsie's life would be no less tragic than Edna's. She was to spend much of her later years in sanitariums and mental hospitals.

15. "Miss Edna Loftus," *The Sporting Times*, 27 October 1906, 10.

16. Miss Edna Loftus," *The Illustrated Sporting and Dramatic News*, 8 September 1906, 6 and 15; "Miss Edna Loftus," *The Illustrated Sporting and Dramatic News*, 10 November 1906, 18. Billie Burke went on to have a long, very successful career in theater and motion pictures

and would be immortalized in the role of Glinda the Good Witch in the 1939 film *The Wizard of Oz*.

17. Don Gillan, "History of Postcards," Stage Beauty, 2007, accessed 2 June 2022, http://www.stagebeauty.net/th-frames.html?http&&&www.stagebeauty.net/th-cards.html. Reproduced courtesy of Don Gillan (copyright), www.stagebeauty.net.

18. "Illustrated Weekly Newspapers," *The Belfast News-Letter*, 1 October 1906, 10.

19. "London Theatre-Goers Pleased with Attractions," *The Philadelphia Inquirer*, 6 January 1907, 39.

20. "Theatrical Notes," *The American Register*, 24 November 1906, 2; "Theatre Royal," *The Scotsman*, 3 December 1906, 1.

21. "Theatre Royal," *The Scotsman*, 13 December 1906, 1; "The Babes in the Wood," *The Scotsman*, 14 December 1906, 9. "Provincial Pantomimes," *The Era*, 22 December 1906, 12.

22. Kate Kellaway, "Babes in the Wood," *The Guardian*, 11 March 2011, https://www.theguardian.com/travel/2011/apr/11/babes-in-the-wood, accessed 27 November 2021; "Babes in the Wood." ItsBehindYou.com, 21 July 2007, http://www.its-behind-you.com/storybabesinthewood.html, accessed 22 November 2021.

23. "Provincial Pantomimes," *The Era*, 22 December 1906, 12.

24. "The Stage Letter Box," *The Stage*, 10 January 1907, 2.

25. "Edinburgh," *The Era*, 16 February 1907, 8.

26. "American Jottings," *The Sportsman*, 11 December 1907.

27. "Rough Voyage for Liner," *The Evening Star*, 30 November 1907, 2.

28. "Jockey's Bride in Peril at Sea," *The Standard Union*, 1 December 1907, 6.

29. Mr. O'Connor and Mrs. O'Connor, lines 12 and 13, p. 14. SS *La Provence* sailing from Havre, 23 November 1907, Passenger Lists of Vessels Arriving in New York, New York, 1897–1957, Microfilm publication T715, 8892 rolls, NAI: 300346, Records of the Immigration and Naturalization Service, National Archives at Washington, D.C.; Amanda Wilkinson, "So wives didn't work in the 'good old day'? Wrong," *The Guardian*, 13 April 2014, https://www.theguardian.com/commentisfree/2014/apr/13/-working-women-stay-at-home-wives-myths, accessed 14 February 2022.

30. "Winfield 'Winnie' O'Connor," National Museum of Racing and Hall of Fame, 2021, https://www.racingmuseum.org/hall-of-fame/jockey/winfield-winnie-oconnor, accessed 27 November 2021.

31. Francis H. O'Connor, New York, State Census, 1905, Population Schedules, Various County Clerk Offices, New York, New York State Archives, Albany, New York; State Population Census Schedules, 1905; Election District: A.D. 03 E.D. 16; City: Brooklyn; County: Kings; Page: 9.

32. Winnie O'Connor, *Jockeys, Crooks, and Kings: The Story of Winnie O'Connor's Life as Told to Earl Chapin May* (New York: Jonathan Cape & Harrison Smith, 1930). Much of the information contained herein concerning O'Connor was derived from this book.

33. "Jockey Sues for $50,000," *The Brooklyn Daily Eagle*, 5 February 1908, 24; "O'Connor to Ride in Germany," *The Chicago Tribune*, 26 March 1908, 8.

34. "O'Connor to Ride in Germany," *The Chicago Tribune*, 26 March 1908, 8.

35. "Miss O'Connor Dead," *The Brooklyn Daily Eagle*, 16 May 1908, 2.

36. "Americans on German Turf," *The New York Times*, 7 June 1907, 28; "Grand Prix Won by Vanderbilt's Northeast," *The San Francisco Examiner*, 15 June 1908, 1; "Rich Suburban Handicap," *The Brooklyn Daily Eagle*, 15 June 1908, 22; "Walker Horses Pass Million Mark," *The Commercial Appeal*, 23 August 1908, 15; "German Horse May Prove," *The Commercial Appeal*, 12 September 1908, 8; "Birds with Sharp Claws," *The Oakland Tribune*, 20 October 1908, 13; "Winnie O'Connor," *The Oakland Tribune*, 24 December 1908, 12.

37. "Bert Dorman in London," *The Hartford Daily Courant*, 14 August 1909, 10.

38. Evelyn Nesbit, *Prodigal Days: The Untold Story* (New York: Julian Messner, 1934), 150.

39. "Is Waiting for Jockey," *The Los Angeles Times*, 20 June 1909, 2.

40. "Rain Dears Come Back Without Fair Neva," *The San Francisco Call*, 20 June 1909, 37.

41. "Dorman's Gossip of Paris," *The Hartford Daily Courant*, 21 June 1909, 10; "Most Beautiful Woman in Paris," *The Hartford Daily Courant*, 8 July 1909, 10.

42. "Is Sore Over Fakers," *The Leavenworth Post*, 23 June 1909, 8.

43. "Careful Edna!" *The Cincinnati Enquirer*, 31 August 1909, 3; "Horsewhip for One Actress," *The Leavenworth Times*, 3 September 1909, 8.

44. "Un divorce," *Le Journal*, 24 September 1909, 5.

45. Hearing in the case of Mrs. Winfield O'Connor, Immigration file for Mrs. Edna Rhinestrom [sic], RG 85, Entry 9, File No. 53575/236, Records of the Immigration and Naturalization Service, Archives File, National Archives, Civil Reference RG 35, National Archives Building, Washington, D.C.

46. Winfield & Neva O'Connor, Sheet 120A, 77, Census Place: Queens, Queens, New York; Page: 20A; Enumeration District: 0319; FHL microfilm: 2341332, United States of America, Bureau of the Census, *Fifteenth Census of the United States, 1930*, Washington, D.C.: National Archives and Records Administration, 1930, T626, 2,667 rolls; "Rites Are Held for Actress," *The Brooklyn Daily Times*, 4 February 1932, 22; O'Connor, 210.

47. "Winnie O'Connor Risks His Life," *The Muskogee Times Democrat*, 18 December 1909, 9; "Mother Orders Rheinstrom in Public Asylum," *The San Francisco Examiner*, 25 September 1910, 29; "May Deport Noted Actress," *The Brooklyn Citizen*, 26 April 1913, 3.

48. "Blame Storm for Fast Train Crash That Killed Three," *The Newark Evening Star*, 14 December 1909, 2; "Three Killed," *The Detroit Times*, 14 December 1909, 1; "Wreck on N.Y. Central," *The Morris County Chronicle*, 21 December 1909, 6; "Heavy Snow Causes," *The Washington Times*, 14 December 1909, 7.

Chapter Three

1. "Charmed," *The Cincinnati Enquirer*, 1 January 1910, 11; W. John Locke, *The Morals of Marcus Ordeyne: A Play in Four Acts* (London: W.T. Haycock & Sons, 1906); "Theatrical News," *The New York Tribune*, 27 July 1909, 4; "New Theater Season Here," *The Sun*, 1 August 1910, 33; "Marie Doro Sailed," *The Democrat Chronicle*, 26 September 1909, 21.

2. "Thought He Was Married," *The Meridian Daily Journal*, 1 January 1910, 7; "Charmed," *The Cincinnati Enquirer*, 1 January 1910, 11; "Leaves Charmer for Sanitarium Following Trial," *The Commercial Tribune*, 1 January 1910, 1–2; "Actress Trying Get Rheinstrom Out of Asylum," *The Dayton Herald*, 3 January 1910, 1.

3. Evelyn Nesbit, *Prodigal Days: The Untold Story* (New York: Julian Messner, 1934), 86.

4. Tracy C. Davis, "Actresses and Prostitutes in Victorian London," *Theater Research International* 13, no. 3 (1988): 221–234, doi:10.1017/S0307883300005794.

5. "Charmed," *The Cincinnati Enquirer*, 1 January 1910, 11; "Leaves Charmer for Sanitarium Following Trial," *The Commercial Tribune*, 1 January 1910, 1–2; "Strange Happenings," *The Stage*, 20 January 1910, 19 (Mrs. Holland was referred to variously as "Minnie" and "May" in the newspapers).

6. "Actress Trying Cet [sic] Rheinstrom Out of Asylum," *The Dayton Herald*, 3 January 1910, 1; "Developments," *The Cincinnati Enquirer*, 4 January 1910, 9; "Makes a Plea for Her Lover," *The Commercial Tribune*, 4 January, 1910, 7.

7. Menachem Kaiser, "Anti-Non-Semitism: An Investigation of the Shiska," *Law Review of Books*, 3 March 2013, accessed 14 May 2022, https://lareviewofbooks.org/article/anti-non-semitism-an-investigation-of-the-shiksa/; Ariela Pelaia, "What Is a Shiksa?" *Learn Religions*, 26 August 2020, accessed 16 May 2022, learnreligions.com/what-is-a-shiksa-yiddish-word-2076332.

8. "Loftus Trial Is Postponed," *The Commercial Tribune*, 5 January 1910, 5.

9. "Freedom," *The Cincinnati Enquirer*, 6 January 1910, 14; "Frees Actress and Companion," *The Commercial Tribune*, 6 January 1910, 5; "My Heart Is Broken," *The Cincinnati Post*, 4 January 1910, 1. The *Enquirer* reported the first witness' name as "J.W. Werden," while *The Tribune* identified him as "J.M. Worden."

10. "Second," *The Cincinnati Enquirer*, 7 January 1910, 14; "Are Steadfast Despite

Court," *The Commercial Tribune*, 7 January 1910, 1–2.
11. "Second," *The Cincinnati Enquirer*, 7 January 1910, 14.
12. "Cupid" and "Lunacy Proceedings," *The Cincinnati Enquirer*, 8 January 1910, 10.
13. Kiddushin 68b from Adin Steinsaltz, Babylonian Talmud, n.d., The William Davidson Talmud, 2019, Sefaria, accessed 15 May 2022, https://www.sefaria.org/Kiddushin.68b?ven=William_Davidson_Edition_-_English&vhe=-William_Davidson_Edition_-_Vocalized_Aramaic&lang=bi&with=About&lang2=en; Tracey R. Rich, "Jewish Attitudes Toward Non-Jews," Judaism 101, 1995–2020, accessed 15 May 2022, https://www.jewfaq.org/gentiles.htm.
14. "Motor Through the Snow to Marry," *The Oakland Tribune*, 8 January 1910, 14; "English Actress in Fight for Husband," *The San Francisco Call*, 8 January 1910, 9.
15. "Effort," *The Cincinnati Enquirer*, 10 January 1910, 13.
16. "Lunacy Experts," *The Cincinnati Enquirer*, 12 January 1910, 8; "Mandamus," *The Cincinnati Enquirer*, 13 January 1910, 14.
17. "Refused," *The Cincinnati Enquirer*, 14 January 1910, 7; "Settlement," *The Cincinnati Enquirer*, 15 January 1910, 20.
18. "Edna Loftus Wins," *The New York Sun*, 18 January 1910, 12.
19. "Withdrawn," *The Cincinnati Enquirer*, 19 January 1910, 8; "Prices and Wages by Decade," Libraries, University of Missouri, updated 22 December 2021, retrieved 28 December 2021, https://libraryguides.missouri.edu/pricesandwages/1910-1919; "Mulqueeny," *The Cincinnati Enquirer*, 20 January 1910, 13.
20. "Sacrifices All for Love," *The Los Angeles Evening Express*, 22 January 1910, 1; "Westward," *The Cincinnati Enquirer*, 24 January 1910, 7.
21. "Asks for $50,000 Damages," *The Cincinnati Enquirer*, 27 January 1910, 9.

Chapter Four

1. "Rheinstroms Here from Cincinnati," *The Los Angeles Evening Express*, 8 February 1910, 5. "Exiled from Eastern Home," *The Oakland Tribune*, 8 February 1910, 3; "Miss Edna Loftus," *The San Francisco Examiner*, 9 February 1910, 1.
2. "Millionaire's Son and Actress," *The Tacoma Times*, 12 February 1910, 8; "Honeymoon Spent in Sylvan Retreat," *The San Francisco Call*, 23 February 1910, 1.
3. E.A. Goldenweiser, "The Farmer's Income," *The American Economic Review* 6, no. 1 (1916): 42–48, http://www.jstor.org/stable/1827810.
4. "Cupid's Aide in Hospital," *The Detroit Free Press*, 24 February 1910, 1.
5. "No Conspiracy," *The Detroit Free Press*, 27 February 1910, 10.
6. "Added Mrs. Rheinstrom to Suit," *The Cincinnati Enquirer*, 2 April 1910, 7; "Harry's Mother Also Defendant," *The Detroit Free Press*, 3 April 1910, 9.
7. "From Lobster Palace to the Farm," *The St. Louis Star Magazine Section*, 17 April 1910, 25.
8. "Coming Back," *The Cincinnati Enquirer*, 9 August 1910, 14; "No Simple Life for Them," *The Washington Post*, 9 August 1910, 3; "Edna Loftus Wins Mama-in-Law Over," *The San Francisco Examiner*, 12 August 1910, 1; "Harry Rheinstrom," *The St. Louis Star*, 12 August 1910, 2.
9. "Edna Loftus Wins Love of Hubby's Mother," *The Oakland Tribune*, 12 August 1910, 2; "Harry Rheinstrom," *The St. Louis Star*, 12 August 1910, 2.
10. "Rheinstroms Come to Seek Forgiveness," *The Commercial Tribune*, 9 August 1910, 1.
11. "Rheinstrom to Fight Father in Home City," *The San Francisco Examiner*, 20 August 1910, 4.
12. "Rheinstrom in Padded Cell," *The San Francisco Examiner*, 22 September 1910, 1; "Millionaire's Son Becomes Manic," *The San Francisco Call*, 22 September 1910, 1.
13. "Rheinstrom Still Kept Locked-Up," *The San Francisco Call*, 23 September 1910, 8; "Rheinstrom Now Manacled in Cell," *The San Francisco Examiner*, 23 September 1910, 5.
14. "Mother Refuses to Assist Son," *The Oakland Tribune*, 24 September 1910, 2.
15. "Rheinstrom's Insanity Unnerves

His Wife," *The San Francisco Call*, 24 September 1910, 5.
  16. "Mother Orders Rheinstrom in Public Asylum," *The San Francisco Examiner*, 25 September 1910, 29; "Mother Abandons Boy Stricken with Lunacy," *The Oakland Tribune*, 25 September 1910, 19.
  17. "Rheinstrom Flees, Raves and Fights," *The San Francisco Examiner*, 26 September 1910, 5; "Youth in Pajamas Runs for Liberty," *The San Francisco Call*, 26 September 1910, 14; "Rheinstrom Escapes from Sanatorium," *The Evening Times-Star*, 26 September 1910, 7.
  18. "Hope Is Given for Harry Rheinstrom," *The San Francisco Examiner*, 27 September 1910, 2.
  19. "Edna Loftus Will Return to the Stage," *The Oakland Tribune*, 16 October 1910, 20; "Edna Loftus Turns to the Stage Again," *The San Francisco Enquirer*, 16 October 1910, 14; "Edna Loftus Goes to Work," *The Commercial Tribune*, 17 October 1910, 1.
  20. "Winsome Edna Loftus Goes to Jail," *The Oakland Tribune*, 17 October 1910, 9.
  21. "Former Edna Loftus Flutters Mothlike Into a Prison Cell," *The San Francisco Chronicle*, 18 October 1910, 4.
  22. "The Popular Sensation," *The San Jose Mercury-News*, 19 October 1910, 6.
  23. Randy Shaw, *The Tenderloin: Sex, Crime and Resistance in the Heart of San Francisco* (San Francisco: Urban Reality Press, 2015), 19–46; Jacqueline Baker Barnhart, *The Fair but Frail: Prostitution in San Francisco, 1849–1900* (Reno: University of Nevada Press, 1986), 14.
  24. "Refuses to Pays Her Chauffer," *The San Francisco Chronicle*, 18 October 1910, 4; Nesbit, 254.
  25. "Rheinstroms Under Arrest," *The Commercial Tribune*, 22 October 1910, 1.
  26. "Edna Forgot Her Assumed Name," *The San Francisco Chronicle*, 19 October 1910, 4.
  27. "Edna Loftus Fails to Answer," *The Muskogee Daily Phoenix*, 21 October 1910, 5; "Edna Loftus Faints, But Goes Free," *The Oakland Tribune*, 21 October 1910, 1. Texas-born Effie Wilson, who was lured to San Francisco's red light district by Guido Varsi, a procurer, shot Varsi to death in his bedroom. Despite the effort of Varsi's relatives to have Wilson arrested for murder, no court officer would sign the warrant. Judge Conlan released Wilson to Mrs. Seaton, who returned her to her mother's home in San Antonio. Effie Wilson's story was found in "A Just Judge," *The Miners Magazine* 9, no. 36 (17 November 1910): 6. Published by the Western Federation of Miners.
  28. "Rheinstrom Jailed; Flees Sanatorium," *The San Francisco Examiner*, 22 October 1910, 7.
  29. "Rheinstrom to Fight for Liberty," *The Oakland Tribune*, 22 October 1910, 1.
  30. "Edna Fails to Visit Husband," *The San Francisco Call*, 23 October 1910, 36; "Loftus Is a Hospital Patient," *The San Francisco Call*, 24 October 1910, 2.
  31. "Edna Loftus Pines," *The Oakland Tribune*, 24 October 1910, 1; "Former Edna Loftus Treated at Hospital," *The San Francisco Chronicle*, 24 October 1910, 3.
  32. "Edna Loftus Near Delirium Tremens," *The Sacramento Daily Union*, 24 October 1910, 1.
  33. "Two People Are Unfortunate," *The Alliance Daily Review*, 24 October 1910, 7; "Former Edna Loftus Treated at Hospital," *The San Francisco Chronicle*, 24 October 1910, 3.
  34. "Asylum for Rheinstrom," *The San Francisco Examiner*, 25 October 1910, 1.
  35. "Harry Rheinstrom Sent to Asylum," *The San Francisco Call*, 25 October 1910, 2.
  36. "New Chapters in Lives of Millionaire's Son and His Wife," *The San Francisco Chronicle*, 25 October 1910, 2.
  37. "A Study in Carelessness of Society," *The Morning Union*, 29 October 1910, 4.

Chapter Five

  1. "On the Pacific Slope," *The New York Tribune*, 30 October 1910, 46.
  2. "Flashes for Femininity," *The Lincoln Star*, 4 November 1910, 6.
  3. "Edna Loftus in Fear of Burglars," *The Oakland Tribune*, 14 November 1910, 2; "Mrs. E. Rheinstrom Sees Man at Window," *The San Francisco Chronicle*, 15 November 1910, 16.
  4. "Edna Loftus Seeks Hubby's

Custody," *The Oakland Tribune*, 22 November 1910, 1; "Edna Loftus Loses Guardianship Fight," *The San Francisco Examiner*, 23 November 1910, 9; "H.A. Rheinstrom Has Guardian," *The San Francisco Chronicle*, 23 November 1910, 8; "Guardian Named for Rheinstrom," *The San Francisco Call*, 23 November 1910, 18.
 5. "The Foolishness of Fools Having Guardians," *The Morning Union*, 27 November 1910, 4.
 6. "Edna Loftus Pulled Out of Park Lake," *The Evening Mail*, 21 December 1910, 5; "Want Drives Her to Try Suicide," *The Oakland Tribune*, 21 December 1910, 5.
 7. "Attempts to End Life of Trouble," *The San Francisco Chronicle*, 21 December 1910, 2.
 8. "Ideal Domestically! Failure Financially!" *The San Francisco Chronicle*, 9 January 1911, 7.
 9. "Edna Loftus in Need of Clothing," *The Oakland Tribune*, 11 January 1911, 13.
 10. "Edna Loftus Found in Rags," *The Sacramento Bee*, 12 January 1911, 10.
 11. "Arise Showgirls!" *The San Francisco Examiner*, 19 March 1911, 19.
 12. "Mother-in-Law Is Anxious to See Son Divorced," *The San Francisco Chronicle*, 21 March 1911, 1.
 13. "Rheinstrom Going East," *The San Francisco Examiner*, 26 March 1911, 1.
 14. "Gets a Job as a Songstress," *The Sandusky Register*, 14 April 1911, 1.
 15. "Golden Vision Too Much," *The Oakland Tribune*, 24 October 1911, 7.
 16. "Edna Loftus Is Freed from Cell," *The San Francisco Call*, 25 October 1911, 8.
 17. "Say Reinstrom's [sic] Wants Balm," *The San Francisco Chronicle*, 25 October 1911, 8.
 18. "Report of Rheinstrom Settlement Is Denied." *The Commercial Tribune*, 26 October 1911, 6.
 19. "Rheinstrom Troubles Aired," *The Los Angeles Times*, 26 October 1911, 5; "No Settlement in Rheinstrom Case," *The San Francisco Chronicle*, 26 October 1911, 8.
 20. Sue Young, "Why No Chorus Girl Can Afford to Wed," *The Tennessean*, 12 November 1911, 38. This article originally appeared in *The American Examiner*, in Great Britain.

 21. "Edna Nervous," *The Evening Times-Star*, 9 March 1912, 2.
 22. "Doctor and Patient Spilled," *The Santa Cruz Evening News*, 9 March 1912, 1.
 23. "Actress and Physician Are Spilled into Water," *The San Francisco Chronicle*, 9 March 1912, 15.
 24. "Actress to Be Named in Suit," *The Oakland Tribune*, 14 April 1912, 16.
 25. "More Woe for Stage Beauty," *The San Francisco Examiner*, 14 April 1912, 1.
 26. "Wife Names Stage Favorite in Suit," *The San Francisco Call*, 15 April 1912, 4.
 27. "Edna Loftus," *The Los Angeles Times*, 21 April 1912, 29; "Edna Loftus Accused of Dodging Auto Bill," *The San Francisco Examiner*, 18 April 1912, 15.
 28. "Edna Loftus Named in Suit," *The Oakland Tribune*, 16 May 1912, 1.
 29. "Joy Ride Has a Sequel in Divorce Complaint," *The San Francisco Chronicle*, 17 May 1912, 3.
 30. "Mrs. Stone Skeptic; Edna Loftus Named," *The San Francisco Examiner*, 17 May 1912, 13; "Divorce Poultice for Cupid's Hurts," *The San Francisco Call*, 17 May 1912, 11.
 31. "Mrs. Wade Stone Granted Decree," *The Oakland Tribune*, 24 July 1912, 4.
 32. "Dr. Stone's Wife Given Decree," *The San Francisco Examiner*, 25 July 1912, 1.
 33. "Edna Loftus as Soul Mate," *The Los Angeles Times*, 25 July 1912, 3.
 34. "Edna Loftus Is Entitled 'Soul Mate,'" *The Commercial Tribune*, 25 July 1912, 12; "More Notoriety for Edna," *The Indiana Gazette*, 25 July 1912, 3; "More Notoriety for Edna," *The Evening Record* (Greenville, PA), 25 July 1912, 1.
 35. "Edna Loftus Told to Leave Town," *The San Francisco Call*, 4 August 1912, 33.
 36. "Actress May Lose Husband," *The Pensacola Journal*, 4 August 1912, 12.

Chapter Six

 1. "Edna Loftus Once More in Public Light," *The Oakland Tribune*, 24 February 1913, 5.
 2. "Edna Loftus Gets Spotlight," *The San Francisco Call*, 25 February 1913, 5.

Notes—Chapter Six

3. "Edna Loftus Figures in Police Episode," *The San Francisco Examiner*, 25 February 1913, 5; "Actress Scores San Francisco," *The Los Angeles Times*, 25 February 1913, 4; "Edna Loftus," *The San Francisco Chronicle*, 26 February 1913, 6.

4. "Edna Loftus Now May Be Deported," *The San Francisco Call*, 10 April 1913, 8.

5. Letter from John A. Robinson to the Commissioner of Immigration; Application for Warrant of Arrest; Official Missive from Charles P. Neill to Samuel L. Backus; Immigration file for Mrs. Edna Rhinestrom [sic], RG 85, Entry 9, File No. 53575/236, Records of the Immigration and Naturalization Service, Archives File, National Archives, Civil Reference RG 35, National Archives Building, Washington, D.C.

6. "Red Light Injunction and Abatement Act," 2005 California Penal Code Sections 11225–11235, Article 2, retrieved 8 January 2022, https://law.justia.com/codes/california/2005/pen/11225-11235.html.

7. "Edna Loftus Is Arrested," *The Oakland Tribune*, 10 April 1913, 1; "Deportation May Be Actress' Fate," *The San Francisco Chronicle*, 11 April 1913, 8.

8. Information about the Angel Island immigration center was derived primarily from Erika Lee and Judy Yung, *Angel Island: Immigrant Gateway to America* (Oxford: Oxford University Press, 2010). Due to overcrowding, the female detainees from China were eventually housed in the administration building. That building burned in August of 1940, but the detention center still stands as an unsettling reminder of institutionalized racism and bigotry in the United States.

9. Hearing in the case of Mrs. Winfield O'Connor, Immigration file for Mrs. Edna Rhinestrom [sic], RG 85, Entry 9, File No. 53575/236, Records of the Immigration and Naturalization Service, Archives File, National Archives, Civil Reference RG 35, National Archives Building, Washington, D.C.

10. "Edna Loftus," *The Sacramento Star*, 17 April 1913, 3.

11. Lee and Yung, *Angel Island*, 56–58.

12. Richard White, *It's Your Misfortune and None of My Own: A History of the American West* (Norman: University of Oklahoma Press, 1991), 321.

13. "May Deport Noted Actress," *The Brooklyn Citizen*, 26 April 1913, 3.

14. "Edna Loftus, Once Theatrical Star," *The Fort Wayne Sentinel*, 23 April 1913, 3.

15. Affidavit of William Littleford, 26 April 1913; H. Edsell to Commissioner General of Immigration, 7 May 1912; Wm. Williams to Immigration Service, 6 May, 1913; Immigration file for Mrs. Edna Rhinestrom [sic], RG 85, Entry 9, File No. 53575/236, Records of the Immigration and Naturalization Service, Archives File. National Archives, Civil Reference RG 35, National Archives Building, Washington, D.C.

16. "Going Home to England," *The Daily Telegram*, 8 May 1913, 1.

17. "Edna Loftus Released," *The Oakland Tribune*, 8 May 1913, 2.

18. "Edna Loftus May Stay," *The San Francisco Call*, 9 May 1913, 4; "Edna Loftus," *The Sacrament Bee*, 10 May 1913, 30.

19. "His Heart Sobs and He'd Wed Edna Loftus," *The San Francisco Examiner*, 10 May 1913, 3.

20. "Edna Loftus Wants Money," *The Long Beach Daily Telegram*, 23 September 1913, 6.

21. "Edna Loftus to Demand Money," *The San Francisco Examiner*, 24 September 1913, 7.

22. "Here's Edna Again," *The Cincinnati Enquirer*, 24 September 1913, 8; "Edna Loftus-Rheinstrom in Limelight," *The Sacrament Star*, 25 September 1913, 5; "Edna Loftus Is Named in Suit," *The Oakland Tribune*, 16 May 1912, 2; "Dr. Stone's Wife," *The San Francisco Examiner*, 25 July 1912, 3.

23. "Index to Divorce Records, 1909–15, 3 vols." and "Divorce Records, 1909–15, 23 vols.," #136 and 137, Dockets, Clerk's Entries, and Record of Trials, Insolvency Court, # 121–137. Held by Hamilton County Courts, Archive & Preservation Department.

24. "Rheinstrom's Guardian Dismissed," *The Sacramento Bee*, 26 February 1914, 3; "Rheinstrom Restored," *The San Francisco Chronicle*, 26 February 1914, 18; "Harry Rheinstrom Is Freed of Guardian," *The San Francisco Examiner*, 26 February 1914, 8.

Notes—Chapter Six

25. "Rheinstrom Freed from Insane Asylum," *The San Bernardino Daily Sun*, 26 February 1914, 2.
26. "Once Star, Is Taken in Raid," *The Oakland Tribune*, 18 October 1914, 17.
27. "Edna Loftus Robbed by Clerk, She Says," *The Oakland Tribune*, 9 November 1914, 3.
28. "Early Research and Treatment of Tuberculosis," 2007, The American Lung Association Crusade, Historical Collections at the Claude Moore Health Science Library, University of Virginia, retrieved 10 January 2022, http://exhibits.hsl.virginia.edu/alav/tuberculosis/.
29. "Edna Loftus Dies, Friendless, Alone," *The San Francisco Examiner*, 16 June 1916, 16.
30. "Edna Loftus Dies in Ward for Paupers," *The Oakland Tribune*, 16 June 1916, 13.
31. "Last Bow Made by Edna Loftus," *The Cincinnati Enquirer*, 17 June 1916, 10.
32. California, San Francisco Area Funeral Home Records, 1835–1979, p. 204, FamilySearch, Intellectual Reserve, Inc., retrieved 3 June 2023, https://www.familysearch.org; Rand Richards, *Historic Walks in San Francisco: 18 Trails Through the City's Past* (San Francisco: Heritage House, 2002), 38.
33. "Friend Buries Edna Loftus," *The St. Joseph Evening Herald*, 17 June 1916, 3; "Edna Loftus," *The Cosshooton Morning Tribune*, 17 August 1916, 4.
34. "Harry A. Rheinstrom Dies," *The Cincinnati Enquirer*, 15 October 1918, 14; "Brewer's Con Death," *The Los Angeles Times*, 16 October 1918, 17; Harry Rheinstrom, Certificate #151188, 14 October 1918, Pennsylvania Historic and Museum Commission, Harrisburg, PA; Pennsylvania (State), Death Certificates, 1906–1968, Certificate Number Range: 150001–153000, ancestry.com, Pennsylvania, U.S., Death Certificates, 1906–1968 [database online], Lehi, UT, USA, Ancestry.com Operations, Inc., 2014.
35. "Boro Jock Was World Idol," *The Brooklyn Daily Eagle*, 11 March 1947, 14; "Winnie O'Connor; Former Topflight Jockey," *The Daily News*, 7 March 1947, 39;

Stephen C. Duer and Allen B. Smith, *Cypress Hills Cemetery* (Charleston, SC: Arcadia, 2010), 70.
36. "Rites Are Held for Actress," *The Brooklyn Daily Times*, 4 February 1932, 22; "Less Than a Score," *The Brooklyn Daily Eagle*, 5 February 1932, 25; Neva Aymar O'Connor, Death date: 1 February 1932, Certificate number 791, New York City Department of Records & Information Services; New York City, New York; New York City Death Certificates; Borough: Queens; Year: 1932, retrieved from Ancestry.com, *New York, New York, U.S., Index to Death Certificates, 1862–1948* [database online] Lehi, UT, USA, Ancestry.com Operations, Inc., 2020.
37. "Gaby Deslys Dies After Operation," *New York Times*, 12 February 1920, 11; James Gardiner, *Gaby Deslys: A Fatal Attraction* (London: Sidgwick & Jackson, 1986).
38. "News from Healdsburg," *The Santa Rosa Press Democrat*, 8 April 1925, 6; Fourteenth Census of the United States, 1920, NARA microfilm publication T625, 2076 rolls; Waid Stone, et al., Records of the Bureau of the Census, Record Group 29. Year: 1920; Census Place: Healdsburg, Sonoma, California; Roll: T625_150; Page: 20A; Enumeration District: 139, Ancestry.com, *1920 United States Federal Census* [database online], Provo, UT, USA: Ancestry.com Operations, Inc., 2010; "Dr. Waid Stone," *The Santa Rosa Republican*, 17 April, 1925, 4; "Waid James Stone," 16 April 1925. Directory of Deceased American Physicians, 1804–1929 [database online].
39. "Pauline Placida Rodrigue," 20 January 1959, Memorial I.D. 145353294, Find a Grave, database and images, https://www.findagrave.com/memorial/145353294/-pauline-placida-rodrigue, accessed 11 January 2022; Find a Grave Memorial ID 145353294, citing Holy Cross Catholic Cemetery, Colma, San Mateo County, California, USA, maintained by Ann (contributor 47099598).
40. "Mrs. Minna Rheinstrom," *The Cincinnati Enquirer*, 2 October 1937, 20.

Bibliography

Baker Barnhart, Jacqueline. *The Fair but Frail: Prostitution in San Francisco, 1849–1900*. Reno: University of Nevada Press, 1986.

Bratton, Jacky. "The Music Hall." *The Cambridge Companion to Victorian and Edwardian Theater*. Cambridge: Cambridge University Press, 2004, 164–182.

Davis, Tracy. "Actresses and Prostitutes in Victorian London." *Theater Research International* 13, no. 3 (1988): 221–234.

Delamont, Sara, and Lorna Duffin, eds. *The Nineteenth-Century Woman: Her Cultural and Physical World*. London: Billing & Sons, 1978.

Duer, Stephen C., and Allen B. Smith. 2010. *Cypress Hills Cemetery*. Charleston, SC: Arcadia.

Gardiner, James. *Gaby Deslys: A Fatal Attraction*. London: Sidgwick & Jackson, 1986.

Gerrard, Steven. "The Great British Music Hall: Its Importance to British Culture and the Trivial." *Culture Unbound: Journal of Current Cultural Research* 5 (2013): 487–515.

Kalifa, Dominique. *The Belle Époque: A Cultural History, Paris and Beyond*. New York: Columbia University Press, 2021.

Lee, Erika, and Judy Yung. *Angel Island: Immigrant Gateway to America*. Oxford: Oxford University Press, 2010.

Mitchell, Sally. *Daily Life in Victorian England*. Westport: Greenwood Press, 1986.

Morrison, James Douglas. *The Lords and the New Creatures*. New York: Simon & Schuster, 1969.

Nesbit, Evelyn. *Prodigal Days: The Untold Story*. New York: Julian Messner, 1934.

O'Connor, Winnie. *Jockeys, Crooks, and Kings: The Story of Winnie O'Connor's Life as Told to Earl Chapin May*. New York: Jonathan Cape & Harrison Smith, 1930.

Powell, Kerry, ed. *The Cambridge Companion to Victorian and Edwardian Theatre*. Cambridge: Cambridge University Press, 2004.

Richards, Rand. *Historic Walks in San Francisco: 18 Trails Through the City's Past*. San Francisco: Heritage House, 2014.

Savanevik, Michael, and Shirley Burgett. *Pillars of the Past: At Rest at Cypress Lawn Memorial Park*. Colma: Cypress Lawn Heritage Foundation, 2002.

Shaw, Randy. *The Tenderloin: Sex, Crime and Resistance in the Heart of San Francisco*. San Francisco: Urban Reality Press, 2015.

Uruburu, Paula. *American Eve: Evelyn Nesbit, Stanford White: The Birth of the "It" Girl and the Crime of the Century*. New York: Riverhead Books, 2008.

White, Richard. *It's Your Misfortune and None of My Own: A History of the American West*. Norman: University of Oklahoma Press, 1991.

Index

Numbers in **_bold italics_** indicate pages with illustrations

actresses 3, 4, 46
Ainsworth, Frank H. 15, 147–152
Angel Island Immigration Station Administration Building 146–147, **_146_**, 154
anti–Semitism 7
author at the grave of Edna Loftus at Cypress Lawn, Colma, California **_165_**
Aymar, Neva 38–41, **_40_**, 168

The Babes in the Wood 28, 30–31, 33
Backus, Samuel W. 143, **_143_**
Barnhart, Jacqueline Baker 110
Barry, Jim 39
The Belmont Hotel, New York City **_87_**
Berger, L.M. 42
Berlin State Archive (Landesarchiv Berlin) 14
Bode, August H. 62
bordellos 111
Bratt, James 74
Bratton, Jacky 16
Britt, James ("Jimmy") 38–39, 91
Britt, Willie 124
Burke, Billie 27
burlesques 17

career, Edna Loftus: *Les Ambaseuders* 12; *The Babes in the Wood* 28, 30–31, 33; *The Catch of the Season* 20–22, **_96_**; and celebrity treatment 9; early career 14; at Folies Marigny 12, 23; *Madame Lengerie* 12; *The Morals of Marcus* 44; in musical comedy 19; *The New Aladdin* 24–25, 27, 28, 31; reviews 23–24, 25, 28, 31–33; *Sergeant Breu* 12, 19
Caryll, Ivan 17
The Catch of the Season 20–22, **_96_**
The Chicago Tribune 36
chorus girls 20
The Cincinnati Enquirer 39–40, 55, 60–61, 95–96
The Cincinnati Post **_50_**, 62–63, **_62_**, **_67_**
Claire, Mildred 29, 31, 33
classism 4–7, 8, 10

College Hill Sanitarium 52, **_69_**
The Commercial Tribune 46, 48–49, **_65_**, 97–98, 112
Conlan, Charles T. 113, 114
Crichton, Madge 22, **_23_**

Dalamont, Sara 3
Dale, Alan 19
Daly, William C. ("Father Bill" or "Pa") 34, 35
Dare, Zena 19, 22
Davis, Tracy C. 3, 46
de Rothschild, Alphonso James 35
Deslys, Gaby: advises Edna against marriage 8, 24; biographical information about 24–25; lying about age 13; photograph **_168_**; review of performance in *The New Aladdin* 26; successful career and death 168–169
Devlin, Robert T. 122, 123
Dillon, John 73
Dorman, Bert 37–38, 39
Dormer, Daisy 29, **_29_**
Doro, Marie 44, **_45_**
Duffin, Lorna 3
Dunbarton, Norman 38–39
Dunne, Frank H. 121, 122, 123, 160

Earl, Lee 164
Edwardes, George Joseph ("The Guv'nor") 17
Elsie, Lily 24, **_25_**, 26, 28
The Enquirer 52–53, 57
The Era 31–32
The Evening Star 33

Featherstone, Alfred 35
Fechheimer, Harry S. 49, 55, 56
Fechheimer, Samuel 56, 75–76, 77
Follies Bergère 16
Freeman, Chuck 45, 51
Freiberg (attorney) 49, 50, 64

Gaiety Theater, London, England **_18_**
Gardiner, James 24

Index

Gerdies, H. 131, 133
German Hospital 115, 116, 118–119, 125
Gerrard, Steven 16–17
the Gibson Girls 22, 25
Gillan, Don 27
Golden West Wine Company 98
Goldenweiser, E.A. 85–86
Greene, Mabel 27
Grossmith, George 24

H. & S. Pogue Company 53, 80
Hamilton, Cosmo 20
Harper, Daniel 33
The Hartford Daily Courant 37–38
Havlin Hotel 46, 48, 52–53
Hayden, Curtis 139
Held, Anna 7
Hereschede, Frank 54
Hermanson, H. 104
Hess, Harry 53
Hicks, Seymour 20
Hiller, Carl 46, 50
Holland, Herbert H.B.: claims hospitalization is result of accident 78; as possible grifter 46–47; proposal to form lumber company with 49; purchases charged to Harry Rheinstrom 52–54; refuses to support wife in lawsuit 88
Holland, Minnie: arrest of Edna Rheinstrom and Minnie for loitering 55–56, 59, 61–62, *62*; purchases charged to Harry Rheinstrom 52–54; relationship with Harry and Edna 46–47; sues Rheinstrom family 83, 88
hot air balloons 44, 48
Hotel Metropole *99*
Howard, John B. 28
Howe, Jessica 14

The Illustrated Sporting and Dramatic News 26–27, 28, *28*
Insane Asylum of California at Stockton *117*

Johnson, Hiram 145
Jorgenson, Peter 101, 117–118, 121–122, 125, 160

Kearny Street, San Francisco, California *161*

Langdon, F.W. 69
Lilliancrantz, Guy H. 100, 101, 103
Littleford (attorney) 64, 67–68
Lloyd, Marie 4
Locke, William 44
Loftus, Cecilia ("Cissie") 11, *13*
The Lords and the New Creatures (Morrison) 3
The Los Angeles Evening Express 84
Lowell, Frank 104, 105, 114–115, 126–127

Lueders, William H. 47, 56, 71, 79–80
Lykins, M.C. 56, 59, *62*

Maid Marion 30
Maloney, William 115–116
marriages, Edna Loftus: and daughter 4, 12, 15, 36, 42; divorce from "Winnie" O'Connor 38, 40–41; to Harry Rheinstrom 7–8, 75, 89–94, *90*; under Jewish law 57, 72; records 14–15; to "Winnie" O'Connor 7, 33, 34, 36
McCarthy, Patrick Henry ("P.H.") 110
The Meridian Daily Journal 33
Meyerfeld, Moses, Jr. ("Morris") 111
middle class 6, 9, 26, 110–111
Millar, Gertie 28
Milliken, Paul 59, *59*
Millington, Thomas 30
Mitchell, Sally 6
Montgomery, Dixie 123, 124
The Morals of Marcus 44
The Morning Union 119, 123
Morris, Froome 48, 60
Morrison, Jim 3
motion picture industry 16
Moulin Rouge 16
Mulqueeny, George E.F. 64, *65*, 66, 83
Murray, Mae 126
music halls 4, 16
musical comedy 16–20

Neill, Charles P. 144
Nesbit, Evelyn: on consequences of notoriety 111; life as show girl 7; marriage as end of freedom for show girl 38; photograph *112*; on placing blame 4; reaction to fame 8–9; on social status of women in theater 46
The New Aladdin 24–25, 28, 31
The New York Sun 82

The Oakland Tribune 96, 102, 106
O'Connell, John 55, 56
O'Connor, Florence 36–37
O'Connor, Winfield ("Winnie"): autobiography 34, 35; biographical information 34–35; daughter 4, 36, 41–42; death of sister 36–37; divorce 38, 40–41; as financially irresponsible 8; later years and death 167–168; marriage to Edna Loftus 33, 34, 36; marriage to Neva Aymar 41; photos *32*, *167*; success as jockey 33–34, 35, 37
opium dens 111
Orpheum circuit 111

Park Emergency Hospital 115
patriarchal culture 3, 4, 110
Pelaia, Ariela 57
The Philadelphia Inquirer 28

photographs, Edna Loftus: from "Catch of the Season" *96*; in *The Cincinnati Post 50*; on cover of *Illustrated Sporting and Dramatic News 28*; on cover of *The Tatler 21*; in custody of immigration officials *156*; in feathered hat *85*; former residence in San Francisco *142*; and George E.F. Mulqueeny *65*; and Harry Rheinstrom *67, 76*; with M.C. Lykins, Minnie Holland, and unidentified police officer *62*; reading letter *2*
postcard trade 4, 27–28
postcards, Edna Loftus: from Dover Street Studios, London *169*; in furs *162*; on ladder *5*; in large hat *45*; lounging in chair *14*; perched on chair *81*; posed on column *131*; with ribbon *108*; with roses *10*; with small unidentified dog *103*; in stockings *121*; in white gown *141*; in yellow gown *166*
Prince Philippe, Duke of Orléans 26, *26*
Prisk, William F. 119, 123
prostitutes 3, 4, 46, 55
prostitution 55, 110–111, 138, 144–145, 152
La Provence (ship) 33, 34

racial prejudice 154–155
Receiving Hospital 100, 114, 116, 119, 128–129
religious intolerance 7–8, 34–36, 56, 57
Rheinstrom, Abraham 52, 118
Rheinstrom, Edna Loftus: announcement of return to employment 106; arrest in deportation case 152; arrest of Edna and Minnie Holland for loitering 55–56, 59, 61–62, *62*; arrested for prostitution 160; arrested for refusing to pay taxi 107, 112, 114; in automobile incident with doctor 131–134; blamed for Harry's mental state 116, 117, 118; charging of goods as reported wife of 53–54; contracts tuberculosis 160, 162; delirium tremens and alcoholism as cause of illness 115–116; education and background 3, 7, 11–12, 63–64, 152–154; evicted from town of San Rafael 137; faints in court 113; gives testimony about Harry's mental stability 50; hospitalized for severe intoxication 115; incident involving stolen watch 139–140, 146; investigation and arrest as undesirable alien 140–144, 152, *156*; "Lobster Palace" newspaper article 89–94, *90*; loyalty to Harry 63, 77–78, 106; moves Harry to Lowell Sanitorium 102, 103; obituary 162–164; perceived as golddigger 61, 72, 117; petitions for guardianship of Harry 121–122; prostitution and part interest in brothel 140, 144–145, 152; purchases farm with Harry 85–86; questions and contradictions surrounding life 15, 42–43; released from detainment in deportation case 156–157; reports of inability to live modestly 102; "Rheinstroms Under Arrest" article 112; secures release of Harry from custody 55; suicide attempts 123–124, 161; transcript of deportation hearing against 147–152; *see also* career, Edna Loftus; photographs, Edna Loftus; postcards, Edna Loftus
Rheinstrom, Harry: accusations of mental illness against 49; accuses family of religious intolerance 48; admits violent behavior 51; admitted to Stockton Insane Asylum 115–116; allegations of violence against 49; application for guardianship 56; attempts to organize reconciliation with mother 78–79, 80–82; checks into College Hill Sanitarium 52; death 167; defends his sanity 58; demonstration of erratic behavior 100; escapes from Lowell Sanitorium 104–105, 114; expresses intention to compete with family business 98; as financially extravagant 102, 117, 118; funeral and grave 164, *165*; gifts to Edna Loftus from 45–46, 49, 50–51; insanity affidavit and application for guardianship dropped against 82; "Lobster Palace" newspaper article 89–94, *90*; lunacy warrant issued for 47, 50; meets Edna Loftus 44–45; moved to Lowell Sanitorium 102, 103; newspaper stories alleging reconciliation with mother 95–96; personal habits 51; photographs *67, 76*; purchases farm 85–86; resumes former position in family business 159, 160; "Rheinstroms Under Arrest" article 112; self-reports of temporary trances 118; takes stand in own defense 50–51; testimony of mother against 49–50; *see also* Rheinstrom, Mina ("Widow Rheinstrom"); Rheinstrom family
Rheinstrom, Mina ("Widow Rheinstrom"): alleges attempted extortion 59–60; attempts to prevent son's marriage 46, 47; as beneficiary of husband's estate 52; blames Edna for Harry being committed to sanitorium 126; concerns that Harry's wine business will compete with family business 98; death 169–170; Harry charged as fugitive from justice on orders of 114; insists that son Harry divorce wife 113; has lunacy warrant issued for son 47; Peter Jorgenson applies for guardianship of Harry at request of 121–122; reasons for opposing son's marriage 72; refusal to intervene in Harry's placement in sanitorium 102–103; swears out arrest warrants 55; testimony against son Harry 49–50

Rheinstrom family 52, 56–57, 91–92, 98
Risque, W.H. 24
Robin Hood, legend 30
Robinson, John A. 143–144
Rose, Ralph W. 128

The Sacramento Star 15, 152–153, *156*
The St. Louis Star and Times 90
saloons 16, 110, 111
San Francisco, California 109–111, *109*, *161*, *163*
The San Francisco Call 85, 140–141
The San Francisco Examiner 98
The Scotsman 28, 30
Seeds, William 59
sexism 1, 8, 10
Shaw, Essie 124–125
Shaw, Randy 110, 111
shiksa 57
show girls 19–20, 26
Smith, John C. 69
Smith, Rufus B. 55, 56, 60
Southwark, London, England *12*
The Sportsman 33
Squire Wheeler 75
Standard Union 33–34
Stanisfer, Elmer 74
Stone, Pauline Placidia Rodriguez 134–136, 169
Stone, Waid J. 131–134, 169

Talmud 72
Tanner, James T. 24
The Tatler *21*
Tedford, William W. 116–117
Tenderloin District 109–111, *109*
Thaw, Harry 4, 46

The Theater Royal in Edinburgh, Scotland *31*
Théâtre de Marigny, Paris, France 22, *23*
Thon, Joseph 53, 54
Torah 72
tuberculosis 162, *163*

underclass 6
US Citizenship and Immigration Services Genealogy Program 15
upper class 6, 7

Victorian and Edwardian culture: anti-Semitism 7; characterizations of self-sufficient women 3, 46; classism 4–7, 8, 10; inherent prejudices 1; middle class women 26, 110–111; role of women 3; and sexism 1, 8
von Weinberg, Carl 35

Walker, George 36
Warner (judge) 64, 68–71
Waste, William H. 114, 117
Wecht, Albert ("Al") 47, 48, 56, 64
Werden, G.W. 55, 61
Wheeler, Judge 74–75
White, Stanford 4, 46
"The White Way" 110
Wilkinson, Amanda 34
Williams, William 156
Wilson, William Bauchop *145*
Wood, J. Hickory 28
working class 6
Wyndham, Frederick W.P. 28–29, 30

Young, Sue 130

www.ingramcontent.com/pod-product-compliance
Lightning Source LLC
Chambersburg PA
CBHW032046300426
44117CB00009B/1213